# EASY RIDER

## My Life on a Bike

## Rob Hayles
### with Lionel Birnie

## BANTAM PRESS

LONDON · TORONTO · SYDNEY · AUCKLAND · JOHANNESBURG

TRANSWORLD PUBLISHERS
61–63 Uxbridge Road, London W5 5SA
A Random House Group Company
www.transworldbooks.co.uk

First published in Great Britain
in 2013 by Bantam Press
an imprint of Transworld Publishers

A CIP catalogue record for this book
is available from the British Library.

ISBN 9780593070604

Addresses for Random House Group Ltd companies outside the UK
can be found at: www.randomhouse.co.uk
The Random House Group Ltd Reg. No. 954009

The Random House Group Limited supports the Forest Stewardship Council® (FSC®), the
leading international forest-certification organisation. Our books carrying the FSC label are
printed on FSC®-certified paper. FSC is the only forest-certification scheme supported
by the leading environmental organisations, including Greenpeace. Our paper
procurement policy can be found at www.randomhouse.co.uk/environment

Typeset in 12½/15pt Ehrhardt by
Kestrel Data, Exeter, Devon.
Printed and bound by
CPI Group (UK) Ltd, Croydon, CR0 4YY.

2 4 6 8 10 9 7 5 3 1

# Contents

# Acknowledgements

To my dad, John, thanks for introducing me into the great world of cycling, and my mum, Mary, for allowing him to take me away on so many weekends in those early years.

To all the hard-working members of staff at *British Cycling* and *UK Sport* for helping us athletes to reach our potential.

A big thanks to all my teammates from all those years, for giving me so many memories and stories . . . with most of them being good ones!

To the new generation of British bike riders for upping the ante, and continuing with the legacy of cycling in Great Britain.

Thanks to Giles Elliott at Transworld Publishers for keeping me on my toes during the writing process, and to Kate Green for publicity.

And Lionel Birnie, without whose help and enthusiasm this book would never have come about.

Finally, to my amazing wife Victoria. For all of her support in life, and our beautiful children Madeleine and Fergus, and for helping me to put things into perspective.

It's only sport, after all.

# Picture Acknowledgements

All images have been supplied courtesy of the author unless otherwise stated. Every effort has been made to contact the copyright holders. We apologize for any omissions in this respect and will be pleased to make the appropriate acknowledgements in any future edition.

*Section 1*

All photos pages 2–8 © Phil O'Connor, except page 2 (Colorado) courtesy of the author and page 8 (with Wiggins) © Johan de Jonckheere.

*Section 2*

Pages 1–3 all © Phil O'Connor. Page 4 (team pursuit) © Getty Images/Bryn Lennon; (Madison) © Francis Specker/AP/Press Association Images. All photos pages 5–7 © Andy Jones except page 5 (hungover) courtesy of the author.

# Foreword by Mark Cavendish

It isn't easy in life to find someone that *everybody* likes. Such people are even more rare in the world of elite sport, where the selfish gene can come to the fore when the pressure of competition begins to take over. But Rob Hayles is one of the few. In victory and defeat, at times of triumph and disaster, Rob is the same guy. There's no side to him.

From the day I first walked into Manchester velodrome to train with the British Cycling Academy squad, Rob was there. Like Sir Chris Hoy, he was in on the ground floor of the sport's revolution in this country. He was one of the people that British Cycling grew up around.

We looked up to those guys not just because they had won medals at the Olympic Games and World Championships but because of the example they set. I'd watched Rob in the track centre during training sessions and marvelled at his ability to strike that tricky balance between appearing relaxed yet remaining focused at the same time.

Because he's so laid back, it would be easy to assume that he's not bothered by things, that he doesn't get worked up about the little stuff. But that would be a mistake because he cares. Deeply.

That's perhaps one of the reasons we get on so well. Outwardly we appear quite different – he's always calm and I'm, well . . . I have my moments, you could say. Inwardly, we have the same eye for detail, the same desire to improve the small things. And we were both born to race. Pin a number on Rob's back now and he'd turn himself inside out to get over the line first.

One of the big lessons young riders could learn from Rob is about taking personal responsibility. The closer to the top of the sport a rider gets, the more people there are to look after the details for you. Obviously, that's fantastic because it leaves you free to concentrate on the important things – racing and training.

Rob had to be self-sufficient when he was starting out because there wasn't the level of support for him that young riders in Britain enjoy today. If he had to, he could build his bike from scratch. Some of the lads today struggle to fix a puncture.

Sometimes he shakes his head and smiles to himself. Sometimes he points out that we don't know we're born and that it was a lot harder in his day.

But he inspires something in people that makes them want to be the best they can be.

In 2005, I won my first World Championship title with Rob. It was in the Madison on the track in Los Angeles. I'd never ridden the World Championships before and was still getting to grips with what it was all about. But I desperately wanted to win.

Rob has a knack of taking the pressure out of a situation, putting everything into context, with a few simple words.

*'It's bike racing. Just do your best. But when we get off that track, let's make sure we have no regrets.'*

In that race I was so desperate not to let him down, not because

I was worried about disappointing him, not at all, but he made me want to do my best for him and for myself.

These days he's one of the people who supports me, keeping an eye on the details so I can concentrate on my training. I trust him completely.

And when I'm getting het up about something, he's always got those simple words to diffuse the situation.

*'Hey, it's bike racing. Just do your best.'*

# Prologue

Copenhagen, 25 September 2011. A few minutes after we came off air, I left the commentary box with Simon Brotherton and we walked down the finishing straight where Mark Cavendish had won the World Championship title, the gold medal and the iconic rainbow jersey half an hour or so before. All the hullabaloo had died down and most of the spectators had drifted away, but after hours cooped up in a stuffy commentary box, trying to keep the late-summer sun off our tiny screen, I wanted to stretch my legs and soak up the atmosphere that continued to crackle in the air.

As Simon and I reached the finish line, which stretched across the road, we stopped and looked down. I moved over to the right-hand side of the road, roughly where Cavendish had crossed the line ahead of the rest of the world's best cyclists, and knew what I had to do.

I knelt down and peeled the plastic tape up from the tarmac, tore off a foot-long strip and, rolling it up, slipped it into my back pocket. It would make the ultimate souvenir.

When I got home from Copenhagen, I trimmed the edges to

neaten it up, and went to an art supplies shop to buy some board. Then I mixed up some paint to get the right, matching shade of grey, and stuck the section of finishing line to it. Then I called Simon to get a copy of his commentary from BBC Radio Five Live's broadcast. Although I'd been sitting next to him, I'd been so caught up in the emotion of that afternoon that I couldn't remember a word he'd said.

Carefully, I transcribed the commentary, typed it up and printed it out on a piece of card.

*'Cavendish goes for gold . . . and he's got it. He dug deep. He delivered. It's gold for Great Britain, gold for Mark Cavendish. He IS the world champion.'*

I had the whole thing framed, then I wrapped it up and gave it to Cav for Christmas.

'Oh, man, it's fantastic. Absolutely fantastic. I can't believe you thought to do that for me. Thanks.'

# 1

# Rainbow Bands

A winter's day on the Isle of Man. It's bleak but beautiful in its own way. Mark Cavendish is training, logging the unseen miles for the coming season. Today we'll do five hours and tomorrow we'll do the same again. Just me, Cav and the cold.

I settle in behind him as we begin to climb a long, steady hill. I watch his legs rise and fall as he turns the pedals. The effect is almost hypnotic and after a while my mind begins to drift.

Cav's reign as world champion ended several weeks ago but he is entitled to wear the rainbow bands around the collar and cuffs of his jersey for life. If you're a cycling fan, you'll know immediately what I'm on about when I talk about the rainbow bands. From top to bottom they go blue, red, black, yellow, green, as if the Olympic rings have been unhooked and stacked on top of one another. Only former world champions are allowed to display the rainbow bands in this way and they are as indelible as any tattoo. I'm proud to say I'm one of that select number too.

As we ride, I think back to that afternoon in Copenhagen when I watched from the commentary box as the Great Britain team dominated one of the toughest and most prestigious single-day bike races in the world from start to finish. They barely missed a beat in 165 miles. For almost six hours they controlled the world's established cycling super powers – the Italians, the Spanish, the Belgians and the rest – until it was time to unleash Cav, the fastest man on two wheels, for the sprint finish.

Was anyone really surprised by the result? The British team had made little secret of the plan and the world knew that if it came down to a bunch sprint, Cavendish would take some beating.

When you looked back ten years, five years, or even three years, it seemed incredible that Britain, for so long a minnow in the cycling gene pool, had grown so powerful.

I started bike racing when I was 12, in 1985, the year Cav was born. At that time, Great Britain had gone sixty-five years without winning an Olympic gold medal in cycling, and the nation would go seven more before Chris Boardman won the individual pursuit in Barcelona.

It would be another eight years before Jason Queally won Britain's next cycling gold, but, since 2000, seventeen different British cyclists have had an Olympic gold medal hung around their necks. In that time there have also been countless British world champions and, in 2012, my old Madison partner Brad Wiggins became the first rider from this country to win the Tour de France.

Where once we trailed miles behind the international peloton, Great Britain is now one of the strongest cycling nations in the world. When I first raced for my country we were virtually penniless, struggling to scrape together the funds to provide riders with enough kit *and* cover airfares and hotel costs. The arrival of National Lottery money, a world-class velodrome at Manchester, and a coaching strategy implemented by Peter

Keen and developed by Dave Brailsford has transformed British Cycling into a world leader.

Now, with Cav bearing down on Eddy Merckx's record of thirty-four Tour de France stage victories, and young riders rolling off the production line to win world and Olympic titles at 20 or 21, as we've seen in Beijing, London and, more recently, Minsk, it's easy to overlook the fact that this transformation didn't happen overnight.

It was a long, gradual and at times frustrating process. I know, because I lived through it. I was there at the start of the journey, when we raced in rags. And although I just missed out on the incredible riches some of the top British cyclists can now command, I like to think I played a part in the rise.

As we reach the top of the hill, a change of direction jogs me back into the present. I roll alongside Cav to ask if he's OK. He nods, so I slip back in behind him and follow. He's not a big talker when he's training on the road and today is not one of his chattier days.

It's fair to say Cav doesn't live for training, but he has the ability to apply himself to the work because he knows that if he cuts corners he won't be able to do what he loves doing best, and that's winning. He lives for the thrill of the race. He's got a competitive streak written through him like the lettering in a stick of Blackpool rock. Put a number on his back and paint a finish line across the road and he is transformed into a different man, like the Incredible Hulk. His ability to see several moves ahead in the hectic heat of a Tour de France sprint finish is a form of genius.

We may be chalk and cheese off the bike but I identify with that killer instinct and desire to get over the line first. I wasn't blessed with Cav's turn of speed (although I was no slouch) but, like him, I was motivated by the intensity of competition, not the slog of training.

I first saw the white heat of his desire when we rode the Madison together at the World Championships in Los Angeles in 2005. We made an odd pair. I was 32 and had just won my first rainbow jersey in the team pursuit after almost ten years of trying. He was 19 and in a hurry to make his mark on the world. There was me: tall, rangy and so laid-back I was almost comatose half the time. And there was him: short, stocky and bristling with electricity.

It didn't strike me at the time, but now I look back I can appreciate how different our respective experiences were at 19. I had been on the longlist for a place at the Barcelona Olympics but my hopes and expectations were relatively modest. I wanted to become an Olympian and I wanted to be the best I could be, but I wasn't setting out on a journey I thought would lead me to world and Olympic medals. I had dreams, of course, but not expectations.

Even when Boardman won in Barcelona, I didn't feel like he'd shoulder-barged down a door for me to follow him through. I thought of Boardman as an exception to the rule – a freak of nature, if you like – a supremely gifted athlete who just happened to have been born in the Wirral, rather than a product of a British sporting system.

A couple of generations later, Cav stormed round the track on his World Championship debut like he owned the place. He'd only been on the scene five minutes but he expected to win. He felt that becoming a champion was his destiny.

It's too easy to say Cav is a freak of nature, because I don't think he is. A force of nature, yes, but that's a different thing. He's obviously talented and incredibly driven and he's got the full menu of attributes a champion needs. He's demanding of himself and others, he's self-analytical as well as self-critical, and he's constantly questioning things.

Cav's personality makes him a winner and you could say that he'd have made it regardless of the era he was born in. When British Cycling's sports scientists first hooked him up to the static bike in the lab to see what he was made of, they didn't think he ticked the boxes required. Later, when he tested in the laboratory with the German T-Mobile team, they were similarly unimpressed. A few years after that, he found out that if they'd gone purely on the test results, they wouldn't have hired him for their women's team, let alone predict he'd turn out to be the fastest sprinter in the world.

And yet, if you put him in a race, he performs time and time again. I get the feeling that had he been born in the sixties or seventies, he'd have taken himself off to France or Belgium, learned the language and thrown himself into the world of professional cycling and become a champion through sheer force of will.

While Cav is clearly one of the greatest riders of Britain's golden generation, you can't really call him a once-in-a-lifetime talent, because he isn't the exception to the rule, he's one of the best of a brilliant crop. So many riders – men and women, road riders and track stars – have emerged from the same system that nurtured him.

When I started out, there was no system, just a loose collection of individuals striving to do their best against odds heavily stacked against them. A few from each generation had a decent stab at it, but there were many times that number who had enough talent but who drifted away without making the most of it because of the obstacles in their way. There were a lot of obstacles. The lack of money and facilities, for a start. After years of banging their heads against a closed door, many riders gave up and got a proper job.

So, as we clock up the miles together, I begin to ponder a question. What is it that makes Cav a champion? What makes anyone a champion?

After more than twenty years in the sport, I think I can offer an answer.

It takes talent, commitment and opportunity.

Talent. That's self-explanatory. If a rider hasn't got the basic raw materials then it's going to be a struggle.

Commitment is even more important. Many a talented rider has failed to reach their full potential because they've been unable to dedicate themselves to the task. Cycling is a tough old sport and there are a lot of distractions.

But even more important is opportunity. A talented, committed rider will eventually run into a brick wall unless there are opportunities ahead of him or her.

Back in the 1980s, there were relatively few opportunities for British cyclists, certainly compared to today. I was fortunate because I had more than most. My dad had been a track cyclist so he encouraged me and because we lived only a few miles from a velodrome in Portsmouth, I had the chance to race frequently and learn quickly.

The revolution we've witnessed in the past decade or so hasn't come about by accident. Nor did they slip something into the water in the 1980s that has led to a generation of kids more gifted at cycling than their predecessors. Cycling's growth in Great Britain has been down to a fantastic increase in opportunities. A British kid coming into cycling in his or her early teens can now see a clear pathway to the Olympic Games. The opportunities are there. It's now a question of having the talent and commitment.

*

Back on the windswept roads of the Isle of Man, Cav and I have got about an hour to go, so I go to the front and pace him the rest of the way home. You thought I was riding a push bike with him, didn't you? No, my training days are over. I never loved training enough to carry on doing it now I'm retired. I love the craic and the coffee stops, but I don't miss the pain.

I'm on a scooter, going just as far and just as fast but for no physical effort. For the past few seasons, I've worked for Cav when he's on the Isle of Man or at his home in Essex, where he lives with Peta and the kids, helping to make his training as efficient and beneficial as possible.

It's the little things that make the difference. I'm his motorized *domestique*. On the scooter I can carry a couple of spare wheels so he doesn't waste time if he has a puncture. I carry water bottles and a bit of food. There's warm clothing under the seat and a spare set of kit in case we stop at a café. That's one of my dad's old bits of advice. Whenever I finished a race on the track at Portsmouth he'd badger me to change into some dry kit. 'You'll catch a cold sitting around in soggy clothes.'

It's not any old scooter either. It's a world champion's scooter. I pimped it up by painting the rainbow bands on it as soon as I got back from Copenhagen.

As we tear through the lanes, with me on the scooter and Cav in the slipstream, we can replicate the effects of racing too. He can train at a higher pace, pushing a bigger gear, simulating the effort of being in the bunch. It's better quality work than battering away on his own. When we get back to his place, Cav can go straight in and get showered and changed while I give his bike a wash down and a check over so it's in mint condition for tomorrow. These may sound like only small savings in time and effort, but they all add up. He's a professional bike rider; all he needs to worry about is his training.

I'm not his coach. It's not down to me to make sure he does the work. But I know his training plans and I'm there to support him, nudge him out of the door if he needs it, keep him company, motivate him a little when he's struggling; help in any way I can.

You'd have to ask him how much he feels it helps, but I'd have loved this when I was training at my peak. In a way, it shows how far cycling in Britain has come. I didn't know it back then, but I was in on the ground floor just as something incredible was about to take off.

This is the story of my sport's revolution, the way I saw it.

# 2

# Giz a Go

I can picture my dad sitting on the sofa dressed as Herman Munster, his face covered in make-up, hair brushed forward and a scar painted on his forehead. He's sitting there, cracking the nuts left over from Christmas in his huge hands, growing more impatient by the minute. It's Saturday, 20 January 1973 and John Ernest and Mary Elizabeth are late for a fancy-dress party. Mary, who will be my mum in a matter of hours, is eight months and four weeks pregnant and dressed as Minnie Mouse.

'So, are we going to this party or not?' Dad asks, between mouthfuls of walnut.

Mum was pretty certain her contractions had started, and decided a party might not be the wisest way to spend the evening, so Dad dropped her off at a maternity home in Emsworth, which is near Havant in the south of England, and went on to the party, just to 'let them know he wasn't coming'. Typical Dad-logic, that. He ended up staying all evening. That was how it was back then. Dads weren't all that welcome at the birth of their own kids in the seventies; they just got in the way and said the wrong thing. The closest they usually got was the corridor outside the ward, hanging around with a celebratory cigar ready to be lit.

At three o'clock in the morning on Sunday, 21 January 1973, I was born. Robert John Hayles. Son of Herman Munster and Minnie Mouse. Aquarius. The water carrier. How apt.

There's quite an age gap between my mum and dad. He was born in 1932 and was 40 when I arrived. Mum is eighteen years younger. My dad had been married before and had two children with his first wife before they got divorced. He was born and brought up on the south coast, did his national service and trained as a fitter and turner for the shipbuilders Vosper Thornycroft. Later he moved into painting and decorating and, by the time I was born, he was working as a chimney sweep. He could do anything that required a precise hand, some elbow grease and a perfectionist's eye.

Not long after the war, he started cycling at the Alexandra Park track in Portsmouth, a big D-shaped track that was exposed to the wind that whipped in off the Solent. He was a sprinter – big and powerful and good enough to win southern area titles. These were the days of Reg Harris, one of Britain's earliest cycling heroes, and the track scene was booming, so Dad could race three or four times a week, either at Portsmouth or by travelling to Brighton or Herne Hill.

He was, and still is, a big unit – 6 feet 3 inches tall and almost 17 stone back then. He wasn't built to head off for hundred-mile rides in the countryside; in fact, he never even owned a road bike. The furthest he'd ride in one go was down to the track in Pompey. He'd attach his best racing wheels to little stands that clipped on to the forks of his bike so that he didn't damage his expensive, lightweight silk tyres on the way.

It wasn't the cycling that fired him; it was the racing, the thrill of speed and competition. He believed track sprinting was about brute force, so he trained in the gym, lifting weights with his legs to build up the strength he needed to get his big frame up to sprinting speed. At the time, that was quite revolutionary thinking. It worked too. He won a lot of races and he was in the mix for a place in the Great Britain team for the 1952 Olympic Games in Helsinki, but didn't make the cut.

Track sprinting was a dangerous game back then; it still is, although they've cleaned it up in recent years. It used to be almost a contact sport – if strength wasn't enough, cut-throat tactics and ruthlessness often made the difference. Crashes were part of the game and, although Dad didn't fall often, when he did, he came off worse. When you're his size and you hit the deck, you can do some serious damage. Time and again he fractured his collarbone. Another time he broke his arm after instinctively putting his hand out to cushion his fall. Each crash meant a lay-off from work, so in the end enough was enough.

After he stopped bike racing, he kept going to the gym. A group of professional wrestlers also trained there and he got friendly with them. One day, someone asked him if he fancied having a go at wrestling. There was a gap on the heavyweight bill at a local bout and, they said, with a bit of coaching from the others, he could fill in.

It was the mid-fifties and the wrestling scene was about to take off. Promoters were putting on wrestling shows at town halls and community centres up and down the country. Even now, when I'm on a trip with Dad, he'll point out some building or another, no matter where we are, and say, 'I've wrestled there.'

Soon British wrestlers were in demand all over the world. Dad's first international job was in Poland in the early sixties. They asked him what his stage name was and he told them he didn't have one. He wrestled as plain old Johnny Hayles back at home. So the Poles came up with a name. There was a famous American wrestler at the time called John 'Killer' Kowalski so, perhaps because they thought it might draw in the crowds, they gave Dad the same name.

Dad winced a bit when he saw his new nickname on the posters because, although he was a big, imposing man, he was the stereotypical gentle giant. Even when he worked on the nightclub doors in Portsmouth and things got a bit hairy, it was usually enough for him to just stand up to his full height and wait for the troublemakers to back down. The only punch he threw was when he was working as a chimney sweep. He turned up to clean someone's chimney and a huge Alsatian came rushing out of the front door, bounded down the path and jumped the garden gate, snarling and with its teeth bared. Instinctively, Dad drew back his arm and punched the dog plumb on the nose, sending it whimpering under the hedge. But even then he probably wouldn't have punched it if he'd had a moment to think.

Dad came to be a fixture on the wrestling circuit in the sixties and seventies. He loved the camaraderie of their travelling circus: the wrestlers would travel together, grapple together and look out for each other. The bouts were not fixed, exactly, but they were loosely scripted. The aim was to put on a good show for the crowd and make sure the good guys, or the crowd favourites, won.

In the seventies, ITV's *World of Sport* programme made the wrestlers Saturday afternoon legends, showing the action from the Assembly Rooms, Derby, or York Hall in Bethnal Green or wherever it was. Big Daddy, Giant Haystacks, Mick McManus and Kendo Nagasaki were household names, and Dad grappled with them all. The arenas were packed with rows of fans and clouds of cigarette smoke. For some reason, wrestling was incredibly popular with pensioners, particularly women, and these old dears used to get quite involved. They had their favourites and they loved to dish out the abuse too. Dad once saw one of the grannies jump out of her seat and wedge her knitting needle in the back of a wrestler's leg because she didn't like what was going on.

Even though some of the moves were rehearsed and the outcome was scripted, it was still a hard sport. A lot of skill, timing and discipline went in to making it look convincing, and some of the slaps, holds and smackdowns could hurt. Dislocated fingers were an occupational hazard. During a hold in one bout, the referee noticed Dad's fingers were sticking out at a funny angle so he grabbed his hand, crunched them all back into their sockets and told him to get on with it. The show had to go on.

They toured around like a theatre company and would often spend weeks, sometimes months, abroad. He wrestled in more than 150 countries. Just about the only place he didn't go to was America, because they wanted the wrestlers to commit to a six-month contract and he didn't want to be away that long. The only country he didn't like was Japan; their wrestlers used to try to hurt the foreigners.

At the peak of his wrestling career Dad was making a very good living, filling in the gaps sweeping chimneys. He was also signed up by an entertainment agency called Uglies, as quite a few of the wrestlers were. They had a lot of big, burly blokes on their books and Dad got a fair bit of work that way. He was an extra in *The French Lieutenant's Woman*, and at some point was in an advert for Kit-Kat, where he spun a little guy above his head, put him down while he ate his chocolate bar, then picked him up and started spinning him round again. Another of Dad's claims to fame: his spare wrestling boots were worn by Darth Vader in *Star Wars*. They were filming at Elstree Studios and didn't have boots big enough for Dave Prowse, the actor in the

Darth Vader costume. The producers rang Uglies and then sent someone to pick up Dad's spare boots. If only we had those boots now. They'd be worth a fortune.

Mum and Dad were introduced to each other by Pat Roach, who wrestled with my dad and later became famous for his role as Bomber Busbridge in the TV show *Auf Wiedersehen, Pet*. Pat and my dad were great friends and Pat knew my mum because they were both from Birmingham. Dad must have charmed her because they got together, got married and she moved down to Horndean, just outside Portsmouth.

With Dad's wrestling career going so well, he was away from home a lot of the time. The phone would ring and he'd put down the receiver and say, 'Mary, they want me to go to India in the morning,' and he'd be away for a couple of months. When I was a toddler, he was away so often I didn't know who he was. I used to cry when he came home. When I was about three, I remember him coming through the front door after weeks away, and I hid behind my mum in the hallway and said, 'Who's that strange man?' I've got a poster at home from his wrestling days. He's top of the bill in Fiji. The date on it is 20 January 1977. The day before my fourth birthday.

So, for much of the time, it was just me and Mum at home when I was young. Mum says I was a joy until the fairies came one night and replaced her little angel with a right monster. I was expelled from playschool. Mum came to pick me up one afternoon and they told her not to bring me back because I'd walloped another kid.

I wasn't a bad child, I was just a handful; a right little sod. I couldn't concentrate on anything and hated being stuck indoors. The only thing that interested me was Lego. Plonk me in the corner of the room with a pile of Lego and I was happy. As I grew older, I got more mischievous: I answered back and I was cheeky. Mum wore out the phrase, 'Wait till your dad gets home.' Often, by the time Dad actually did get home, whatever it was I'd done wrong had all been forgotten, although I do remember making Mum cry once and Dad chased me all the way up the stairs and into my bedroom. I scurried under the duvet but he grabbed me by the ankles and held me upside down with one hand while he gave me a good hiding with the other.

At infant school I spent almost as much time in the headmistress's office as I did the classroom. When I moved up to junior school, I'd frequently get the head's Dunlop Green Flash slipper round my backside. On the last day of my first year at junior school, we were given our classes for the following year and I found out I was moving up to the dreaded Mr Peake's class. When I think of him now, I see a wizened old guy like Mr Burns from *The Simpsons*. Knowing I was going to be in his class ruined my summer. I had a horrible feeling of butterflies in my stomach throughout the holidays, because I knew he wouldn't like me and I wouldn't like him.

The kids at school all knew my dad was a wrestler, which helped if I ever got into any scrapes.

'I'm going to get my dad on to you,' someone would say.

'Well, I'm going to get my dad on to your dad,' I'd reply.

That usually settled it.

I used to dream about getting my dad to sort out Mr Peake.

We lived on the Cowplain estate in Horndean. My parents' house is on the brow of a hill and if I stood on tiptoes, I could see over the bungalows on the opposite side of the road and for miles around. Behind our garden fence was an area of rough grassland that backed on to Waterlooville golf course. The local kids would all play there and everyone knew it as 'the humps and bumps'.

I was about to turn ten when the film *E. T.* came out and the BMX craze gripped every schoolboy in Britain. One by one, as their birthdays came round, my friends got a BMX. My parents made me wait for what seemed like an unkind eternity before they bought me one. In the meantime, I got the nickname 'Giz a go' because I used to stand on the side of the humps and bumps waiting for one of my friends to let me have a go on their BMX.

Eventually, I got a second-hand Raleigh Burner with a Grifter back wheel. Any child of the eighties will feel my pain here – it's like getting a Porsche with Ford Escort alloys – but I was just happy to have a bike. We'd race round the humps and bumps, hold longest-skid competitions, see who could wheelie the furthest, or dig jumps and see who could get the most 'air'. I didn't even need anyone to compete against. If it was just me out there at twilight trying to beat my personal best, I'd be happy.

When I got to secondary school, my behaviour calmed down a lot, although I was hopeless in the lessons. 'Sportsman hated school' is hardly a surprising revelation. I'm sure a lot of kids feel the same way I did. I just couldn't see how any of it was relevant to me. Most of the academic lessons went over my head and I was too laid-back, or lazy, to take it in. I enjoyed wood-work, metalwork and technical drawing, but that was about it. I wasn't even any good at PE. I tried cross-country running, and wasn't any good at that either, and I was hopeless at anything involving a ball because I had no hand-to-eye coordination. But I had at least worked out that being disruptive and getting into trouble was an even bigger waste of my day than sitting tight and waiting for home time.

As a teenager, I became more aware that my dad was an older dad, and his values were old-fashioned. Dad was never cold or distant, but he was quite reserved, proper and upright, at a time when, as a teenager, fashion became much more important and what you wore defined who you were. Unfortunately for me, I was the son of an Edwardian gentleman.

Dad would take me shopping for my clothes, and I used to dread it because there could be no arguing with him. He'd pick out the most sensible of sensible shoes: black with clunky last-you-a-lifetime soles. My school bag was from a military outlet shop, green and canvas. It was all good utilitarian stuff. When I started cycling to school, he bought me some rubber galoshes and huge wellies like it was the 1920s.

The thing was, he couldn't see it through my eyes. He didn't want me to get picked on; he genuinely thought he was buying me the best gear – which he probably was – it just wasn't the *right* gear. A bit like the Raleigh Burner with the Grifter back wheel; he just couldn't see the problem.

'There you go, son, that'll do the job.'

One day he took me to get a school coat, and we got a girl's coat by mistake. I didn't realize until I noticed a girl in my year had the exact same coat. I ripped out the label, which had a bust size on it, and then I just hoped no one would notice, because otherwise I'd be known as Girl's Coat for the rest of the year. If you didn't have the right gear, you got singled out. I'd never been picked on before, so it was strange to take so much ribbing because of my gear. Everyone else was wearing Farah slacks and Lacoste pullovers.

It wasn't until I saw Feargal Sharkey on *Top of the Pops* that I managed to give myself a bit of a makeover. It was coming up to Christmas 1985, and I remember deciding that I wanted to look like Feargal Sharkey, so I went shopping with Mum and got kitted out.

Dad thought there were ways you did things. I was getting ready to go to the doctor's one day and he was horrified because

I was wearing jeans. He said, 'Put some proper trousers on, Rob, you're going to see a professional person.'

When I was 14 I was standing at the kitchen sink doing the washing-up, which was a rare enough occurrence that I remember it vividly. I was wearing ripped jeans, as every teenager did in the late eighties. That cracked my dad. He just couldn't get his head around someone wearing jeans that were deliberately torn. You either patched them up or put them in the bin. At a push you might do the garden in them. Anyway, he got his hand in the hole and ripped the lower half of the leg clean off.

Even now, if I visit home with a day or two's stubble on my face, he can't resist saying, 'Are you growing a beard there?' He just can't help it. Mind you, Mum's always reminding me: 'Make sure you iron your shirt before you go on the telly.'

It's the little things that make you the person you turn out to be. I've inherited my perfectionist's streak from my dad. He used to bring stuff home from his wrestling trips. Airfix models were a favourite when I was eight or nine. We'd make them together over a number of days, taking turns to do a bit. We had a model tank that we were working on. He was so painstakingly precise, I was practically hopping up and down with impatience. He was using a pinhead to dab just the right amount of glue on and leaving each piece to stick properly before doing the next bit. I just wanted this thing finished, so I got up early the next morning and whacked it together any old how. There were big, ugly globs of glue all over the place, but it was finished.

'You didn't want it done properly, then?' he said when he saw it.

But a few years later, after hyperactive Rob had been replaced by laid-back Rob, I started to understand where he was coming from. At school, we were given a project to make a balloon-powered boat. The brief was simple – the boat which completed the most lengths of a water trough would win.

I sat down and designed a catamaran, then went to the art and craft shop to buy balsa wood. I followed my blueprints and put my craft together with the skill and expertise that would have got me a job as a shipbuilder at Vosper Thornycroft. It was a proper catamaran with a flat top. I carefully fixed the balloon in place and used a fine sandpaper to make sure all the joins and surfaces were smooth before testing it in the bath. She sailed well and I was feeling pretty confident.

On the day of the competition, my boat did a length and a half of the trough and looked like winning. The only boat that beat mine was a crude thing made from half a washing-up-liquid bottle, a pen and a balloon. I watched as this thing did length after length before the balloon went flat.

What annoyed me was that no one commented on the thought, the engineering skill and the effort that had gone into my craft. The prize went to something that had taken a couple of minutes to knock up.

Perhaps I learned a valuable lesson that day.

Sometime in the early eighties, Dad began to help run the cycling sessions at Portsmouth track with a man called Jack Smith. I'd never seen Dad race but there was something about cycling that grabbed hold of me. It was the only sport I was any good at. I'd go to the track to watch the races and would be itching to have a go. The problem was, back then, you couldn't easily get track bikes in kids' sizes. I would have to wait until I could swing my leg over the crossbar and reach the pedals. It felt like an agonizing wait. Every now and then I'd get on a bike with its saddle dropped right down and see how many inches I still had to grow.

Alexandra Park was not, in all honesty, a glamorous place, but it seemed so cool. The D-shaped track looked almost unfinished. Unlike a modern velodrome, which has curved banking, Alexandra Park is half athletics track, half curved banking. Only two of the corners are banked, and even they are very shallow. The back straight is flat.

Portsmouth's big race meeting was held at Easter, and for me it was like the FA Cup final. The cut and thrust of the races, the shouts, crashes and near-misses held my attention like nothing else. When it was all over I climbed over the barriers and tentatively stepped on to the tarmac, feeling almost as if I shouldn't dare set foot on the hallowed ground.

Eventually, after what seemed like an age, when I was 12, I found I could ride one of the smallest adult bikes they had at Portsmouth, and I was away. I wasn't an instant success or anything – no one looked at me and said, 'Hey, lads, we've got one here' – but I could hold my own. And I loved it. Cycling was the first thing I felt I was any good at. Even though Dad didn't ever push me, I know he was glad I got into it so deeply. I quickly became a regular at the Portsmouth and Southampton track leagues, and I got my own bike, second-hand, of course.

There is something about track cycling that pulls children in. It's racing at its purest. You know how kids race each other to the end of the street, or round the garden; how the instinct to try to be first is just in them? That was what track league was like. It was hectic. It was fast. It was exhilarating and it was dangerous. There were different types of races – long bunch races that continued to push you deeper than you'd gone before, with a dozen or so riders all banging elbows, jousting for position and using the banking to try to get a jump on everyone else. Or there were the sprint races, just me against another lad, winner takes all.

Although I had never seen Dad race, I gravitated towards

sprinting, as he had done. Track cycling wasn't trendy back then, it was something that got handed down from father to son. My grandad had raced, then my dad, now it was my turn. Almost all the riders I began racing with had got into cycling because of a parent or an uncle. There were very few 'first generation' bike riders who had discovered the sport on their own. It was like cycling was hidden behind a magic door and someone had to lend you the key to let you in.

Dad wasn't pushy but he was quietly supportive. Without his support I wouldn't have been able to travel to Portsmouth or Southampton, and I certainly wouldn't have been able to go further afield as I got older. Dad's willingness to give up his evenings and weekends gave me my opportunity. We spent hours in his van, travelling to training sessions or races. He didn't coach from the sidelines like some of the dads. He had enough racing experience of his own to tell me where I was going wrong, but he almost never did. He just wanted me to have fun. 'Just go and enjoy it, son.'

I crashed heavily once and bashed myself up badly, spending two nights in hospital with concussion. When we got home he said to Mum, 'Right, that's it, he's not racing again. He's going to end up getting seriously hurt.'

Mum replied, 'You can't say that to him. He's got to make that decision for himself.'

Dad tried to influence me in more subtle ways, though. If I was going to be a track sprinter, I needed to be big, like him. He was always trying to feed me up. He was self-employed and would be finished from his rounds as a chimney sweep before Mum left work – she was a secretary at Gales, the brewery in Horndean – so he'd cook dinner. He'd pile up the pasta, chicken and tomato sauce and say, 'Come on, son, have some more, you need to bulk up.'

We trained together at the gym, pumping the iron with my legs, and he had a real downer on me joining a road racing club because he thought their long Sunday rides – 60 or 70 miles into the Hampshire countryside – would kill my speed. They used to hold centre-of-excellence training camps along the coast at Bournemouth during the school holidays, but Dad didn't like me going because they did too many road miles which, he thought, were the enemy for a sprinter.

Even then, in those early days, I had a bit of a love-hate relationship with cycling. I'd be stuck at school all day, barely paying attention to what was going on, gazing out of the window, desperate to be on my bike and praying it wouldn't rain. If it rained, track league would be off and we'd have to train indoors on the static bikes.

And yet, on the way to the track league, I'd be in the passenger seat in Dad's van, head lolling against my shoulder, half-asleep. I'd complain that I didn't want to ride, wasn't in the mood, but when we came over the hill and could see the whole of Portsmouth ahead of us, I'd wake up. My eyes would dart across the sky, checking for dark clouds, sensing the likelihood of rain and hoping that Alexandra Park would stay dry. Suddenly, the prospect of missing a night's racing would make my heart sink.

There was a six-month period when I stopped cycling altogether. I just began to drift away until something happened to reignite my passion. There was a professional circuit race in Portsmouth one evening and Dad managed to get some grandstand tickets. We sat right above the finish line and I can't remember anything except being impressed by the giant East German sprinter Olaf Ludwig, who had been Olympic road race champion in Seoul in 1988. It was as exhilarating as my first trip to see the racing at Alexandra Park. The speed, the aggression, the vibrant colours all sucked me back in. From then on I was hooked again.

In my teenage years, I was one of the strongest riders in the south of England, but I wasn't the top dog. There was always someone who was stronger than me. First it was Mark Armstrong, a very talented lad from the Isle of Wight, who slowly drifted away, perhaps because he had to travel across to the mainland every time he wanted to race. Then there was Andy Mummery, a big, strong rider who seemed to have the beating of me for a while. But racing against people who were better than me dragged me up.

I became more and more immersed in cycling, so schoolwork faded even further into the background. It even got to the stage where the school let me pull out of PE lessons if they were on the same day as track league. I don't think the teachers really understood what I meant when I said I needed to save my legs for cycling, but they tolerated it. Cycling wasn't a hit with the other kids either. It was a bit of an oddball pursuit.

One rainy day when I was about 15, we had to do PE indoors in the school gym. (It can't have been a track league day.) They put all the boys and girls together and we were sitting on benches waiting to be split into teams.

I could sense the girl sitting next to me was staring at me in that hyper-judgemental way that comes naturally to most teenage girls.

'Rob,' she said.

Here it comes.

'Do you shave your legs?'

I tried to explain that cyclists shaved their legs for a number of reasons – aerodynamics is one – but the main one being that it made it easier to have a massage after races. I knew it was no use, though. By lunchtime it was round the school that I was the weirdo who rode a push bike and shaved his legs.

I was starting to get recognized in a small way. I entered the National Track Championships at Leicester when I was still a schoolboy, but I broke my collarbone during one of my last training sessions before the championships. I was up on the banking with another sprinter called Brian Fudge. We were doing track stands, which is where you stop still and balance the bike by shifting your weight. It's a tactical ploy. The idea is to try to lure your opponent to the front so that you have the element of surprise and can launch your sprint from behind, where your opponent cannot easily see you. The only rule is that you're not allowed to roll backwards. I pulled my foot upwards and it came out of the toe straps, which should have held my foot tightly to the pedal, and I went over the handlebars, breaking my collarbone.

So I had to wait another year before I could ride the National Championships, but when I was 16, I won a silver medal in the sprint and a bronze medal in the time trial.

As the racing began to take over, my schoolwork was suffering even more. I read *Cycling Weekly* from cover to cover every week. 'If you spent half as much time reading your school books as you do that magazine . . .' Mum used to start to say, but realized before the sentence was over that it was futile. Dad tried a different tactic: 'You should pay more attention in French. You might ride the Tour de France one day.'

I had no idea what I was going to do with my life. There seemed absolutely no way I could make a living from cycling, not in Britain. It was an amateur sport. It was rarely on television – only the Tour de France made it on to our screens. I was one of the best young riders in the country – I was a regular in the national junior squad – but no one was going to pay me to ride a bike.

There was a vague thought in the back of my mind that I'd stay on at school to do A levels, but only because I couldn't think of anything else to do. I certainly didn't get as far as choosing which subjects I'd take. I wondered about physiotherapy because the only thing I'd been interested in during science lessons was how the muscles of the body worked.

While I waited for my GCSE results, and to prevent me staying in bed until lunchtime, Mum got me a summer job in the technical services department at Gales, the local brewery. I learned a bit about the dispense equipment they used in pubs, how the barrels of beer were kept at the right temperature and pressure. Most of the time was spent rolling beer kegs about.

When my exam results arrived, I opened the envelope and hoped for a split-second that F stood for French and E stood for English. But the collection of other Ds, Es and Fs could not be allocated to the other subjects. It didn't make promising reading. Suddenly, my only academic option was to do retakes at the local college. That didn't appeal too much, so I was happy when, at the end of the summer, Gales offered me a full-time job.

The secretaries in the office called me Mummy's Little Soldier. Mum gave me lunch money to start with, but I saved it all up and then went to Guildford and bought a Dolce & Gabbana suit in the sales, so there was no more money after that. One of the supervisors at Gales decided he didn't like me much, so he asked Mum to 'sort me out'. Mum's reply was brief: 'He's nothing to do with me between nine and five-thirty; he's your problem until he comes home!'

A few months later, when I turned 17, they booked me on an intensive two-week driving course, so I passed my driving test a fortnight after my birthday. That meant I could drive one of the vans and make myself a bit more useful. I'd travel to pubs delivering things or doing minor repairs. Although I was surrounded by beer all day, I wasn't a big drinker. My vice back then was baked goods. I'd swing by the bakery and load up the passenger seat of the van with doughnuts, pasties and sausage rolls – all buttery and flaky fuel for the big sprint engine I was developing.

When athletes look back on their teenage years, or their twenties, they often talk about the sacrifices they made to get to the top of their sport. I often think, 'Sacrifices? What sacrifices?'

I loved what I was doing. I raced as often as I could, but I went out with friends when I wanted, too – I just didn't do it every Friday and Saturday night like they did. They'd wake up with the same hangover they'd had the previous weekend, while for me that would happen only once or twice a month. But if I was going out, I'd go for it and have a whale of a time.

In the early hours of one Sunday morning, when I was almost 17, I woke Dad up because I was pissed out of my head, jabbing the key repeatedly at one of the half-dozen keyholes I could see dancing in front of me. When he came down in his dressing gown and opened the door, he was not amused, particularly as I was supposed to be racing the next morning.

He woke me up earlier and more noisily than was necessary to make his point, but I hauled myself out of bed, stinking of booze and, with a pulsing headache, slumped beside him in the van.

We went to a race at the airfield at HMS *Daedalus* near Gosport. It was always hard racing there. The airfield was completely open and the wind would cut you in half. The bunch of cyclists would be in a long line, all bent double over their bikes and grovelling for shelter behind the rider in front of them.

Despite the thumping head and washing-machine stomach, I returned to the van with an envelope of prize money. I knew Dad was dying to say something about my boozy, late night, but he couldn't. I'd won!

# 3

# The Need for Speed

I'm not sure you could even describe the way I trained as actual 'training': I just rode everywhere flat out. There was no subtlety or sophistication to it. Whenever I rode my bike, I wanted to go faster than the last time; it was as simple as that. I was going to be a track sprinter, so the clock was my only friend or foe, and speed was all that mattered.

I devised a number of circuits near my house and I'd race against myself. They were all short circuits – never more than ten miles or so – and I knew my personal best time for each one. I would role play, pretending I was riding in the Tour de France with the commentary running in my head.

*'And here comes Hayles . . . He's leading at the first checkpoint . . . Can he hold on to the finish?'*

After setting off at full pace, within a mile my calves would be stinging and my lungs rasping, but I was never frightened of hurting myself. What annoyed me was when I felt as if something was holding me back. I always wanted more. If I felt I wasn't pushing hard enough, I'd get so frustrated that I'd lift my handlebars and thump the front wheel on the road, as if trying to jump-start an engine that was already running.

The clock would make or break my day. If I recorded a good time, I was happy. If not, I wanted to go out and do the circuit again. It was another symptom of my love-hate relationship with cycling. It didn't matter if I'd been slowed by a raging headwind, I didn't take that into account, because as far as I was concerned, the clock didn't lie.

Looking back, it's easy to conclude that I didn't really know what I was doing. I was making it up as I went along. My theory was that if I pushed harder, eventually I'd get faster. That seemed to make perfect sense to me.

When I went for longer rides, I'd often come to grief miles from home. I'd ride off with one small bottle of water, no food, no money (and there was no mobile phone in those days, of course). I'd set out hard, usually riding up the A3 for an hour and a half, before turning round and heading for home again. My rides were not leisurely excursions into the lanes and hills, they were brutal battles against myself. How often did I fly along on the outward leg, only to find I'd been given an invisible helping hand by a tailwind? I'd turn and head for home, against the wind, and every turn of the pedals would hack another huge chunk out of my dwindling energy reserves.

So many times I'd be crawling towards home, counting down the miles and feeling sorry for myself. Every cyclist knows the horrible, desperate feeling when there's nothing left. Your legs feel as if they're no longer attached to your body, and your stomach is so empty you feel sick.

As I struggled on, my mind would drift. I'd begin to fantasize about getting home and stuffing my face with huge sandwiches. I can remember once being overtaken on a gentle hill by a middle-aged woman on a bicycle with a full shopping basket. Two things crossed my mind. One: 'Perhaps I could lean over and pinch myself something to eat?'; and, two: 'She doesn't realize she's just passed a member of the Great Britain junior cycling squad.'

The last ten miles would always be haunted by thoughts of the hill leading up to my house. I'd crawl towards Horndean thinking, 'I'm never going to get up it this time,' but I always did.

Then I'd get home, chuck my bike in the garage, raid the kitchen and lie in a steaming, hot bath, eating digestive biscuits until the shakes went away.

I didn't learn. The next time I went out, the same thing would happen. I just wasn't a natural trainer. Pacing my effort was not my strong point and I didn't see the value of long, steady rides. It was all about the need for speed.

But put me in a bike race and I was transformed. There was a point to it. Whenever I pinned a number on my back my attitude was: *'This is mine.* How dare anyone try to take it from me?' I raced with a controlled anger and aggression that just seemed to rise up in me.

When I was 16 I was invited to train with the Great Britain junior sprint squad for the first time. It was during the winter time, so the weekend sessions were held at Calshot track near Southampton, which was almost my second home. Back then, in 1989, Calshot was the only indoor velodrome in Britain. Now we have Manchester, Newport, London and Glasgow, with another on the way in Derby.

Calshot was the only place where track cyclists could train or race when the weather was bad, and there it was, right on the south coast, out of easy reach for more than half the country. See what I mean about opportunity? I lived forty minutes away and had another velodrome that was practically on my doorstep.

Calshot's track is only 143 metres round, about as short as a track can be, and it was like racing inside a washing-machine drum. In those days the wooden track had a gritty, grippy coating on it that made it easy to ride up on the steeper parts of the banking, but also meant it was incredibly painful if you crashed. Fall and you skidded over the coarse, sandpaper-like surface until you were red raw. Mind you, the fear of crashing helped improve my bike-handling skills. I'd do anything to get out of trouble and avoid a stack.

The track was built inside a big, draughty hangar, so it was always freezing cold in winter. As the cyclists raced and generated heat, the warm breath from their lungs ballooning into the icy air, condensation collected on the ceiling and dripped on to the floor in the track centre, making it treacherous to walk on and impossible to ride a bike on. So between turns on the track, we had no option but to sit in the centre, each rider tucked into a sleeping bag, trying to keep warm until it was your go again.

When winter gave way to spring, the national squad's training camps switched to Leicester's Saffron Lane velodrome. Compared to Calshot, Saffron Lane was like Wembley Stadium to us. It had hosted the World Championships in 1970 – when Hugh Porter won the professional 5,000-metre individual pursuit – and again in 1982, and the National Championships were held there every summer. The velodrome was relatively new – built in the late sixties – and had two grandstands that could seat three thousand spectators between them, but by the late eighties it was already beginning to wear badly. The main problem was that the wooden track was exposed to the elements.

As soon as there was a hint of drizzle in the air, it was too dangerous to ride on. The wooden boards would become incredibly slick and slippery, like untreated decking in your garden. Race meetings and training sessions would often be cancelled or shortened because of the weather. Too often Dad would drive me up to Leicester in the van for a weekend's training with the squad and I wouldn't even get on the track because of rain. Instead, we'd do a couple of indoor sessions on the static bikes or rollers, or go for a ride on the road, none of which was doing our track craft much good. So many hours were wasted because of the weather – time we could have spent racing, honing our tactics and building our strength was lost. Can you imagine the best young cricketers in England getting together for a long weekend's training only to find there weren't any bats or balls to play with? It wasn't the British Cycling Federation's fault – Leicester was the best facility we had – but it was far from ideal if the goal was to try to compete with the rest of the world.

Even if we didn't get to ride on the track, I loved those weekends away. We'd stay in dormitories, ride our bikes on the road and eat in the canteen. Full English for breakfast, sausage and mash for tea followed by jam roly-poly; all proper school-dinner-style grub, with not a nutritionist or sports scientist in sight to monitor our intake or advise us what to choose.

Dad would often come up to stay in Leicester for the weekends too. My cycling took up almost as much of his time as it did mine, but I never heard him complain. It wasn't as if he was putting me on to a career path with a potential pot of gold waiting for me on the finish line, but he encouraged me quietly. Cycling's profile was at an all-time high in Britain in the late eighties, but it was still a minority sport. The Tour de France was shown on the telly in July, but there was more darts, snooker or wrestling than cycling on the box. Even crown green bowling got more airtime. And if road cycling was a minority sport, track cycling was practically a backwater. But Dad supported me because I was good at cycling and because I enjoyed it, not because he necessarily thought there was a future in it.

On the way back from those weekends in Leicester, I'd be physically exhausted but mentally alert and wide awake, my mind replaying little moments that had gone well and others I could learn from. Sometimes on the drive down the M1, Dad would pull over at the services, and we'd swap seats, even though I didn't have a driving licence at the time. I'd start the engine and he'd do the gears as I accelerated gently up to speed – 'Steady away, son, don't let the needle go over 3,000 revs' – then I'd pull off the slip road and on to the motorway and drive for a bit so Dad could get some rest. When I told Mum about that, she went absolutely spare at him.

The British Cycling Federation, as British Cycling was known back then, was a pretty threadbare organization. It was the governing body for a sport that struggled to attract major sponsors. There was hardly any money about. Cycling's benefactors were people who had an ingrained love of the sport and had made a success in business. They sponsored teams to support the riders, without expecting a penny's return on their investment.

The Federation had only one full-time coach who earned a salary: Doug Dailey. Everyone else was a volunteer, giving up his or her time for nothing more than a love of the sport and some expenses money.

To call Doug Dailey a mere coach is to do him a great disservice. He is one of British cycling's unsung heroes. For more than thirty years he served generation after generation of young bike riders, before he retired after the London Olympics. Any British rider representing his or her country over the past three decades has had their movements planned and plotted by Doug. He spent almost twenty years as British Cycling's logistics guru and got to know every airport's three-letter code and every hotel chain's good and bad points. He's spent hours negotiating with airlines over excess baggage rates, planning training camps and racing trips down to the last detail. I wonder how many riders appreciated the fact that, on important trips, Doug had travelled ahead of them to ensure the British riders were allocated rooms on the quietest side of the hotel, away from the main road or lift shaft?

Of course, as British Cycling benefited from a big increase in funding in the late nineties, Doug's job got slightly easier, but back in the late eighties, Doug did absolutely everything. For the riders, whether senior or junior, he *was* the British Cycling Federation.

He typed the letters telling riders they'd been picked to race for Britain. He'd collect some of them from their homes and drop them off again after a trip abroad. He booked the flights and accommodation – bear in mind it was not easy to plan a week behind the Iron Curtain in the days before the internet – and he drove the minibus. He was our mentor, masseur and, if there was no one else, sometimes even our mechanic too. And he did it all on a shoestring budget, not that I appreciated how hard that must have been at the time. We didn't feel deprived because there was nothing else to compare it to. We didn't know any different.

Sometime in the summer of 1989, a weekend's training at Leicester was drawing to a close. It was our last session on the track and Alan Sturgess, a former Great Britain international who was national junior coach, told us to do a ten-lap race with attacks all the way. He wasn't interested in a cagey, tactical battle, and he didn't care who crossed the finish line first, he just wanted to see all-out aggression. He wanted us to attack each other over and over again until we were on our knees, no holding back. This was music to my ears.

Alan was one of the coaches we perhaps looked up to a little more than some of the others because he had a prodigiously talented son, Colin. Colin was only 20 but was already a professional and, later that summer, he would win the professional world individual pursuit title in Lyon, just as Hugh Porter and Tony Doyle had done before him. Everyone knew what a great rider Colin was and we wondered if a bit of the Sturgess magic might rub off on us if we were coached by his dad.

Alan was pretty old school, even for the late eighties. To him, cycling was simple. There was no mystery to it: to go faster, you pedalled harder, which was a philosophy that chimed with me at the time. So, when Alan told us to give it some welly, I knew what he meant.

We started riding round at a decent pace, with Alan yelling at us to attack, attack, attack. The other riders would lift the pace, hit the front for half a lap of the track and then swing up the banking, their effort spent. I suspected Alan was getting frustrated because he wanted to see us give everything until the tank was empty.

With about five laps to go, I rode to the front of the group, wound the pace up and up so that no one could get level with me, let alone go past, and I held the speed high all the way to the finish line. One by one, the other riders dropped away, until no one was able to challenge me in the sprint finish.

Alan didn't say much to me, as I slumped, gasping for air on the grass in the track centre, just a brief 'well done', but before we left Leicester later that afternoon, I was handed an envelope. When I got back to Dad's van, I opened it. The letter inside informed me I'd been selected to race for Great Britain at a Junior Five Nations meeting in Brno. I had to ask Dad where Brno was. (It was in Czechoslovakia and, surprisingly, Dad hadn't wrestled there.) I was buzzing all the way home but Dad was typically reserved. 'Just see how you get on, son. You can only do your best.'

*

Brno was an eye-opener. Going to Eastern Europe then, before the Berlin Wall came down, felt a bit like travelling back in time, which made the whole trip an adventure. It was the first time I felt like cycling was offering me something that I couldn't have dreamed of experiencing otherwise. It wasn't about money or medals – it was never about the money – I was travelling to another country to race a bike for Great Britain. How cool was that?

I'd only been on a plane once, and that was on a family holiday to Spain when I was a toddler. I'd screamed so loudly that we holidayed in Britain or, at a push, took a ferry to France after that.

When I look back now, I think of that trip to Brno and can realize that not everyone had the temperament for travel. I seemed to take everything in my stride, whereas some of the other lads were on edge with the travelling, sleeping in an unfamiliar bed, and the strange food. They spent a lot of energy adapting to the change in their surroundings before they even got on the bike. Over the years, I've seen plenty of good riders fall short because they couldn't cope with the absence of tomato ketchup, Rice Krispies or other home comforts.

Having said that, the food in Brno took some getting used to: unidentified things in soup, a lot of gherkins, and meat-based products in breadcrumbs. One night we had steak and the lads were winding each other up that it was probably horse meat. Doug said: 'Well, let's hope it's a thoroughbred then, eh, boys?'

We knew we were going to be up against it in the races. Our opposition was France, Germany and Italy – three of the giants of European track cycling – and the hosts, Czechoslovakia. Everyone looked bigger, fitter and better kitted-out than we were. It took me back to the school playing fields and that moment of trepidation when the boys from the other school came out of the changing rooms and you clocked them for the first time. 'Look at the size of that one!'

Everyone looked stronger and more experienced than we were. To be blunt, we were a bit of a rag-tag outfit.

I'd been handed my first Great Britain skinsuit – the skin-tight one-piece jersey and shorts that track racers wear – in the national colours of red, white and blue, with a British Cycling Federation logo on the chest and Great Britain lettering on the shorts. I couldn't have been prouder.

'Here you go, Rob. Whatever you do, don't crash in it.'

There was so little kit to go round, we were using old hand-me-downs. The skinsuits had been through the wash so many times, the chamois leather pad stitched into the crotch to offer some protection against the bike's hard saddle was old, rough and cracked. I rubbed handfuls of Vaseline and sun cream into it to try to soften it up, and tried not to think about how many pairs of balls had been on it in the past.

The track at Brno was outdoors and was made of sections of concrete that jarred as you went round. Donk. Donk. Donk. It was a horrendous track but that was no excuse for our performance that weekend. We were taken to school. And you know how badly I did at school.

That trip abroad, and the ones that followed it, dragged me up quickly. Just as being beaten time and again by Mark Armstrong back at home made me a better rider, seeing how good the Europeans were showed me what I should be aiming at.

The following season there was a Junior Five Nations meeting at Kirkby in Merseyside. I was a year older, a bit stronger, and it was probably the first time I impressed anyone.

Kirkby track was a huge great thing – 486 metres long – because it went round the outside of an athletics track. I was beginning to become a more versatile rider and was developing into a sprinter with a diesel engine. I suppose I was becoming a rider a bit like Ed Clancy is now – fast off the line but with plenty of endurance. I could sprint but I could also sustain a high speed for longer than most track sprinters.

One of the last events at Kirkby was the scratch race, which is basically a free-for-all bunch race: first over the line at the end wins.

I punctured midway through but after getting a wheel change from our coach, Dave Le Grys, I was back in the thick of things and feeling like I owned the track. At the start of the last lap, I sat halfway down the line of riders waiting for the right moment, then I made my move down the back straight and powered past everyone. As I came round the final bend, I found I still had more to give, so I started my sprint and held off the rest.

We, the British team, won that Five Nations meeting overall on points, which was a pretty big deal at the time, but I was the only one of our team to win an individual event, so the rest of the boys decided I should keep the trophy. It was my first international victory and my mum and dad have still got the cup at home.

The Junior World Championships were held in Cleveland in the north-east of England that summer. Home advantage didn't count for much and we were brought back down to earth. Although I still thought of myself as a sprinter, and considered the kilometre time trial to be 'my' event, I continued to improve over longer distances, so I got a ride in the 4,000-metre team pursuit alongside Rod Ellingworth, Matt Charity and Nigel Simpson. We finished tenth.

*

On my eighteenth birthday, in January 1991, I was eating breakfast in the kitchen at home when I thought, Christ. I'm 18. An
adult. I'd better hurry up and do something.

It wasn't easy to see a future in cycling at that time. There
were three options. Go to Europe and join a club, stay at home,
or give up and start thinking about a career. I was happy working at Gales when it was a means of supporting my cycling but I
wasn't sure I wanted to stay there for ever.

Rod Ellingworth, who was a really gifted road racer, went off
and joined a club in France. I'd spent hours on the Leicester track
staring at Rod's back wheel as we did lap after lap, wondering
when the suffering was going to stop. He was a real talent and
he was tipped to make it. When he moved from the junior ranks
to senior status at the age of 18, he was immediately among the
top-ranked riders in Britain. Rod and I got on right from the
start because he had a similar mentality to me. He lived for bike
racing and had a pragmatic approach to the sport. 'It's a bike
race, let's get stuck in.'

As I mentioned, Mark Armstrong drifted away from cycling.
He was one of the best riders of my generation but that addi-
tional hurdle he had to overcome – travelling over from the Isle
of Wight for every race, track league or training session – forced
him to pack it in. There just wasn't the infrastructure or money
to make life easier for a young cyclist.

As for me, I was committed to the track, which ruled out going
to France like Rod. In my three years as a junior I concentrated
on track racing, criteriums (short, fast circuit races on tight
town or city centre courses) and ten- and 25-mile time trials. I
only did three 'proper' road races in my entire three seasons as
a junior. To remain part of the track squad, you had to stay at
home. It was quite a cliquey set-up then, and riders who went off
to Europe were out of sight and out of mind.

I had the 1991 Junior Track World Championships in my sights but I can't honestly say I had any kind of career plan. Perhaps if I'd had a picture in my mind of what I wanted to do, I'd have achieved more, but the horizons were a lot narrower then. No British rider had managed to win a gold medal at the Olympics since Harry Ryan and Thomas Lance won the two-kilometre tandem at the 1920 Games in Antwerp. World titles were few and far between. Britain had a reputation for producing a brilliant, world-class rider every couple of generations or so. There was Reg Harris in the 1940s and 1950s; Tom Simpson, Barry Hoban and Hugh Porter in the 1970s; and Tony Doyle in the 1980s, but you couldn't say they were the products of a system, because there was no system. They were exceptions to the rule, people who had the talent or doggedness to overcome the barriers in their way. I couldn't honestly say I thought of myself as a once-in-a-generation talent like those riders, or like Colin Sturgess or Chris Boardman.

Years later, Rod devised and ran British Cycling's academy that nurtured and developed Mark Cavendish, Geraint Thomas, Ed Clancy, Ben Swift, Peter Kennaugh and a host of other talented young riders. Rod created a system and moved the rungs of the ladder so that they were much closer together. When I was 18, the canyon that stood between me and an Olympic medal was deep and the stepping stones worryingly far apart. There wasn't a pathway to success for me to follow.

A year or so after Cav turned professional he sat down with Rod, his coach, and wrote out a checklist of things he wanted to win. The World Road Race Championships, the green jersey at the Tour de France and a hatful of stages, the points competition at the Giro d'Italia, the Milan–San Remo Classic, an Olympic gold medal . . . basically a list of the biggest prizes in the sport. The fact it was realistic, rather than pie-in-the-sky, for Cav to do that showed not only what a talented and confident rider he was, but also how far cycling in Britain had come.

If I had written a similar list of goals in 1991, people might have admired my ambition but most would have written me off as a dreamer. If I had a goal, it was to become an Olympian, by which I mean race for my country at the Games. Yes, I thought I could win a medal, but only in the same way I thought I owned every bike race I ever started. If you look at the results, the reality of bike racing is that even the very best riders lose a lot more than they win. A medal was something to aspire to, not necessarily a realistic aim.

The 1991 Junior World Championships were originally supposed to be held in Trexlertown, Pennsylvania, but the organizers ran out of money, so the event was switched to Colorado Springs in Denver. Gales gave me five weeks of paid leave from the brewery so I could travel with the Great Britain squad for a pre-Championship training camp. Our home for those five weeks was a university campus on the outskirts of town. This was to be my college experience crammed into a few weeks and I was determined to make the most of it.

On the first day, we went out for a ride in gorgeous sunshine. It was so hot that I pulled my jersey up, and rolled up my sleeves so the lower half of my back and my shoulders were exposed to the rays. I didn't want the traditional cyclist's tan, which makes you look like your arms, legs and face have been dipped in mahogany wood stain, while the rest of you is a sort of translucent blue. Stupidly, I didn't put on any sun cream.

When I got back to my room and had a shower, the water stung a bit. I turned and looked in the mirror and my lower back was bright pink and already beginning to blister. Poor Doug spent the next week rubbing ointment into my back to heal the burnt skin. Whatever he was paid, it was nowhere near enough.

Colorado was such a blissful few weeks it was easy to forget we had the World Championships at the end of it. We rode our bikes in the sun, spent a fair bit of time watching the American women's team training at the track, and laughed a lot.

As you'd expect of a bunch of teenagers away from home, we were on the look-out for mischief. Booze was out of the question but we'd heard some old nonsense that you could smoke banana skins if you dried them out, so we hoarded a load of them and put them on top of the wardrobe for the month. Eventually we shredded and rolled the banana skins into rubbish cigarettes and lit them. The harsh smoke hurt the backs of our throats and in the middle of a coughing fit someone shouted, 'Doug's coming!' so we threw them out of the window.

The British junior road team were in Colorado at the same time so we trained with Roger Hammond and Jeremy Hunt some days. Both Roger and Jez went on to have very good pro careers on the road, riding well into their late thirties before retiring. Both of them did it their own way, following the well-beaten track to Europe for years of suffering and surviving. Roger went to Belgium and made it on to the podium at Paris–Roubaix, one of the toughest one-day Classics there is. Jeremy headed to Spain, then France, and lived a nomadic life moving around Europe. Neither of them were products of a system either. They made it because they were prepared to stick at it in a foreign country. You wonder how well they'd have done if the current system had been in place when they were coming through.

In the afternoons we'd head into town for a coffee or hang out in a bike shop that was like a cross between Santa's grotto and Aladdin's cave. The stuff they had in there had my eyes out on stalks. I spent a small fortune and could have spent five times more. The early nineties was an exciting time if you were a nerd about bicycle equipment: a technological revolution was going on, carbon fibre was taking over the world and designers were pushing the boundaries. And everything was fluorescent yellow. It was all achingly cool.

I had recently bought a pair of expensive Oakley sunglasses with gold-mirrored lenses that cost about a week's salary, but when I bought another new pair in the Colorado Springs bike shop, I lent them to Jez. We were riding down a sweeping descent and I could see Jez up ahead of me. As he went round one corner, I could tell he'd got the line wrong and was going to come a cropper. He missed the bend and instead went straight on down a dirt track and fell off. I panicked and rode down the track after him.

'Jez . . .! Jez . . .! If you've scratched those glasses . . .!'

It's good to think back and know I had my priorities straight.

Expectations were low at an event like the Junior World Championships, but that didn't mean we rode like losers. A good performance in an event like the individual or team pursuit was enough to qualify for a second ride in the knock-out rounds.

We didn't have the resources that some of the major cycling nations enjoyed. We were training at the track one day and Jon Stacey, who was our rider for the individual sprint, was going through his drills. He was repeating his 200-metre sprint efforts. He had a stopwatch hanging round his neck and, at the start of each sprint, he pressed the button – then, when he crossed the line, he'd reach down to press the stop button. He was attempting the impossible trying to time himself like that – he must've been seconds out – but there was no one spare to help him, so he had to do the best he could.

On one of my frequent trips to the bike shop, I bought some

triathlon-style handlebars. They set me back a couple of hundred dollars, which was still a lot cheaper than they were at home. Greg LeMond made tri-bars famous when he used them during the final time-trial stage of the 1989 Tour de France and turned a 50-second deficit to Laurent Fignon into an eight-second victory in under 25 kilometres. Afterwards, he credited the tri-bars for making that possible. Triathletes had been using them for a few years and, after LeMond's heroics, everyone started using them in time trials on the road, but they hadn't really caught on among track riders.

Tri-bars, for those who don't know, enable a rider to get into a much more aerodynamic, tucked position. Instead of having regular handlebars, which mean your hands are the width of your chest apart, making your body into a big fleshy parachute that creates drag, the tri-bars help you get into an arrow shape. The arms point directly out in front of the body, the head comes down and there's a smaller frontal area hitting the wind. The result is that it's more efficient and helps you go faster.

I put the tri-bars on for a training session at the Colorado track. I could feel the positive effects immediately and I was desperate to use them in competition. There was no way I could use them in the 4,000-metre team pursuit because the other three lads didn't have a set, but I could still use them in my individual event.

So I said to Alan, old-school Alan, 'I'm going to use these in the kilometre time trial.'

'You can't use them, Rob, they're for road riders. They're no good for the track; you'll hamper your breathing.'

So I rode on my standard track bike and finished a pretty decent seventh in the kilometre time trial, 0.9 seconds off a medal, a shade over a second off gold. On that big, 333-metre track, tri-bars might have made a significant difference, perhaps as much as a second over the other riders. Perhaps I could have been world junior kilometre champion if I'd used those handlebars?

During the qualifying round of the team pursuit, I pointed out to Alan that the Danish squad were all kitted out with tri-bars. Around halfway through the race, the Danes overlapped wheels, there was a crash and they went down like skittles.

'See, there you go,' said Alan. 'They're no good on the track those bars.'

We got our second ride in the team pursuit. Andy Forbes, Paul Jennings, Chris Newton and I finished fourth, beaten to a bronze medal by the Australians, who had Stuart O'Grady and Henk Vogels, who both went on to be top professional riders, in their team. A few days later, Sally Dawes got a silver medal for us in the women's road race, which was a fantastic result and had our whole team smiling.

I didn't want it to end. If I could have stayed in Colorado another month I would have done. I wasn't dreaming of Olympic medals or world titles, but I'd experienced enough to know that I wanted to keep doing this for as long as I possibly could.

After the World Championships and with my graduation from junior to senior ranks just around the corner, I was named on the longlist of riders in the frame for the 1992 Olympic Games in Barcelona.

By then, a young sports scientist called Peter Keen, who had begun working with the British Cycling Federation a couple of years earlier, was the national coach. Keen was not only a sports scientist but also an exercise physiologist, based at University College, Chichester; but he was better known as Chris Boardman's coach.

It's fair to say that the British cycling revolution owes as much to Keen as it does to the influx of National Lottery money that was to come in a few years later. Keen completely revolutionized the way things were done. He based everything he did on evidence. There was no guesswork. He didn't go on hunches or superstition. He had no time for the phrase: 'But that's how we've always done it.' If you thought a particular technique worked or didn't work, he wanted to see the evidence to support your view. If science didn't prove something, he disregarded it until there was some research to prove the case.

Dad and I went to a coaching seminar that Keen was talking at once, and Dad stood up and said, 'After exercise, you need plenty of protein.' He was basing it on his own experiences as a track sprinter and a wrestler. He'd always eat plenty of meat or chicken after a race or a bout. Keen didn't agree or disagree; he simply said the science didn't back it up. A couple of years later, Keen gave us some boxes of protein powder to take after training and my dad said, 'See . . .?' But Keen's point was that he needed to see evidence of something before applying it.

This isn't knocking the coaches who were involved before Keen took charge at the British Cycling Federation, but an awful lot of the knowledge, the skinsuits and equipment, was hand-me-down stuff: techniques that riders in the fifties and sixties had sworn by filtered down through the generations. The way we trained, the way we raced, it was all based on what riders who had gone before us had done. All the old wives' tales and the accepted dos and don'ts were rarely challenged.

Now here was Peter Keen to tear all that down (but not in a destructive because-I-say-so way), before rebuilding it using only the pieces that science proved actually worked.

At the start of my final year as a junior, Keen had approached me and said he was looking for another rider to coach. I was about to become a senior rider and would be on the fringes of the Olympic squad. Part of the reason he was interested in me was no doubt practical. I lived in Horndean, he was in Chichester, only half an hour away. Boardman was up in the Wirral, so perhaps he was looking for a guinea pig closer to home.

I was keen, but I was also loyal. I liked Alan Sturgess and, as he was the national junior coach, I felt I should stick with him – at least in part. My dad and I said to Peter, 'I'm sure between you and Alan we can find a way to make it work.'

Peter said: 'No, I'm sorry. It's all or nothing with me. I either coach you completely or we leave it.'

Part of my hesitation was that Keen was a man in a lab coat. I was interested in his methods but I thought I needed to work with people who understood bike racing. So I stuck with Alan.

When you think of the pivotal decisions in life, that is one that stands out. I wonder how things would have worked out if I'd chosen Peter Keen as my coach. I can't say I would have been another Chris Boardman, but it would be fascinating to be able to go back and see how it might have gone.

Back then, I thought of Boardman as a freak: our generation's outstanding individual who bucked the trend and succeeded despite the lack of a system. He was the Reg Harris, the Hugh Porter or Tom Simpson: a British rider who had reached the top in isolation, rather than as the result of a broad-based improvement in coaching techniques. I was in awe of Chris and just accepted that he was much more gifted than me, which he undoubtedly was, but what I didn't realize at the time was that Keen had devised a system. Boardman was brilliant, yes, but he wasn't throwing darts blindfolded, hoping to hit the bull's-eye. Keen and Boardman had planned carefully and they worked methodically. They had devised a pathway, working backwards from the goal they were trying to achieve. Keen studied every aspect of Boardman's performance and improvement and was in the early stages of building a system that was to kick-start the revolution in British cycling.

In those early days, I found Boardman quite daunting company. I liked things light, breezy and informal. I was laid-back. Boardman walked around with a permanent frown and a crinkled forehead, as if he was trying to work out a really complicated mathematical equation in his head, which, I guess in some ways, he was. He wasn't one for small talk or jokes. It took me about fifteen years before I completely got his dry sense of humour. It wasn't just dry, it was arid. Since he's retired, he's relaxed a lot and his sense of humour, though still dry, is right on my wavelength.

We shared a room after a race one time in the lead-up to the Barcelona Olympics and I was treading on eggshells the whole time. I didn't want to do or say anything that would annoy him. It was well after midnight, we were lying there in our separate beds with the lights out, listening to some dog nearby barking on and on.

Eventually I'd had enough of it, so I got out of bed, opened the window and shouted: 'Will someone please shut that fucking dog up!'

Boardman said, completely deadpan, 'I was just thinking the same thing meself.'

I was still caught between two stools. Was I going to be a kilometre rider or should I switch my attention to the longer pursuit events? A pre-Olympic selection meeting at Leicester in the early autumn of 1991 began to push me in one direction. I won the kilometre time trial in a time of one minute and seven seconds, but because I hadn't met the official qualification time of 1-06.9, which would have guaranteed me a place in Barcelona, they left me out and gave the place to Anthony Stirrat, a more experienced rider who was national champion. I argued that it had been a windy day and that, in the conditions, the time was a good one, but it didn't make any difference.

Instead, I was added to the longlist for the team pursuit. I was about to turn 19 and I was in the Great Britain Olympic squad.

At the start of 1992 a stalwart of the British cycling scene called Ed Taylor, who owned a company called Taylor's Foundry, offered to cover my expenses for the season, and that was all the incentive I needed to call it a day at Gales brewery. On 14 February 1992, I did my last proper day's work and became a full-time cyclist.

Although I was part of the squad, I don't think I ever convinced myself that I'd actually go to Barcelona for the Olympics. We'd been there for a training camp at the back end of 1991 and I felt like the junior member of the squad all week. Boardman, Simon Lillistone, Bryan Steel and Glen Sword were all older and more experienced than I was, and I knew that if I was going to get into the squad, one of them would probably have to get ill or be injured.

On that trip to Barcelona, we went out training as a group, and it soon dawned on me that I had a slow puncture, so I stopped to change my tyre. They waited for a bit then said they'd roll on at a slower pace to give me a chance to catch up. Once I'd fixed my tyre, I set off after them at race pace, thinking every time I went round a corner that they must be just up ahead. Eventually I saw a rider so I sprinted to close the gap. It took me ages to get close – I thought they were pushing on to make me chase them harder as a joke. Eventually, I got close enough to realize I'd been chasing some bird on a scooter.

By this time I was completely lost, the sun was beginning to dip down behind the hills and it was getting chilly. I had no idea what our hotel was called, where it was, or where I was.

'*Ciclista, Inglés?*' I asked people in the street, hoping they'd guess I was looking for the British cycling team's hotel and know where it was.

Eventually, after dark, I got back to the hotel, tired, embarrassed and cold, and saw the rest of the squad were having dinner. They took the mickey out of me all night, which is pretty much the initiation ceremony for any athlete in a group situation. Once your teammates are ripping the piss out of you without mercy, you know you've been accepted.

I knew I wouldn't be going to Barcelona as soon as Keen announced the squad for another pre-Olympic training camp that was to be held in Ghent. We had just competed at a World Cup meeting in Hyères, near Toulon in the south of France, when he sat me down and told me his decision. He explained that he felt I'd struggle to cope with the workload he had prepared for the pursuiters at the Ghent training camp. It was the first time anyone had talked me through a selection decision. Before that you were either in or you were out; now here was someone giving me a reason.

Not everyone saw that as a significant step forward, but it was. When we arrived back in Britain after the Hyères trip, Spencer Wingrave's dad, Keith, was waiting for Keen at the airport. Spencer was on the longlist with me and thought he should ride the points race in Barcelona, but he'd not made the cut for the team pursuit and so the points race slot went to Simon Lillistone.

Keith was furious and I saw how uncomfortable Keen was with a confrontational situation. As far as he was concerned, the facts said all that needed to be said. Dealing with an emotional parent was completely alien to him because he was so used to a clinical, analytical approach.

*

On Wednesday, 29 July 1992, we all got to Alexandra Park velodrome in Portsmouth an hour or so earlier than usual. It was track league night but we weren't so gripped by the prospect of an evening's inter-club racing that we felt the need to arrive so early. It was the evening of the Olympic individual pursuit final in Barcelona. Chris Boardman of Great Britain versus Jens Lehmann of Germany. Boardman had been the fastest rider in qualifying and had stormed through to the final almost unopposed.

Tim and Sue Knight, the stalwarts who dedicated so much of their time and energy to the riders, young and old, at Alexandra Park, had brought in a television set, so we all gathered in the club room, eagerly awaiting the final.

Boardman was riding his futuristic bicycle that had been designed by Mike Burrows and made by Lotus, the car manufacturer, from carbon fibre. It was a fusion of science and art that not only looked beautiful but rode brilliantly. At the time it felt like the moment that the combination of Keen's vision and knowledge and Boardman's athletic gift had been building towards. Looking back, it's clearly far, far more significant than that.

As Boardman bore down on Lehmann, the group of club cyclists stood to roar him on. Boardman caught and overtook the German before the end of the 4,000-metre race to become the first British cyclist to win an Olympic gold medal in seventy-two years.

This is the bit where I'm supposed to say that, as I watched Boardman win his gold medal, I thought, 'One day I want to do that.'

The truth is, I didn't. I know Brad Wiggins says that seeing Boardman win in Barcelona that night was the spark that fired his ambition. Perhaps that's because Brad was a 12-year-old kid then.

I was 19. I'd raced with Boardman, I'd seen how supremely gifted he was. I'd almost wangled my way on to the plane for Barcelona. And I knew the gulf there was between him and me. I couldn't honestly say to myself, 'Well, if Chris can do it, so can I,' because I didn't believe it then.

I watched Boardman win gold that summer's evening through the eyes of a cycling fan, and then I got warmed up for our track league races. I felt so detached from it all. I didn't feel like Boardman was paving the way for me, or for anyone. I was delighted for him that he had won a gold medal, but he still felt like the exception to the rule rather than the product of an improving system.

Boardman came to lunch at the team hotel during the National Championships after the Games and he brought his gold medal with him. I remember refusing to touch it because I didn't want to jinx anything.

# 4

# Six Days of Hell

At the end of the 1992 season my sponsor, Ed Taylor, gave me a cheque for £670 to cover my expenses for the year, and I gave a big chunk of it back to him in exchange for a Ford Escort with a hundred thousand miles on the clock. That car was going to see us through an epic road trip that would put hairs on my chest, so to speak.

Bryan Steel, who had ridden the team pursuit at the Olympics, had been offered a place in the amateur Six-Day race in Ghent, Belgium, at the end of November, but for some reason he couldn't take it, so he asked me if I'd like to go with Paul Jennings.

So we were going to head off to Europe to see whether we would sink or swim. Either way, the learning curve was going to be as steep as the banking at the famous Kuipke velodrome.

Belgium, and particularly the Flanders region, is crazy about cycling and Ghent is the sport's spiritual home. When Tom Simpson went to see if he could make it as a professional rider in the late 1950s, he headed to Ghent. The region is famous for the Tour of Flanders, one of the toughest and most prestigious single-day Classics, which zigzags across the farmland seeking out as many of the short, steep hills and stretches of cobbled roads as it can. The weather and the harsh roads made the Flandrians tough.

A passion for cycling oozes from Ghent's pores. Go into any bar in the city and you can guarantee three things: a selection of excellent beers, an atmosphere thick with cigarette smoke, and a simmering debate about the latest events in cycling. (Well, you could: there's a smoking ban in place now.)

The Kuipke velodrome is situated in the Citadelpark, a short walk from the city centre, and it hosts one of the most iconic Six-Day races on the winter track programme, which used to span from Copenhagen to Bremen and from Bordeaux to Munich. The list of riders who have won the Ghent Six reads like a who's who of Belgian cycling legends: Rik Van Steenbergen, Rik Van Looy, Eddy Merckx and Patrick Sercu, the granddaddy of them all, on the track at least. Sercu won the Ghent Six-Day eleven times in his career and after he retired he took on the role of organizer. The typical Six-Day organizer combines the panache of a theatre director and the showmanship of a circus ringmaster, with a hint of a mafia don's ruthlessness lurking just below the surface.

In the old days, Six-Day racing was not for the faint-hearted. It still isn't, but until the 1960s it was brutal, perhaps unnecessarily so. In the 1890s and early 1900s the riders raced individually and the competition was to see who could ride the furthest in six days and nights. The race went on non-stop and riders would snatch a bit of sleep here and there when they could, choosing their moment to get off the track strategically. Those early events were popular in the United States, with the old Madison Square Garden establishing itself as a regular venue.

After the turn of the century, rules came in to restrict the amount of time the riders could spend on the track. That's when the Six-Days became two-man races, enabling the riders to take turns. The races still went on twenty-four hours a day for six days, and each team had to have one rider on the track at all times, but at least they could alternate, which allowed one rider to go and grab some proper rest while his teammate held the fort. Eventually, the organizers realized that racing twenty-four hours a day was a pretty pointless exercise. At four o'clock in the morning, there'd be hardly anyone watching. The European Six-Days did away with twenty-four-hour racing in the 1960s, but the sessions could still be very long, starting at 8 p.m. and lasting well into the early hours.

The modern Six-Day race is an event for pairs of riders. The programme varies from track to track, but the bulk of the racing is made up of long, energy-sapping Madison races. The Madison gets its name from Madison Square Garden, where this two-man event was first popular, and if you have never watched one, here's a quick explainer.

A Madison race at a Six-Day usually lasts about forty minutes. The idea is to gain laps over your opponents, which makes it a test of both speed and endurance. (The Madison at the World Championships and Olympic Games is slightly different, with sprints every twenty laps, so the game becomes even more complex as riders try to improve their points total by winning sprints, while others focus on lapping the field.) In the Six-Day Madison, the riders take turns in the race. You could say it's like tag-wrestling on a bike. The resting rider has to stay above a line halfway up the track and rolls round getting a bit of respite from the fierce pace below. The rider in the race then propels his teammate back into the action with a handsling. A Madison race is exhilarating, stressful, exciting and intense. The physical toll and the mental concentration required make it incredibly demanding. Often I'd step off the track and it would take a moment for the world to stop spinning.

With so many riders on the track – some of them 'in' the race, others resting – it can be hard for spectators to keep track of what's going on. In fact, even when you are in the race, it can be very hard to know exactly where you are in the standings. If you switch off for a minute you can miss one of your opponents trying to gain a lap. You can lose a handful of places in the blink of an eye and suddenly find that you're playing catch-up again.

On the Six-Day circuit, the Madison race is also known as a 'chase', probably because no matter where you are in the field, you're always chasing someone. If you're at the front trying to gain a lap, you're chasing the tail of the bunch; and if you're down at the back, you're chasing just to keep up.

Anyway, the races are unforgiving. There are only a dozen or so teams on the track, which means there's never anywhere to hide. The moments when you can pull out of the action and catch your breath and let the pain in your legs simmer down are uncomfortably brief. Before you know it, your teammate is coming round the bottom of the track looking to throw you back into the furnace again.

On a typical night at a professional Six-Day, there will be two Madison 'chases' interspersed with other crowd-pleasing track races. There are often flying laps, where riders get up to sprinting speed and see who can do the quickest lap. There are also motor-paced races, where each cyclist rides behind a motorized bike, known as a Derny. Another popular one is the devil (as in devil take the hindmost, also known as the elimination race, which Laura Trott has made her speciality in the past year or so) where the last rider over the line every second lap is eliminated until only the winner is left.

As exhausting as the racing can be, the idea of the Six-Day races has always been to entertain the crowd. The racing isn't fixed, exactly, but there's a hierarchy to be observed, so what you get are a number of races within the race. The top teams battle against each other, but look after each other's interests too, while the smaller teams concentrate on beating the other small teams. The crowd expects to see their favourites win and the organizers want the spectators to go home happy. The stars get the biggest pay cheque and the rest know to play their part. The organizers don't take too kindly to some unknown upstart coming along and spoiling things. That's one way to ensure you never get invited back.

There are quite a few similarities to the wrestling circuit from my dad's day. The Six-Day riders make up a small, close-knit group of professionals who travel round Europe together. They look out for each other in the races, they make sure no one gets ripped off and they ensure the crowd is entertained. But if you think the races are easy, you're mistaken.

Paul and I were heading to Ghent to take part in the amateur Six-Day event, which lasted about an hour each night and was held in the early evening, before the main professional event. The idea was that there'd be a race on the track as the spectators filled up the velodrome – we were the hors-d'oevre. The aim for us was to try not to get chewed up and spat out.

Paul picked up my 'new' motor from Ed Taylor on his way down to Horndean and the next morning we packed up the car for a couple of weeks in Belgium. There were a few warm-up races at the Kuipke track in the week leading up to the Six-Day and we'd been entered for those too.

We put our track bikes in the back of the car, then our mountain bikes, which we were taking so we could train even if the weather was lousy. Then we counted out our money on the kitchen table – we had a couple of hundred quid between us – and prepared to leave for the ferry port.

Just before we set off, Dad persuaded me to pack the Calor gas camping stove and some pots and pans. I tried to tell him we weren't going on a Boy Scout's trip, we were going bike racing, but he said, 'Take it just in case. You never know.'

By the time we'd bought our ferry ticket, the kitty was already running pretty low. We burnt through another wedge of cash when we stopped for petrol on the motorway to Ghent. Paul wasn't too worried because he was the self-sufficient type. His trick was to turn up at road races with the needle on his petrol gauge hovering just above empty, knowing that he'd have to win some prize money just to get home.

We arrived in Ghent with nowhere to stay. Once the Six-Day race started, our accommodation and food would be paid for by the organizers, but we had almost a week to survive before then. We drove round town looking for the cheapest hotel we could find and booked a twin room for two nights in a grim-looking place.

Then we headed to the supermarket to stock up on provisions. We filled a trolley with the cheapest stuff we could find – tins of baked beans and tuna, packets of sweet Belgian waffles, chocolate biscuits and fruit. We scooped up anything that was on special offer. By the time we'd done that, we had barely any money left.

We couldn't afford to eat in a restaurant, so our trick was to get up very early and raid the breakfast buffet, filling our bags with croissants, bread rolls, ham and cheese and anything else we could squirrel away for later.

Having so little money put the fear in us. During the first warm-up race at the Kuipke velodrome, we won a couple of sprints to add a few hundred Belgian francs to the pot. It wasn't much, but it was enough for us to go to the supermarket for another game of bargain hunt.

During the day we trained on the track or we rode our mountain bikes on the cycle path that runs alongside the canal to the south of the city. In the evening, we raced, hoping to earn a bit more cash to see us through another day.

After two nights, we had to check out of our hotel because we couldn't afford to stay any longer, even though it must've been the cheapest place in town. Later on, at the track, we saw Spencer Wingrave, who was also racing the Ghent Six. We got chatting and he asked where we were staying.

'Funny you should ask that . . . Do you know anywhere?'

Spencer suggested we follow him back to his place, which he said was great, and really cheap, so we set off, driving for what seemed like miles, until we'd left Ghent and were out in the countryside. As soon as we saw the list of prices on the board in reception we knew we couldn't afford it, so we got back in the car and drove back to Ghent, wasting more of our precious petrol.

We'd run out of options, so we headed back to the track, where it was at least warm, to hang out for the afternoon. We'd got to know one of the old boys who worked as a mechanic during the Six-Day. He seemed to have the run of the place and he let us keep our mountain bikes in one of the store cupboards near the changing rooms.

It was then that we hit on an idea. We hung around in the changing rooms for a bit and when no one was around I opened one of the windows and left it so it was slightly ajar but still looked closed. The plan was to wait until night, climb in through the window and sleep in the changing rooms, which were warm and dry. We'd have the toilets and showers to use. What more could we want?

So we waited in the car park next to the velodrome until it was dark. We could see a light was on in the changing room and when we climbed up and looked through the window, our mechanic friend was in there with a woman who was quite a bit younger than him and, ahem, quite glamorously dressed.

We scarpered and that night we slept in the car. Dinner was a mixture of tuna and baked beans cooked until they were just past lukewarm on the Calor gas stove. I opened the car door and crouched down to protect the flame from the freezing wind. Thank goodness for Dad's last-minute suggestion, because although tuna in brine and baked beans do not go together, it would have tasted even worse stone cold out of the tins.

Although we'd reclined the seats as far as they'd go, it was an uncomfortable night's sleep, and in the morning the car was steamed up and smelled pretty funky. When we saw Spencer again he asked where we'd stayed. We told him we'd slept in the car in the park on the other side of the velodrome.

'Oh, you don't want to sleep there. That's where the drug addicts and prostitutes hang out.'

The next night we drove down to the canal and parked up there. In the next couple of races we managed to get our hands on enough prize money to pay for another night in the hotel, which was the last night we had to get through before reporting to the Six-Day organizers and being given a couple of bunk beds in a breeze-block dorm at the outdoor velodrome on the other side of Ghent.

By the time the Six-Day race actually started, I was exhausted. We were two unknown Brits, and it seemed like we were not to be trusted by the other competitors because an unknown rider on the track might turn out to be a dangerous rider. Most of the riders in the amateur race were aspiring pros, so they weren't putting on an exhibition for the crowd, they were trying to kill each other and get noticed by any pro team managers watching.

I'd ridden a few Madison races that year – my first one was during a trip to South Africa with the British team in the spring – and they'd been enjoyable, but this was completely different.

The track at the Kuipke is small, only 166 metres round, and although I was used to racing on a tight velodrome – I'd learned my craft at Calshot – the aggression and the cut-throat manoevres the other riders pulled off were in another league. Paul and I took a kicking. We were only on the track for an hour at a time but I was on my knees by the end of the first night.

No one spoke to us around the track or during the down time at our breeze-block dormitory, except for one young Belgian lad whom I'd met on that trip to South Africa. It was clear we still had a way to go to earn anyone's respect, let alone make an impression.

That Belgian lad was Tom Steels, who went on to become a formidable sprinter and who won nine stages of the Tour de France in his career. He went out of his way to be friendly and kind to a couple of Brits who had found themselves out of their depth. He had a few words of encouragement: 'Don't worry, you'll get stronger.' And, 'Do your best.'

On the second night, though, I ran up his backside in the middle of a 'chase' and we both hit the floor, so even he didn't speak to us after that.

As the week went on, Paul and I were struggling to keep our heads above water. It was amazing how long an hour could feel as the laps slipped away from us. It was hell.

When the last night was over, we packed our stuff back into the car and headed home without staying to watch the pro race. We drove back to the French coast and got the late ferry back to Portsmouth. The next day I slept until well into the afternoon and it took me days to get back to normal. It wasn't just the racing, it was having to live on our wits that did us in. Wasting energy worrying about where we were going to stay, grabbing a few hours of interrupted kip in the car, not having enough money to eat properly, it all added up. We'd been living hand to mouth and there was nothing left when it came to actually racing. I learned that week how important it was to recover properly and how a bad lifestyle can undo all the good work you do in training.

But it was a great experience. It was fun and we survived it, although I wouldn't necessarily recommend it. Every older generation loves to tell the younger ones how much tougher, and therefore better, things were in their day, but that's not often the case.

When Rod Ellingworth developed the British Cycling academy in 2004, one of the first things he did was take a couple of lads to Ghent for the under-23 Six-Day, which had replaced the amateur event.

Rod has always believed that track racing can make a bike rider better, and he's right. The bikes are simple – there are no gears or brakes to get you out of a tight spot, so you learn how to ride fast and close. The skills and drills, as he calls them, that can be honed and perfected on the track stand a rider in great stead on the road too. Before a rider realizes it, track racing has started to give them a smoother pedalling stroke, a more powerful acceleration and a bit of tactical nous.

Over the years, the number of British riders who've ridden at Ghent and gone on to make it in the professional ranks is impressive. In 2004, Matt Brammeier, Mark Cavendish, Tom White and Geraint Thomas rode at Ghent. Three of them are established riders. After them Andy Tennant, Ian Stannard, Steven Burke, Jonny Bellis, Peter Kennaugh, Adam Blythe, Andy Fenn and Luke Rowe have raced in Ghent. There's a couple of Olympic champions and another host of professional riders among them. It is probably the case that they were the cream of the crop and many of them would have made it anyway, but Rod's trips to Ghent were all part of a structured learning experience. Rod worked them hard – he'd make them do the map-reading on the journey and plan their own itinerary, and he'd also get them training in the morning before the under-23 Six-Day race in the evening.

In 2005, I went back to Ghent to ride the elite race with Cav, when we were the reigning world Madison champions. Geraint Thomas and Ian Stannard were riding the under-23 race and Rod had them out on the road for a couple of hours in the morning. As they got back to the hotel they saw a couple of the Belgian under-23 riders heading down for breakfast and complained to Rod: 'They're not out training every morning. Why are we?'

'No. But they're winning this event,' Rod replied.

I've often joked with the young lads who've come through the academy and been spared the ritual of having to fend for themselves in a foreign country without money or a mobile phone. 'You don't know you're born!' Without sounding like a grumpy old man, they can't appreciate what it was like before the present British Cycling system existed. And why should they?

Sleeping in the car and eating tins of beans for dinner isn't part of a process. So Rod made life hard for the young riders, not unnecessarily so, but in a structured way. They washed their own bikes and cleaned the Great Britain team car, but they weren't left to fend for themselves, which made a huge difference.

As fondly as I look back on our survival camp in Ghent in November 1992, and as resourceful as it perhaps made me, it didn't make me a better cyclist.

I saw Tom Steels in Calpe, in southern Spain, not long ago. He's one of the sports directors at Cav's new team Omega

Pharma–Quick Step. I reminded him of that trip to South Africa and the time I crashed into him at the Ghent Six and we had a laugh about it. He must've remembered what a state we were in because he shook his head and said, 'That week made you a man, eh?'

# 5

# Have Bike, Will Race

Did I mention that I once beat Chris Hoy in a Keirin race? OK, so he was only 17 at the time, and whenever I mention it to him, as I frequently do, he pretends not to remember. But I did beat him. It was at Leicester velodrome during the National Championships, it was a support race rather than a title contest, and he was far from being the rider he eventually became, but, as they say, a win's a win.

The Keirin was a pretty good event for me back then because it married my sprinting speed, my endurance and my ability to find that sixth gear at the sharp end of a race. For those who have only a basic grasp of the intricacies of track racing, the Keirin is 'the one with the motorbike'. Between six and eight riders line up behind the little motorized Derny, which sets the pace, gradually increasing the speed to about 50 kilometres per hour, before pulling off the track with 600 metres to go, leaving the cyclists to fight it out. Keirin racing originated in Japan and is hugely popular there. Spectators bet on the races like we do on the greyhounds here.

The Keirin wasn't added to the Olympic Games programme

until 2000, so in the early nineties, in Britain at least, it was more of a crowd-pleaser than a career choice.

As we've seen in recent years, Chris Hoy made the Keirin his own, winning Olympic gold in Beijing in 2008 and again in London. He's a beast on the track and, when he gets up to top speed, other riders find it almost impossible to get past him. I was not the same type of rider as Chris, but I do wonder whether I would have remained a track sprinter if the Keirin had been an Olympic event when I was in my early twenties.

At the start of 1993, my route to the Atlanta Olympics looked so simple. I was a kilometre time-trial specialist and, as far as I was concerned, that discipline was my ticket to the Games. The 4,000-metre team pursuit was more than a solid back-up. I figured I had a good chance of making the squad, but I still considered myself first and foremost a kilo rider.

I won my first senior national title in the kilometre time trial at Leicester velodrome in 1993 and my times were steadily improving, to the extent that I was becoming a world-class rider. Looking ahead to Atlanta, I roughly mapped out the next four seasons. I wanted to win national titles, establish myself on the international stage, go to the Olympics and, above all, get faster.

But so much was to change in the four years between Barcelona and Atalanta that, by 1996, my career had already started to turn in a different direction. There were a number of things that happened in track cycling in that period that subtly influenced my career. In 1993, the 'Berlin Wall' that had divided the professional riders from the amateurs came down and the open era began. The Atlanta Olympics in 1996 were to be the first Games open to professional cyclists. Until 1992, all the riders had been amateurs, officially at least, although some nations were able to make their riders professional in all but name. They were paid and well supported. The best British riders had to ignore the carrot of a professional contract and remain amateur in order to compete in the Olympics. Colin Sturgess and Tony Doyle could have lifted the British team pursuit squad into medal contention in 1992, but they were ineligible because they were professionals. In a small way, the open era would begin to level the playing field for a country like Great Britain.

The completion of Manchester velodrome towards the end of 1994 was the second of three big developments that began the revolution. (The first being Peter Keen's appointment as national coach, the third being the arrival of National Lottery funding in 1997.) Once Manchester opened, we had a super-fast indoor velodrome to rival the best in the world, and cancelled training weekends would be a thing of the past. Instead, the number of available training hours was multiplied by hundreds. Riders could train from early in the morning until late at night and the weather was never a factor. I remember Doug Dailey saying it would take a couple of years for 'the Manchester effect', as he called it, to take hold, but the benefits for us were immediate. Three days of training at Manchester meant three days of good-quality work.

I was 20 in 1993, still the young boy of the squad, and with my horizons firmly fixed on Atlanta I was committed to doing everything I could to make sure I was selected for the Olympics. It probably sounds quite blasé now, but I coasted through those years a bit. I went from race to race, championship to championship, and took things in my stride. Nothing felt like it was make or break, partly because I always felt I was doing enough to justify my place in the national squad, and perhaps because there wasn't the depth of competition for places there is now. The goal was to become an Olympian, because I suppose I thought that was a realistic aim.

I was still an amateur, but I was doing OK riding for Team Haverhill, which was run and funded by Ed Taylor. He paid enough to cover all my main cycling-related expenses and he helped make sure I was never short of good bikes – Ed fixed me up with some Condor bikes – and equipment. It was a huge help and before the arrival of Lottery funding, so many athletes relied on people like Ed. Without the support of volunteers, willing benefactors and (sometimes not so willing) mums and dads, it would have been a struggle to field a British cycling team in the Olympics at times.

As I was living at home with Mum and Dad, I didn't need a lot of money to survive, which was a good thing, because the British Cycling Federation's coffers were still pretty bare. I applied for a grant from the Sports Council, which gave me about £1,000 a year, so I had just about enough to be a full-time cyclist without having to get a job, which would have eaten into valuable training and resting time. I probably took liberties at home, and Mum would say I treated the place like a hotel at times, but athletes quickly learn to pull the get-out-of-jail-free card: *'But Mum, I'm racing tomorrow!'*

In August 1993, I was picked for the senior World Championships for the first time. The Worlds were in Hamar, Norway, on the track where Graeme Obree had broken Francesco Moser's nine-year-old and seemingly unbreakable World Hour record by 445 metres a month earlier. Six days after Obree, in Bordeaux, Chris Boardman became the first man to break the 52-kilometre barrier in an hour-record attempt. In one crazy week, British track cycling had grabbed headlines, and the contrast between Obree and Boardman had captured the public imagination.

I first met Obree in Hamar and immediately I liked him. When we sat down in the hotel one evening and had a chat, it was obvious he was bonkers, but in a completely brilliant way. He had the creative genius of an absent-minded professor. He spoke so quickly, in a broad Scottish accent, giving the impression that his mind was a jumble of ideas all competing for attention. I found him absolutely captivating. Here was this guy who had come from nowhere, who had designed his own bike, nicknamed Old Faithful, who had shunned convention and embraced innovation. His position on the bike was radically different to anyone else's. Instead of using tri-bars to get himself into an arrow shape, his bike had upturned handlebars, like a New York City courier, that meant his arms were folded and tucked under his chest. It looked uncomfortable and awkward, and when he first got his big gear rolling he seemed unsteady, like a new-born foal taking its first steps, wobbling away from the line. But when he got up to speed, he was fast. Incredibly fast.

Outwardly, Obree appeared scatterbrained, completely unable to conform, determined, in fact, to upset the applecart. The suits at the UCI, cycling's world governing body, were so appalled at Obree's ungainly position on the bike and the stories about how parts of his bike were made from old washing-machine bits, that every time he unveiled a new piece of homemade equipment, they banned it.

In fact, the only bits of Obree's bike that came from a washing machine were the ball bearings in the bottom bracket (the part the cranks attach to the axle and revolve around). Obree apparently thought a washing machine's ball bearings were an improvement because they were used to spinning a drum at 1,200 revs a minute. A couple of decades later, 'conventional' bike design had caught up with Obree with the development of ceramic ball bearings, which everyone thought were more efficient and which cost a fortune.

The bottom line was that the establishment didn't like Obree. I've always suspected that if he'd played the game a bit more and let one of the major, traditional bike manufacturers make his bike (or at least put their logo on the frame), he'd have been allowed to use Old Faithful. When the UCI banned his hunched position, Obree went to the opposite extreme, inventing the 'Superman' position, using extended tri-bars that stretched him out even further. The UCI banned that position too, but not before Boardman had used it to break the hour record again in 1996.

On the face of it, Obree and Boardman were polar opposites. Boardman was quieter and more reserved. Obree's techniques appeared to be based on hunches or instinct and then proven through practice, whereas Boardman and Keen were used to putting everything to a rigorous scientific test. It was a bit like the film *Rocky IV* and the contrast between the boxers played by Dolph Lundgren and Sly Stallone. Boardman was in the lab poring over flow charts while Obree was out chopping down trees and throwing logs, and drinking raw eggs and Tabasco sauce for breakfast.

Actually, I think they were far more similar than that. They were both trying to solve the same problem: how to ride a certain distance in the fastest possible time. And they were both thinking laterally. Boardman and his team were just as radical and unconventional when it came to bike design and training techniques too.

I've always been fascinated by the way people from all corners of the world find different ways of doing things and then, when they come together to race, they are split by seconds, sometimes fractions of a second. Obree and Boardman weren't from different corners of the globe, but their ideas and inspirations came from different corners of the mind.

I probably didn't appreciate then the importance of what they were achieving that summer, because neither Boardman nor Obree were part of my team pursuit squad. I was a bit of an outsider, watching what they were doing, fascinated by their success, but more concerned with my own performances. Obree won the individual pursuit world title in Hamar that week, with Boardman taking the bronze medal. Two British riders in the top three at a World Championships was unheard of then. I thought, 'Wow, that's brilliant,' but then got on with what I was doing.

Actually, Great Britain had three riders in the top nine of the individual pursuit – Shaun Wallace was ninth, only a couple of seconds off a medal – but none of them rode the team pursuit, which probably seems a bit strange now but made perfect sense then.

With his precarious position on the bike, there was no way Obree could have ridden the team pursuit. He'd have been a liability swinging up the banking each time he came to change from first to fourth position. Wallace had been based in the United States for a few years and was not truly integrated in the British squad. His girlfriend, Tina, was his track-side support, rather than one of the British coaches. Boardman perhaps could have ridden with us but the overall benefit to the team would have been minimal. He was a good bit quicker than the rest of us, so he'd have been forced to hold back to avoid blowing the team apart.

In the team pursuit, you're only as strong as your weakest man, so it was better to have a team of four more evenly matched riders: Gary Coltman, Bryan Steel, Jon Walshaw and I made up the quartet. We reached the second round and eventually finished seventh in a competition won by the Australians. They were 11 seconds quicker than us over 4,000 metres, which is the track cycling equivalent of a country mile. I was also 13th in the kilometre time trial that week, which wasn't a bad result in my first major championships as a senior.

\*

My first experience of a major Games was at the Commonwealths in Victoria, Canada, in 1994. They call the Commonwealth Games the friendly games, and everyone in the village seemed to get on well, particularly towards the end as more and more athletes finished their events and let their hair down.

I loved just sitting in the village, having a coffee, people-watching. We'd play 'spot the sport', guessing whether someone was a swimmer, weightlifter or runner, judging by their physique and the way they walked. You could spot the cyclists a mile off, with their distinctive tans and shuffling gait, but the game was harder, and more amusing, than it sounds.

The level of competition at the Commonwealth Games has never been as high as at the Olympics, for obvious reasons, so there was an element of expectation around the England team. The Australian cyclists were top dogs pretty much across the board but, really, if we hadn't got a medal in the team pursuit there would have been something wrong.

As professional riders were now allowed to ride in the previously amateur Games, Tony Doyle came into the squad alongside Chris Newton, Bryan Steel and me. We reached the final without too much trouble, only to be overtaken by the Australians in the gold medal race. In our defence, they had a pretty formidable line-up, with a young Stuart O'Grady and Brad McGee in the team.

The final was the first time I took bicarbonate of soda, or baking powder, before a race. Bicarb is alkaline and so it helps deter and delay the build-up of lactic acid in the muscles. We'd mix about half a gram for every kilogram of body weight in water and drink it. The main side effect is that it goes through you like the proverbial dose of salts, which I suppose is exactly what it is. I spent quarter of an hour in a Portaloo, feeling like the bottom was falling out of my world. Pre-race nerves and bicarb have never been a pretty combination.

In 'my' event, the kilo, I was fifth, half a second off a bronze medal, in a competition dominated by the Aussies. Shane Kelly, who was still young then but would go on to dominate the event for a number of years, won gold. Fifth place and a silver medal was a good return for a 21-year-old at his first Commonwealth Games.

Because of our success in the team pursuit, Bryan Steel and I were invited to a series of races in Australia run by the promoter Mike Turtur, who is director of the Tour Down Under these days. We went down under for a couple of months at the end of the year, taking part in exhibition races all over the country. We travelled with a group of Six-Day riders, including the Dane Michael Sandstød and Dutchman Rob Slippens, and did a couple of track meetings here and there, before going to the Formula One street-racing circuit in Adelaide. We did a couple of motor-paced bike races on the F1 circuit on the Friday and Saturday before the Australian Grand Prix. It was brilliant to race, but I'm not sure the crowd were too impressed. We felt like we were flying, but after watching the Porsche race or the grand prix qualifying round, the spectators were probably a bit underwhelmed by the sight of a bunch of blokes on pushbikes trundling around.

After that I flew to Tasmania for a race that was billed as a Commonwealth Games rematch with Shane Kelly.

Before our kilometre race, I'd been tinkering with my bike and I must have over-tightened the bolt holding my rear wheel in the frame because when I started my effort, I knew something was wrong. My wheel had pulled right over so it was at a funny angle, wedged against the frame, so I stopped, thinking I'd get a restart. It was an exhibition race, after all, not a major championship. But the chief judge wasn't interested in my explanations.

Shane tried to get them to give me another go but as far as the judge was concerned I was a Pommie, he was an Aussie, and it was my tough luck, mate.

My other event, the devil catch the hindmost, was just as embarrassing. We were riding round the track and I was waiting for the starter to fire his gun to signal the start of the race, not realizing we were already underway. I was last over the line at the end of the second lap and they called me out of the race. The first two riders eliminated were the only two not to get a share of the prize money, so I managed to miss out on the cash in both my events.

The races had been televised and the other lads had been watching in Adelaide. When I got back they were merciless. 'That went well, Rob,' was about the gist of it.

At the end of 1994, Tony Doyle persuaded me to take out a professional licence and offered me a place on his team. I say 'team', but it was actually just Tony and me, and my role was to be Doyley's training partner and general dogsbody. He lived about an hour up the A3 from me, so, three times a week, I'd drive up to his place and we'd go training on the road.

I had been used to my track training, which was tailored towards the kilometre time trial. Dave Le Grys, the national sprint coach, used to have me riding round the track at full pelt with a huge truck tyre tied to the back of my bike. Doyley's form of punishment was to go out and smash himself for four hours while I hung on grimly.

I was constantly outside my comfort zone, riding at a tempo that wasn't far off road race pace for hours. I didn't question it because Doyley had been a world professional pursuit champion and was one of the regulars on the Six-Day circuit, so I thought this was what you had to do.

As soon as we got back to his place, he'd be on the phone making call after call, talking to race organizers, sponsors, the media, while I staggered around and climbed, cross-eyed, into the shower. He was constantly busy and totally self-involved. My needs weren't secondary to his, they were much less important than that. And I don't mean that in an unkind way, because it was probably the attitude that had made him successful.

In early spring 1995, Doyley was invited to the Six Hours of San Sebastián track event in the Basque Country and he asked me to go with him. The event was basically a condensed version of a Six-Day held at a track that had room for about fifteen thousand spectators. It was a huge venue and the atmosphere was electrifying. It was like a football match. The crowd passed wine around, sang and chanted.

We flew in the night before the race and there was a steak dinner for all the riders. We had breakfast the following morning, steak for lunch and then raced at the track from mid-afternoon until about 9 p.m. Another steak meal was consumed before flying home the next morning with a thousand quid in appearance money in my pocket.

Suddenly, being Doyley's wing man wasn't so bad. Three steaks in four meals, a grand in cash and the chance to race with some of the Six-Day circuit's biggest stars – among the riders was the Swiss legend Urs Freuler and his equally legendary moustache, Jimmy Madsen and Jens Veggerby – was fantastic.

I learned a little more about how the Six-Days operated when we went down to the track with our passports to meet the organizer and collect our money. Doyley introduced me to the boss, who counted out my money, took back a handful of notes for tax, and handed me my envelope. When we got back to our hotel, Doyley said: 'We need to hide this money.' One of the old stories about unscrupulous Six-Day organizers was that they liked to pay the riders before the race, knowing they'd have to leave the cash unguarded in their hotel room while they were on the track. Then someone would let themselves into the riders' rooms and collect all the money.

We were in our room and Doyley was looking for a place to hide the cash. Eventually, we lifted up the heavy sideboard and slid the envelopes underneath. It was then I noticed how much fatter Doyley's wad was compared to mine.

The riders knew how to put on a show. The racing was incredibly fast. We did a couple of Madison chases, an elimination race and a points race, and the pace was relentless throughout. It was a whirlwind couple of days, and lucrative too, and I was already thinking that perhaps there was more to cycling than the kilometre time trial.

Although I had won back-to-back national titles in the kilo, I'd also branched out and cycled the longer events like the pursuit, the points race, the scratch race and the Madison. I was riding more and more on the road, training with Doyley and entering more races. I loved the variety and enjoyed the fact that I could race more often.

A coach had once told me that if I wanted to achieve my maximum potential in the kilo, I'd have to dedicate myself solely to it. The thinking then was that the kilometre was such an explosive event, you could only peak for one or maybe two major races a year. The rest of the time was spent training and in the gym. Those words stuck in my head, and the idea of racing for a minute or so, a few times a year, did not appeal at all. I still didn't love training – that wasn't why I rode a bike, it was the buzz of racing that got me fired up – so why restrict myself to only a handful of races?

*

Once Manchester velodrome was up and running, there were more and more races to do. There was a two-day event to officially open the velodrome, then the National Championships moved there in 1995, and Alan Rushton, the race promoter who had organized the Kellogg's Tour of Britain in the eighties and brought the Tour de France to the south coast of England in 1994, put on Superdrome, which brought all the excitement and razzmatazz of a Six-Day to our doorstep. The place was packed, the crowd was jumping, and Rushton understood what elevated a bike race into a spectator event. There were dancing girls between the races and music during them. It was brilliant to be a part of but I remember seeing a reader's letter in *Cycling Weekly* complaining about the girls and the music. I wondered if he'd ever been to a Six-Day in Germany when the oompah band and the strong lager is in full flow.

The 1995 World Championships in Bogotá, Colombia, were a really important marker on the road towards Atlanta. There were only ten months to go until the Olympics and, although there wasn't a queue of riders snapping at my heels, waiting to take my place, I wanted to perform well to book my ticket to Atlanta.

Bogotá was a disaster from start to finish. I went to have my jabs for yellow fever, and whatever else we were supposed to be in danger of contracting over there, a week later than the rest of the squad. Everyone had a bad few days where they felt groggy, like they had a mild dose of the flu, but they were over it by the time we flew out. Unfortunately, having had my jabs the day before our flight, I knew what was coming.

In order to acclimatize to racing at altitude which, in Bogotá, could be at 2,600 metres, we went to Colorado in the United States for a training camp. First, we went to Boulder, Colorado, which is 1,600 metres at the foot of the Rocky Mountains. Then we spent a few days at Vail, at 2,400 metres, before going higher to Breckenridge – 2,900 metres, or 9,600 feet. The idea was to do it in stages to make it easier to get used to.

I was in all sorts of trouble, trying to cope with the side-effects of my inoculation jabs and suffering with full-blown altitude sickness. If I'd thought about it, I would have taken a couple of days off to recover and then start training, but because we only had this short period at Breckenridge, and because everyone was wary about what effects racing at altitude in Colombia would have, I felt the pressure to go out on my bike. We didn't have a coach with us either; to save money, they would all join us in Colombia. We had one mechanic, a lovely guy called Geoff Shergold, whom we nicknamed Captain Cholesterol because of his fondness for food. He ran up a bill of a couple of thousand quid on his own credit card buying food for all the riders in Colorado. He took us out to diners, where the portions were huge. When we'd finished eating, he'd ask around the table: 'Are you going to finish that burger?'

A day or two after we arrived in Bogotá, I started to come round and was feeling like I was back to normal. We were training on the track, which was a horrendous concrete velodrome – a dead track with no life in it at all. It also wasn't in the best condition. Jon Clay, Bryan Steel, Matt Illingworth and I were going through our team pursuit drills one afternoon and I bumped it down the back straight. There was a dip in the track and I ran into the back of the rider in front of me and took Illingworth down with me.

I wasn't too badly hurt and was in no danger of missing the championships – until I chose the fish for dinner at the hotel one night and went down with a violent bout of food poisoning.

I was away from home for a month and I didn't even get to race. Another valuable lesson was learned. You never have the fish on the eve of a major championships.

Towards the end of 1995, I went on another Six-Day road trip. Although I was technically a professional in Britain, I was still eligible for the amateur Six-Day races in Europe, so I was able to fix up a place at events in Dortmund and Munich.

I took our road atlas of western Europe off the shelf and Dad highlighted the route to Dortmund. By now I had an old but reliable Ford Sierra estate that was perfect for the long drive, but I thought I might need a phone in case of emergencies, so I went and bought this great big mobile before I set off.

At the end of a tough but uneventful Dortmund Six, I hooked up with the Danish riders Freddie Bertelsen and Tayeb Braikia, who were also heading to Munich for the next race. I said I'd follow them down. Fortunately, I'd filled the Sierra with petrol, because they drove at 110 miles per hour all the way, without stopping, and despite a torrential rainstorm that meant I could barely see beyond the length of the bonnet. I had no idea where I was going, so I didn't dare back off; I just gritted my teeth and followed the trail of spray to Bavaria.

When we got to Munich, I was told there was no partner for me to race with. The Dortmund organizer had told me the people in Munich had someone lined up for me; but now the Munich organizer was telling me the guy in Dortmund should have sorted it out. Either way, I was partnerless. They told me to head to my hotel and they'd see what they could do.

The next morning, they introduced me to a guy called Markus Köcknitz, who'd been a junior German champion on the track and was a decent team pursuiter. The only problem was, he'd been in semi-retirement and had been working in a bank for the past three months.

During the first handsling change in the first Madison, I pulled him clean off his bike. The poor guy suffered like a dog that week, and I tried to nurse him through as best I could. His family were so kind, they invited me to lunch every day and really looked after me. Towards the end of the week, he was coming round a bit and he managed to tough it out to the end. I think he was even beginning to enjoy it.

I came off the track and made one of my frequent calls home to friends or family, only to be tapped on the shoulder and told I was due back on the track again. 'Sorry, got to go, I'm doing some sprints now.' Not long after I got home, I got my first mobile-phone bill. I gawped at the number at the bottom of the last page. It was more than £250, almost a quarter of my Sports Council grant for the year.

No, it wasn't all glitz and glamour being in the Great Britain Olympic cycling squad back then. No one gave you a free phone and picked up your roaming charges when you were away.

# 6

# Love in the Olympic Village

In Olympic year, everything got more serious and more organized. There was a bit more money available, so we could race and train abroad more often. Government funding was weighted towards Olympic seasons, and the British Cycling Federation tried to save in non-Olympic years so there'd be more to spend in the final countdown to the Games. We started to have training seminars, talks by nutritionists and coaches from other sports. Former Olympians came to tell us about their experiences of the Games so we would have an idea of what to expect.

By now, competition for places in the team pursuit squad had heated up quite a bit because we knew that only four riders would be going to Atlanta for the event. Chris Boardman had moved on to the road and was winning prologues at the Tour de France, so he was going to do the time trial in Atlanta. Graeme Obree took our individual pursuit place and he was no more suited to the team pursuit now than he had been in Hamar three years earlier. Normally, a nation's points race rider would be the reserve for the team pursuit. However, we hadn't qualified for a place in the points race. The World Championships in Bogotá was the last opportunity to qualify and Jonny Clay got wiped out in a crash by a rider from Barbados in the first heat.

So Doug had a bit of a selection headache for the team pursuit. He had to choose four from five of us – Chris Newton, Bryan Steel, Matt Illingworth, Simon Lillistone and me.

We had a selection meeting at the velodrome one afternoon and sat round in a semi-circle as Doug handed round paper and pens. He asked each of us to write on a piece of paper the four-man line-up we'd pick if it was up to us to decide. I suppose it was a bit of a cop-out by Doug, but I can see why he did it, and in the end we got the right result and the best team went.

Lillistone was the one who got the chop. Objectively speaking, the rest of us made up the fastest four. Whether Doug was trying to make a difficult decision slightly easier, I don't know, but one thing is certain: if you ask the riders to select a four-man team, they will put themselves in it and then pick the three other riders they consider to be the fastest. So Doug could take the temperature of the group and, by a process of elimination, pick the right team.

But it was slightly awkward, because Lillistone was a nice guy and it was not pleasant to have to publicly reject someone you'd raced and trained with. That should be the coach's job. Steely was another nice guy and he chirped up and said he'd voted for Lillistone. Whether he did or not is neither here nor there, but it took the sting out of things a bit.

Training for the team pursuit has changed radically since 1996, but back then we still did it the old-fashioned way. We trained below race pace and then expected to step it up when we got into the heat of competition. That sounds logical enough, but if you think about it, you're setting off on a journey into the unknown if you do it that way.

Over the next decade or so, the thinking completely changed.

We trained harder, beyond what we were hoping to do in the race, trying to acclimatize our bodies to the feeling of going faster. We'd push beyond where we'd been before and then, on race day, we reined it back to a point that was sustainable over four kilometres. Eventually we got to the stage where our scheduling was so good for the team pursuit that we could predict, give or take a couple of tenths of a second, what time we would record in competition, because it was all planned for. Successive British team pursuit squads at the Beijing and London Olympics have taken that on in huge great strides.

Some nations still haven't caught up. You see the Belgians training on the track in a nice small gear, twiddling away, looking smooth, no doubt feeling comfortable and in control. Their confidence is sky-high. But when they put the bigger gear on for the race it feels alien and it's harder for them. I'm not just singling out the Belgians: a lot of countries still do that, and back in 1996 we were still working that way. It wasn't until a bit later that the British Cycling coaches broke down the team pursuit into the scientific equation it really is. If we know the size of the gear on the bike, we know how far one revolution of the pedals will take us. If we can spin that gear at 125 revolutions per minute, we can work out exactly how long it'll take us to cover four kilometres. Then it's simply a question of finding four compatible riders and training them until they are capable of doing it. There. Easy. Honest!

A couple of months before the Atlanta Olympics, a sports psychologist called John Syer came to see us. His speciality was team-building exercises and he had us crawling round on our hands and knees, doing role plays and stuff. Those kinds of sessions are always embarrassing to start with and people are reluctant to throw themselves into it, but you can gradually feel the inhibitions melt away. While I wouldn't say I embraced it

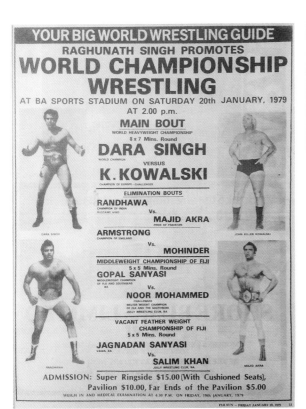

**Left and above:** This poster of my dad, wrestling in Fiji the day before my fourth birthday, is on my wall at home. John 'Killer Kowalski' Hayles kept me in line, most of the time!

**Below left:** Messing around on my BMX on 'the humps and bumps' near Horndean. I think it was my teammate-to-be Paul Jennings who took this picture.

**Below:** Racing in an early criterium in Winchester, alongside Ben Wilson and Mark Pearce.

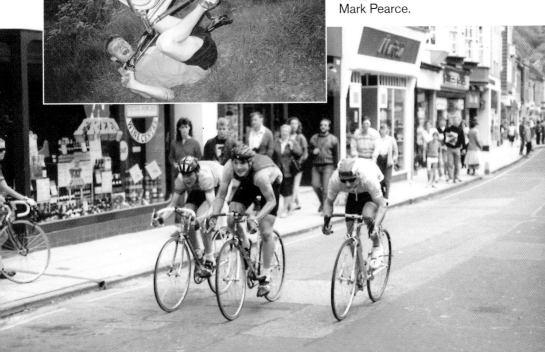

**Left:** The Junior World Championships were held in Colorado Springs in 1991. We had lots of fun and too much sun, which was more than you could usually say about Leicester's Saffron Lane velodrome **(below)**.

Winning the National 10 mile title in 1994 **(above)** followed by the kilo **(right)**. I've still got that bike, and use it for my coffee run.

Crossing the line first at Herne Hill, in the Good Friday meeting in 1995 on my trusty Columbus Max **(left)**, and in the 10 mile race in 1997 **(below)**.

I was National points race champion five years in a row, starting in 1996, and here I am with my Ambrosia teammate Russell Williams and Phil West on the podium.

**Above:** The 1994 Commonwealth Games in Victoria, Canada, were my first experience of a major Games.

**Middle:** Showing off my medal with Bryan Steel (far left) and Chris Newton (far right), although Tony Doyle typically just had to run off and put his sponsors' top over his England one.

**Left:** At the start line of 'my event', the kilo. Fifth place, along with that silver in the team pursuit, was good going for a 21-year-old, at least in those days. It would be twelve years before I got a Commonwealth gold medal.

We entered the 1996 Olympics with high hopes of a medal – at least I did – but Chris, Bryan, Matt Illingworth and I ended up a disappointing tenth. More importantly, it was in Atlanta that I met my future wife Vicki.

From about that time, I felt I could make it on the road too, and Stage 7a of the PruTour from Carlisle to Edinburgh in 1999 saw one of my biggest wins, holding off Stuart O'Grady (in the green) and Pascal Lino in the rain.

**Left:** Giving it everything (including home-made bars on my bike) in the individual pursuit at the 2000 Sydney Olympics.

**Below:** Chris Hoy roared me on but despite a personal best in the bronze medal race, the home fans inspired Brad McGee to nick it from me. Did I mention I once beat Sir Chris in a Keirin?

**Above:** A smile on my face at the start of Paris–Roubaix in 2001, my first year as a road pro. I was warned that despite being 28 and an Olympic medallist, I'd get my head kicked in.

**Above:** My three years with Cofidis were tough but enjoyable, especially living in Biarritz, where David Millar held court.

**Above:** Riding in Six-Day races was always a blast or just plain crazy. This was one of the fun ones, in Dortmund with Brad Wiggins in 2003.

with both hands, I didn't dismiss it either. I was open to anything that might make us better.

We had to sit round with our eyes closed, visualizing every phase of the team pursuit competition: arriving at the velodrome, warming up, going to the start line, strapping my feet to the pedals and waiting for the gun to go off. Then I had to think about the race itself, powering away from the line and settling in behind Steely, getting close, but not too close, to his rear wheel. Over and over again we visualized doing the perfect changeovers, getting every stage of the manoeuvre spot on.

At the time, it was pretty radical. I'd never been asked to do that before and, even if I wasn't convinced it would make us faster, I couldn't see it doing us any harm.

Later on, not long before we flew to the United States for our pre-Olympic holding camp, we had another session and Syer asked us how we thought we were going to get on. He went round the group and, although I can't remember specifically what Newton, Illingworth or Steely said, I know they didn't have any wildly ambitious expectations.

When it came to my turn, I thought about what I was going to say and decided to just say what was in my gut: 'We're going to get bronze.'

I felt all three heads turn to me.

'I don't know why, I just have this feeling we're going to get bronze.'

I'd been scared to say it in front of the group because I was almost embarrassed and because I didn't want to put the others on edge. It was strange, but it was the first time I'd ever been asked to say how I thought I'd do in a competition. As an athlete, there's a peculiar battle going on in your head. I've said that part of my approach to cycling was that I always thought I could win every race I took part in. That is the mentality of an athlete.

You have to believe you can win, because if you don't, what's the point in taking part? What are you doing there, just making up the numbers?

And yet it's also an act of self-deception. You can't win every race and, if I was to be blunt, there was no chance we could win the Olympics. When someone asked me a straight question – 'How are you going to do at the Olympic Games?' – I couldn't say we were going to win it, because that wasn't realistic. We weren't close to being the best team pursuit squad in the world. We were a decent, and improving, team but we were a way off being potential Olympic champions.

I've often wondered why I thought we'd finish third. Was it a measure of my own growing self-belief? Did I think: 'If there were four of me, we could get bronze'?

Really, we didn't know what we could achieve in Atlanta, because we were looking forwards, trying to improve and hoping for the best possible result. I didn't know it then, but the way to win an event like the team pursuit is to work backwards. Identify the target – in this case the time you think you can do on a particular track in certain conditions – and then work through the steps you need to take in order to achieve it.

In a way, Atlanta was the last journey into the unknown. We travelled in hope.

And we finished tenth.

The result may not have gone as I had hoped, but everything else about the Atlanta Olympic Games was brilliant. From the moment Steely and I set off in my new Ford Fiesta van to collect our official kit in London, to the moment I stepped off the plane after flying home, it was fantastic. Imagine the best family holiday you've ever had and multiply it by ten. It's not an exaggeration to say Atlanta changed my life.

Knowing I was going to represent my country in the Olympics had me bursting with pride. After our final training camp at Leicester, we headed down to London in my van. I drove at 60 miles per hour on the motorway, sitting in behind the big trucks to save fuel by driving in their slipstream. I was only 23, and I'd turned into my dad. It cracked Bryan, because he used to tailgate cars in the outside lane and flash his headlights until they moved over.

It was a burning hot day and it was the closest I'd come to that first-day-of-the-holidays feeling since leaving school. We parked up at the college in west London where the British Olympic Association were dishing out the official Great Britain clothing and headed inside.

They had soldiers from the army running the operation, with typical military precision. They were ticking off the names on a clipboard and handing out the right quota of kit. It was like reporting for our first day at Sandhurst. I'd take four red T-shirts, four blue T-shirts and four white ones from one soldier, then step to the side, where I'd be given a couple of tracksuits. On and on down the line we went, until we had a couple of huge official Great Britain Olympic team suitcases full of swag. There were two pairs of trainers, a rain suit, a kit bag and rucksack, several pairs of shorts, flip-flops, sun hats, baseball caps, sun visor, sweatbands and my Great Britain blazer and slacks for the opening ceremony. We also got a BOA Olympic Games Swatch watch, which I've still got somewhere.

Sports people are often easily pleased, but heading down to London to be given a year's supply of Adidas clothing took some beating. It was like a couple of Christmases and birthdays rolled into one. For me, the Games started there.

*

Being part of the Olympic team was like being in a bubble. For months, everything I did related to the Olympics. I was either racing, or training, or resting, or I was planning for Atlanta. Living inside that Olympic bubble was great, but there was a major drawback. There's only room for one in there.

It was Atlanta, Atlanta, Atlanta, Olympics, Olympics, Olympics – all year. The Olympics didn't just dominate my life, it dominated the lives of the people around me.

I was engaged to a girl called Michelle, who lived not far away in Hayling Island. We met when I was 20 and we'd been together for a couple of years or so. After a while, I had proposed, because that was what people did, wasn't it? You went out for a year or two and then you got engaged. It seemed the right thing to do at the time, but I suppose I was approaching life the way I approached cycling. I was wandering down the middle of the road seeing what came my way, rather than getting the map out and picking my direction.

Michelle was a great girl but she didn't love cycling. It was something I did; it took up a lot of my time and energy and meant I didn't have a proper job or much money. It dominated the weekends and, not surprisingly, she got fed up with hearing me say, 'I can't this weekend, I'm racing.'

'What about next weekend?'

'I'm racing.'

It got to a point where she was sick of me being away all the time and when we were together we were beginning to argue. The six months leading up to the Olympics weren't much fun for either of us, but at least I could avoid the issue, because I was looking ahead to Atlanta. Instead of talking about where the relationship was going, I used the Olympics as an excuse.

Not long before the Games, Michelle got a job up near Reading and, although we didn't say it, I think we thought that would be a convenient way to end it. Having said that, we didn't actually get round to ending it before the Games, but we both knew it was inevitable. Well, I did.

A couple of weeks before the Games, we flew to Tallahassee, Florida, for the Great Britain team's pre-Olympic holding camp. It was a chance to get used to the humid weather, train together and get into an Olympic frame of mind before heading to the village in Atlanta.

We quickly got into a routine. Bryan, Chris Newton, Matt Illingworth and I would train in the morning, then we'd relax at our apartment in the afternoon. A lot of the other British teams came in and out of Tallahassee on their way to Atlanta. The British swimming team was already there when we arrived, so after training we'd spend our time gawping through the wire fence as the women's team relaxed by the outdoor pool. I was too shy to go and hang out at the pool, so I kept my distance. They were loud, confident and looked like they were having a great time. I was a slightly gawky cyclist.

One afternoon, Bryan and I went down to the little communal laundry room in our apartment block to put our cycling kit through the wash. When we got there, three of the women's swimming team were in there sorting out their underwear.

'Whose bra is this?'

'Are these your knickers?'

Brian and I giggled and legged it, like a pair of schoolboys, completely out of our depth.

Later I found out that the three swimmers we'd bumped into were Karen Pickering, Claire Huddart and Vicki Horner, and it was Vicki who had caught my eye.

*

We flew to Atlanta, Georgia, for the Games of the Twenty-Sixth Olympiad, which also marked the centenary of the modern Olympics. I was going to become an Olympian. I was determined to make the most of it and find out what the Olympic experience was all about. That's not to say I wasn't taking the cycling seriously – I was, but for all I knew this could be it, my once-in-a-lifetime opportunity. The Olympics are so bewildering, it takes a set-up like the one the British Cycling team has now to keep people's heads on for their event. There were so many distractions in the village.

The Olympic village was like a cross between a university campus and a holiday camp. We were staying in blocks, organized nation by nation. Cuba were over the road from us and everyone hung out their flags, which was handy when it came to finding our way home after a night out once the competition was over. 'Remember, turn left at France, go past Germany and we're on the right.'

Everything was very American. The fixed smiles and have-a-nice-day attitude didn't feel a hundred per cent real, they were brought to you in conjunction with McDonald's or Fuji. Security was red-hot, which was probably not a bad thing considering a bomb went off in the Olympic park, but before that terrible event it seemed very heavy-handed. Our block was right near one of the entrances to the village, but the security guards wouldn't let us exit that way with our bikes, so every time we wanted to go somewhere we had to go all the way across the village to leave on the other side.

There were golf buggies all around which were meant for the staff and officials in the Olympic village, not the athletes. We didn't have a key to start the motor, but we found that if you lifted the seat and wedged a ring pull from a Coke can between the battery and the metal body of the buggy, the contact was enough to start it up. So if we needed to get around the village, we hijacked a buggy, hot-wired it and raced around.

The bus system laid on for the athletes was chaotic and the buses were always late. Stories of athletes only just getting to their events in time because the bus hadn't turned up, or the driver had gone the wrong way down the freeway, went round the village in double quick time and made everyone edgy about getting around. If you saw a bus going where you needed to go, you got on it: there was no guarantee another one would turn up.

Turning up for the opening ceremony was like joining the army for the day. I put on my uniform, the Great Britain blazer and slacks, and we were all directed into the baseball stadium next to the Olympic stadium.

'This way, sir.'

'That way, ma'am.'

They gave us a lunch box and drinks, and we sat in the stadium watching the opening ceremony on a big screen until it was our turn to go across the car park and into the stadium for the athletes' lap.

We were waiting there for hours and it turned out that the swimmers were in the same row as us, just a little further along. They kept getting up to go and get soft drinks, because it was a pretty warm day, and when they came back we had to shuffle in our seats and shift our legs to the side to let them go past.

After they'd been back and forwards a few times, there was a bit of joking between us. One of them was Vicki, although she had no idea who I was or that I'd seen her sorting through her washing in Tallahassee. As they were coming down the row towards us, I deliberately left my leg in the way when Vicki came past so that she walked into it.

And when she did, I faked injury like a Premier League footballer.

'Agggh, my leg! You've walked straight into my leg.'

'Oh no, I'm so sorry!' she said in her Geordie accent.

'I'm a cyclist. That's it, my Games are over.'

When she realized I was winding her up, she smiled the most amazing smile, and I think that was the moment I fell in love with her. I did a Hugh Porter and fell for a swimmer. Hugh, a cyclist, met his wife, Anita Lonsbrough, when they were travelling to compete at the 1964 Olympics in Tokyo.

Eventually, someone with a clipboard and headset shouted 'Great Britain' and we all got up and left the baseball stadium and headed over to the Olympic stadium. We walked up the tunnel into the stadium and the sight in front of us had me almost gasping for breath. It was so vast, the camera flashes were going off all over the place like twinkly lights, and the atmosphere was electrifying. I was only one member of a huge Great Britain team, and we were only one nation, but as we walked around the athletics track, I felt like the eyes of the world were on us.

We stood and watched as Muhammad Ali, one of those legendary sportspeople who leaves everyone awestruck, stepped out with the Olympic torch to light the flame. Ali was suffering with Parkinson's disease and his step was unsteady and his hands were shaking. To see such a great boxer diminished like that, yet acting with such dignity, was very moving. Ali had the attention of the entire stadium and probably everyone who was near a TV watching it.

The stadium was silent. I stood and stared at the cauldron and then Ali lit the touchpaper and a flame shot across the night sky and rose up towards the red cauldron. The yellow flames went up and they danced in the cauldron, and as soon as it was lit, I couldn't help myself.

'It's a carton of McDonald's fries!'

Vicki turned round and whacked me playfully in the chest. But she had to accept that now it was alight, it was impossible not to see the likeness. The red cauldron was almost a perfect replica of a McDonald's chip carton and the flames were like fries; the only thing missing was the golden arches logo. Only in America. The corporate Games.

After the opening ceremony had finished, there were hundreds of athletes outside the stadium. We were left to fend for ourselves. Suddenly the guys with clipboards and headsets were nowhere to be seen. There was no 'This way, sir,' or 'That way, ma'am.'

There was a line of buses and they were crammed full of Olympic athletes. It was a huge scrum to get on to one of those buses and I found myself holding Vicki's hand, guiding her through the mêlée, trying to get her safely on board. The bus looked like it couldn't possibly squeeze anyone else in but I put Vicki in front of me, pushed her on to the bus then got in behind her and wedged myself in between the doors.

When we got back to the village, we said goodnight and went our separate ways and that was it until after our events. She was going to swim in the 4x200-metre freestyle relay and I was in the team pursuit. Even our events were sort of similar.

I've said pretty much all that needs to be said about our race. Put simply, we didn't ride fast enough. We were tenth, so we missed out on reaching the quarter-finals. My Olympic Games lasted four minutes and 15 seconds, but we did beat the Germans, who sacked their coach immediately afterwards. The French squad won the final in a time of 4-05. Ten seconds was a big gap.

The only other cycling event I made a point of watching was the kilometre final, because I wanted to see Shane Kelly. We'd got to know each other a little bit during that trip to Tasmania, and since then he had developed into the best kilometre rider in the world. He was the reigning world champion, having won in Bogotá the previous year, and a lot of people expected him to win Olympic gold.

When I'm not racing, I love watching the very best do what they do best, so I headed to the velodrome on the day of the kilometre final. I was used to the Atlanta weather by now. The day would start warm and get more and more humid as the morning gave way to afternoon. By the middle of the afternoon the sky would be heavy and oppressive and, at about four o'clock, we'd have a thunderstorm. It would rain hard and go almost dark for half an hour or so, before clearing up to the extent that you wouldn't even know it had rained. It was as if the sky was in the habit of rebooting itself.

But that afternoon, the expectation was tangible in the velodrome. Everyone wanted to see what Shane Kelly could do.

He pulled out of the start gate and immediately I recognized something was wrong. He wasn't powering away like he normally did, instead he was pedalling tentatively and looking down at his bike. He'd pulled his foot out of the pedal.

The kilometre rules, as I knew from my exhibition race in Tasmania, are unforgiving. If you mess up the start, that's it. It was a huge downer not to see Kelly race, but I could only imagine how bad it was for him. Four years of work down the drain in a second. This was *his* time, *his* race. A foregone conclusion. That was another lesson learned. Never take anything for granted.

Once the team pursuit was over, we still had a couple of weeks to enjoy the Olympic village before it was time to go home. Everything you've heard about the Olympic village is true. Once the competition is over, it's party time. The longer the Games go on, the more athletes finish their events, and the years of training, stress and tension are released in a variety of ways.

The queues at the three McDonald's restaurants in the village got longer and longer every day. But even though the party started, there was a sort of code of honour among the athletes, even when they were completely hammered after a night out. Not everyone had finished their events, so people staggered round in a silent drunken stupor. There was lots of shsss-hing. No one wanted to keep awake someone who was competing in a final the next morning.

The cycling and swimming events finished at around the same time, so as soon as we were free, we met up with Vicki, Karen, Claire and the others again. These were the days before everyone had email, and our mobile phones wouldn't work in the United States (although we heard Linford Christie had a mobile that worked in America and thought that was the coolest thing). But there was a room in the village that had two computers in it and there was an internal email system. Every athlete had a user name and password, so you could send private messages. That was how we coordinated everything: 'Where are we meeting? Where shall we go?'

The British team had a place just outside the village where we could meet friends and family who didn't have Olympic accreditation. They had the BBC on the TV, some British newspapers, Cadbury's chocolate and a pump doing British beer. It was a little piece of home. Bryan, Matt, Chris and I would head there and wait for the swimmers and then we'd head out to Buckhead, Atlanta, to drink.

Buckhead was brilliant. There were loads of bars and it looked like something out of a western. We'd order fishbowl-sized cocktails and then head to a club, where I'd impress absolutely no one with my moves on the dance floor. I'm pretty sure Vicki stood and laughed at me when I tried to dance, which just made me like her even more.

And at the end of the Games, when it was time to go home, Vicki and I swapped numbers and told each other to keep in touch. I don't know what I was expecting. It felt like the best holiday romance was coming to an end, but I wanted it to be more than a holiday romance.

I remember getting the road map out as soon as I got home to Mum and Dad's and tracing my finger over pages and pages of Great Britain from my house in Horndean to her place near Newcastle. I could have wept. There was almost 350 miles between us. We might as well have lived in different countries. Then there was the fact that we were both athletes. She'd be training and racing, so would I. When would we see each other? Oh, and she had a boyfriend too.

I knew my relationship with Michelle was over. We talked on the phone and there were tears, but we decided we wanted to end it on good terms, so I said I'd go up to Reading to see her. We went to a pub to chat and while I was there my phone rang.

Vicki and I have never agreed on exactly what happened next. I was in a busy pub and I was sure that the voice at the other end of the phone said, 'Is Bryan Steel there?'

I said no, and hung up, not realizing it was Vicki.

She must've thought, 'Charming, he's had his fun, now he's avoiding me.'

Later on, the penny dropped that it must have been Vicki calling, so I rang the number she'd given me in Atlanta, which was her home number. Her mum answered, so I asked her to pass on a message. It turned out Vicki was down in London with some friends, and was heading to see the Rolling Stones play. Had I known that, I'd have driven over to see her.

The next time we met was at the Leeds International Classic

road race. It was a round of the World Cup and half the field was made up of riders who'd just done the Tour de France. Although I'd done some road races, I was an 86 kilogram track rider, a big unit. I felt like Gulliver as I stood on the start line surrounded by all these tiny roadies with skinny legs and sparrow's chests. I knew I wasn't going to finish a 150-mile road race that took us up every hill in West Yorkshire. I was in the race because I'd been to the Olympics and because the pro team I was riding for that year managed to wangle an invite.

Our team was sponsored by the company that makes tinned rice pudding and custard: Ambrosia Desserts. Our manager was Micky Morrison, a real character who had been a rider himself, but his true calling was as one of life's duckers and divers. Look up 'loveable rogue' in the dictionary and it says 'Morrison, M'.

Micky was one of the people who helped Tony Capper put together the ANC–Halfords team that rode the 1987 Tour de France. They did that on a wing and a prayer, and Micky's methods hadn't changed much. Micky had stumped up the entrance money for a series of city centre races organized by Alan Rushton. For some reason, the races didn't happen, so Micky said that instead of having his money back, he'd take a place in the Leeds International Classic, which was also being run by Rushton.

The Ambrosia team was only small and hadn't been registered with the world governing body to ride international events, which meant we were ineligible. Rushton pointed this out and Micky said, 'Don't worry, I'll sort it.'

In order to qualify for international clearance, the team had to have a minimum of twelve riders. We only had six, so Micky had put down the names of the mechanics and even his own dog to complete the paperwork. He went back to Rushton with his registration documents and we were given our place. (Years later, when I went to Belgium and France, the fans who collect autographs would ask me if so-and-so was still riding. I didn't have the heart to point out that the rider they were after was a 40-year-old mechanic or Micky Morrison's dog, so I just said they'd retired.)

On the start line, the announcer introduced Chris Boardman to the crowd. Boardman was the star of British cycling by now. He'd worn the yellow jersey at the Tour de France in 1994. Then the announcer introduced a few more notable riders before calling out my name, which took me a little by surprise.

*'Ladies and gentleman, just back from riding the team pursuit at the Olympic Games . . . Rob Hayles!'*

I rolled up to the start line alongside Boardman and then we were told to roll out. Road races like that always start with a neutralized section where the riders just cruise along casually for a few miles, usually until they are out of town. Then the chief judge will wave a flag to indicate the proper start of the race.

So I was rolling along as we headed out of the city, enjoying the applause and cheers from the crowd, but aware that I couldn't see any other riders in my field of vision. I was becoming more self-conscious, but I daren't look round. I didn't realize that I had drifted ten or fifteen bike lengths ahead of everyone else.

Boardman came up alongside me and said, 'It's very calm back there. It doesn't bode well.'

I knew there was very little chance I'd finish the race, but I also knew that I had to hang on as long as I possibly could and that doing so would be painful. I was crapping myself and yet when a few riders broke away from the bunch, I instinctively followed them. I raced like an unbridled horse. I saw the move going and off I went. Unless you held me back, I couldn't help myself getting stuck in. *Cycling Weekly* took the mickey, of course, saying: 'Who was the home hero trying to get in the early break?'

That night, I met up with Vicki, and a few weeks after that she moved to Stockport to train at the Stockport Metro pool. Her friend Claire said, 'It's destiny, Vic. You'll be at the pool in Stockport, Rob will be at the velodrome in Manchester. It can all work out!'

Claire was right. Whenever I went up to Manchester I'd go and see Vicki for a few days; and whenever it was time to go home I'd sit outside in the car in tears before composing myself enough to drive off.

When you think about the way life turns out, you realize how often events that seem important in their own right and for one particular reason are also important for a completely unconnected reason. Imagine if my team pursuit teammates had voted me out of the Olympic line-up when Doug handed round those pens and paper. I would never have met Vicki.

# 7

# It Could Be You

No one rested on their laurels after the Atlanta Olympics, because there were no laurels to rest on. Compared to Barcelona, Atlanta had felt like a bit of a step backwards. Four years earlier, Chris Boardman had ridden his specially developed super bike to gold; this time round, we'd sent our own bikes to the Liverpool-based frame-builder Terry Dolan to have them sprayed blue in time for the Games.

Although there wasn't a gold medal in America, the British cycling team actually did pretty well in Atlanta, just not on the track. Boardman won bronze in the road time trial and Max Sciandri got another bronze in the road race. Until about a year before the Games, the Derby-born Sciandri had been competing as an Italian, but he took out a British racing licence so he could race for us in Atlanta.

Across the other sports, Atlanta had been a let-down for the British team – the worst since 1952 in terms of gold medals. The rowers Steve Redgrave and Matthew Pinsent won our only gold and the press and politicians decided 'Something Must Be Done'.

That something was the formation of UK Sport in early 1997, followed by a flood of National Lottery money into Olympic sports. The £300,000 annual budget Doug Dailey had managed to spin out so it lasted a season was more than trebled, and Peter Keen was appointed director of the new World Class Performance Plan. National Lottery money changed everything. It was the third big building block to be lowered into place, and now we had the crucial foundations that would at least provide a platform for success. We had the money, the facility (Manchester velodrome) and a man with vision at the head of it all.

Keen's first job was to put together an application for funding and a detailed eight-year plan that would take us past the 2004 Olympics. Looking back now, it's easy to forget just how significant the arrival of that funding was. Although I'd had brilliant, unwavering support from my parents, I couldn't have carried on living at home for ever. At some point, I'd have had to earn some money, either by trying to get a better contract with a road team in Europe, which would have taken me away from the Great Britain track squad, or by getting a proper job. I knew I was in a better position than most. My parents had the means and the patience to give me enough support to get by. The rest I made up in whatever government grants were available and in the bits of sponsorship money I could attract. Lottery funding would enable the next generation of young riders to view riding for their country as a career choice rather than a hobby. OK, it wasn't a king's ransom at the start, but it meant young athletes could concentrate on racing, training and recovery without having to squeeze in a part-time job to make ends meet.

Although we knew the lottery money was coming, it took a while before it filtered through to us in the form of a monthly pay cheque. We had to fill out forms to get our grants, and the funding was split into three grades: A, B and C, depending on your sport and your level of competition. Everything was allocated according to your past experience and future potential, but you also had to jump through hoops to qualify. There were no cash cows. To get any money, you had to deserve it and then perform well enough to keep it.

Peter Keen set out the qualifying criteria, and we had to go to Manchester velodrome to do a series of timed tests on the track. One was a three-kilometre time trial from a standing start, but you also had to complete the first kilometre within a certain time. The idea was to demonstrate your sprinting power at the start then your endurance over the rest of the distance. The times required to qualify for funding weren't ludicrously quick, but neither could you just roll out of bed with a hangover and tick it off. It was like exam day at school, with a bunch of cyclists milling around waiting for their turn on the track, confident that they would pass the test ahead of them but nervous nevertheless.

Bryan Steel never actually made the kilometre time. He was plenty fast enough over three kilometres, but on his own on the track, without a rider to follow off the starting line, he just couldn't get that first thousand metres under his wheels quickly enough. Keen showed a bit of discretion there, because he understood the event and he knew Bryan's role in the team pursuit squad. Bryan was our diesel engine, our powerhouse, and he never underperformed in races; he just wasn't the quickest off the line. But he didn't need to be, because all he had to do was get on the wheels and then he did his bit – his vitally important bit – once we were up to speed. Fortunately, although we had forms to fill in and boxes to tick, common sense came into it too, and Bryan was given his money.

I qualified for B-category funding, which meant I got just under £1,100 a month. When Vicki got her paperwork back,

British Swimming had made a mistake: she'd been allocated under half the amount she thought she was due. She rang me up in tears because that money meant even more to her than it did to me. For the best part of a year, since she'd moved to Stockport to train at the pool there, her parents had been covering her rent. Although her parents were happy to help, the silent, self-generated pressure of taking money from them was tough for Vicki. It was a relief when it all got sorted out and Vicki got the grant she was due.

The lottery money meant that at the start of 1998 I could move up to Stockport, so Vicki and I could get a place together. It was a small house that backed on to the A6, but it was home. There we were, two elite athletes looking ahead six months down the line to the Commonwealth Games in Kuala Lumpur, and then past that to the Olympic Games in Sydney. We loved each other and, because we were both used to the rhythm of racing and training, we understood each other but, as we were to find out, having two self-centred athletes living in a small space together wasn't always bliss.

The World Track Championships were held at Manchester for the first time in August 1996. I walked into the velodrome on the first day of competition feeling a great sense of pride that we were able to welcome the rest of the world to our place and put on a top-class event. Track cycling was quite a small world and, after competing all around the globe, it was nice to be able to welcome the Aussies, the French and Italians to Britain and show them we meant business. The rest of the world looked at us differently after that, as if being able to host the World Championships made us more worthy. Our performances were improving too, albeit not enough for anyone to really notice. Even if we had pulled something out of the bag, we'd have been overshadowed by Boardman that week. He broke the world record in the 4,000-metre individual pursuit with an astonishing time of 4-11.114 – a record that stood for fifteen years until Jack Bobridge, an Australian, broke it in Sydney in 2011.

There was a bit of razzmatazz in Manchester because the event was organized by Alan Rushton, who produced some of the music and dancing girls from the Superdrome. The traditional, quite staid era of the World Championships, where the blazers from the UCI liked to hear only the ticking of the clock when the riders were on the track, was over. In Manchester, the crowd was encouraged to get involved and roar – it was the dawn of a new era for track racing.

At the start of the following year, I was 24 years old and still riding for a small British team sponsored by Ambrosia Desserts. The team didn't actually pay me a salary but, as the manager Micky Morrison pointed out, 'At least you know I'll never flick you, because at the start of the year, you know you're not getting any money!' Micky did make sure we had decent bikes; he provided me with a car and all my expenses were covered. I was also free to bring in my own sponsors, which I did, although they did 'flick' me by not paying for the final six months of my contract. At times it was harder for a 'professional' cyclist in Britain to get the money they were owed by sponsors than it was to actually win races. But at least we were never short of rice pudding once the Ambrosia truck arrived and lowered a palette of tins into the garage.

I always loved racing on Britain's roads. By 1997, the Premier Calendar – the elite series of domestic road races – was enjoying the tail-end of its heyday. We had sixteen elite events that season (down to half a dozen these days) and there was a really good level of competition. You'd see the same core group of guys week in, week out, all over the country. There was the Essex Grand Prix, the Girvan stage race in Scotland and the Tour of Lancashire in the early part of the season. The Lincoln Grand Prix remains one of the most prestigious races, because it goes up and over the cobbled Michaelgate hill in the shadow of the cathedral several times. Then there was the Tour of the Kingdom – another stage race in Scotland – the Tom Simpson Memorial in Harworth, on the border between Nottinghamshire and South Yorkshire, before the Manx International, held on the famous motorcycle TT circuit on the Isle of Man. After the National Championships in June, we'd have the Tour of the Cotswolds and Tour of the Peak. Add in the Archer Grand Prix, Romford–Harlow, the Welwyn Grand Prix and a host of other events, and we could race every weekend from early spring to late summer.

We may not have been on the telly or made the sports pages, but the racing scene was still thriving. It wasn't glamorous but it was great fun. I'd put my bike in the back of the car and drive to a race. The headquarters and changing rooms would be at a community centre, sports hall or secondary school, and the air would reek of Deep Heat and anticipation. There was a lot of banter and joking around, but the races could be brutal. No one held back and nothing could beat the feeling of going to the front of the bunch and winding up the pace. I used to ride those races flat out, whether I was in good form or bad. It was pure, hard racing, and when it was over we'd go back to the community centre, or wherever, and have a cup of tea and a slice of cake before driving home.

By the late nineties, the difficulties of organizing a bike race on Britain's busy roads – with an army of volunteers and little more than a couple of motorcycle outriders and a team of marshals with flags and goodwill – were becoming apparent. The Sunday trading laws began to strangle the bike-racing scene. More and more drivers were out on a Sunday morning, heading to the shops or the garden centre, and because the races took place on open roads, it could get dicey.

One by one the events began to disappear, either because the organizers were finding it increasingly hard to ensure the riders' safety, or because the police were intervening and telling them to stop. One year at the Archer Grand Prix in Buckinghamshire, there was a car boot sale in the field next to the finishing straight, which made it a nightmare. Without significant funding or an Act of Parliament to allow the organizers to close the roads for a morning the races were living on borrowed time.

Fortunately for me, there was enough money around for the Great Britain squad to go abroad to take part in stage races, and we did a few of them each season. In 1997, we were still a bit of a ragged outfit. Our white British Cycling Federation jerseys had been through the wash so many times they were baggy and slightly grey. Our Volvo estate team cars had seen better days too.

We went to the Olympia's Tour in the Netherlands and it rained every day. We'd get covered in muck from the roads and then have to wash our kit in the bath to try to get it as close to white as we could because we only had one spare set each. One morning I lined up at the start next to the Italian Andrea Collinelli, who was the star of their Olympic and world champion team pursuit squad. The Italians always looked immaculate and had brand new kit, fresh out of the packet, each morning. He looked me up and down with a horrified expression on his face. A day or so later, I had been dropped from the bunch and was in about the fourth group on the road, grovelling along, when we saw a bright yellow Italian Pinarello bike leaning up against a tree. Then we saw Collinelli, who was leading the race overall, jump out of the trees and get back on his bike. Someone shouted 'Piano', meaning to roll along easy to let him catch up. The poor sod had a dose of the shits and it was all down his shorts. 'He doesn't look so pristine now,' I thought, although he could at least drop back to his team car and change into some clean shorts.

On some of those foreign trips we used to have a hard time in the races, without having to get a debilitating stomach bug. The gap between the top nations and us was still a chasm. During one European stage race, I was sharing a room with Wayne Randle, one of the toughest British amateur riders I've ever raced with. Wayne was good enough to have made it as a professional, but the opportunities were few and far between, so he remained stuck in the no-man's-land between amateur and semi-professional status. Over the years, he'd been all over the world racing for Great Britain, making do with the few resources we had, and now we were witnessing a new breed of young rider who was being paid. Wayne said, with a wry smile, 'The number of kickings I've taken over the years for these lads.'

The World Track Championships, held in Perth towards the end of 1997, were instantly forgettable for me. I pulled my foot out of the pedal after a lap of our team pursuit qualification ride and had to leave the other three lads to it. Once the regular season died down, I headed to Europe for another round of gruelling Six-Day races that I thought would stand me in good stead for the Commonwealth Games the following summer.

At the start of the new season, I had a new team, one that was pretty groundbreaking at the time. Team Brite was sponsored by a telecommunications company owned by Stuart Hallam and run by Graham Weigh, the bicycle-frame builder, and most of the riders were part of the Great Britain team pursuit squad. There was Jonny Clay, Matt Illingworth, Chris Newton, Bryan Steel, Colin Sturgess – who was making a comeback after a few years away from racing – and me. We also had a stick-thin 18-year-old junior rider called Bradley Wiggins, who fancied himself as a pro in the making.

Brite was quickly dubbed a super team – the Red Machine – by *Cycling Weekly* because we won just about every domestic race going, until Chris Lillywhite of the Harrods team took the Lincoln Grand Prix in May. The fact we won every week was starting to rub people up the wrong way, so it probably wasn't a bad thing to let someone else have a few crumbs.

We rode the first PruTour of Britain, which was an eight-day stage race sponsored by the insurance company Prudential, and went abroad as the Brite team quite a few times, and as a result there was a lot more cohesion for the team pursuit. We were coming together as a unit, getting on well and building an understanding. For the first time, we also had a squad of five or six competing for the four team pursuit places, and that was propelling us to quicker times.

At the World Championships in Bordeaux a month before we were due to fly to Malaysia for the Commonwealth Games, things were going better than ever. We finished fifth in the team pursuit but the important thing was we went the quickest we'd ever gone – 4-06.360. Sturgess may have had a few seasons out of top-level competition, but he was still a class act and he'd slotted in with Jonny, Matt and me really well. We also had Bryan to come in if we needed to rest someone. The biggest boost, though, was that we went faster than the Aussies in Bordeaux, which gave us a genuine feeling we could win the Commonwealth title.

A couple of days later, I crashed in the points race and injured my ribs. With the Commonwealth Games only a month away, and a week's training at the outdoor track in Bordeaux to do, I gritted my teeth and tried not to let on how much it hurt.

When we arrived in Kuala Lumpur, I was still suffering. The pain in my ribs was inhibiting my breathing every time I tried to ride on the track. We still didn't have a full-time physio with the England team, or if we did, they hadn't arrived in Malaysia yet, but I knew I had to get myself checked out. I was talking to Lucy Tyler-Sharman, one of the Aussie track riders, and mentioned I had a problem. She got me an Australia tracksuit and smuggled me into the Aussie holding camp to see their osteopath. He took one look at me, diagnosed dislocated ribs and cracked them back into place. The pain was sharp but the relief was instant, like having a tooth pulled.

I saw Steve Paulding, who was our national track manager, and he asked, 'How are the ribs?'

'Yeah, fine,' I replied, without letting on I'd been behind enemy lines to get it sorted.

Those Commonwealth Games were when I first got to know Bradley Wiggins. He'd been on the Brite squad, but I hadn't really bumped into him too much because he was still a junior. All I heard was Graham Weigh, our team manager, complaining, 'Who the hell does this Bradley Wiggins think he is? He wants this bike, that bike, these wheels, those wheels.'

Of course, when Brad won the individual pursuit at the World Junior Championships in Cuba that summer, Graham couldn't do enough for him.

Brad was the son of a former Australian professional, Garry, a hard-as-nails survivor of the Six-Day circuit who did what he had to do to keep afloat. Brad didn't have much of a relationship with his dad back then. But he did have a clear idea of how a professional cyclist was supposed to behave.

In a way, Brad was the first product of the World Class Performance Plan, part of that first year's intake and a beneficiary of a system that improved every year for about a decade. He acted like he knew cycling was going to work out for him. He had an air of confidence I'd not seen in a young rider before. Perhaps that's what winning a world title as a junior does for you. His mum, Linda, would get his kit out of his bag and lay it out for him. His stepdad would be busy sorting things out, and he had his coach, Sean Bannister, doing whatever he could to make Brad's life easier. Brad was living like a young pro already.

Before we flew to Malaysia, we went to collect our kit for the Commonwealth Games and Brad asked Paulding for two pairs of arm and leg warmers. Brad had this image of professional riders training in full kit. He'd probably read Sean Kelly saying that you didn't take your arm and leg warmers off until the mercury was in the mid-20s. Knowing that Kuala Lumpur would be 40 degrees Celsius, humid and oppressive, Paulding ventured, 'If you want two pairs of arm and leg warmers you can have them, but you can bloody well pay for them yourself.' Brad did, but they never saw the light of day in the heat of Malaysia.

Brad had a level of expectation that none of those who had gone before him had. After a training session on the Kuala Lumpur track, we all headed out of the track centre to go back to our apartments. Matt Illingworth turned to Brad and said, 'Where's your bike?'

'Oh, Marshall is looking after it,' Brad replied, referring to our coach Marshall Thomas.

Matt exploded: 'Oi, he's not your dogsbody. Go and get your fucking bike and look after it.'

Matt didn't care who you were or how good you thought you were, he would say it like it was. We were a team and we were self-sufficient. We weren't yet good enough to have people wheel our bikes around for us.

We qualified third in the team pursuit, which was a bit of a disappointment after our fine ride in Bordeaux, but we knocked out New Zealand in the semi-finals to set up the final against

Australia. We pushed them close, but the Aussies had too much for us at the end and they beat us by just under a second. I won a second silver medal in the points race. Meanwhile, over at the pool, Vicki won silver in the 400-metre freestyle, so it had been a pretty decent Games for the Hayles–Horner household.

Once the 1998 season had drawn to a close, I decided to plan for the future more than I'd ever done. I had my eyes fixed on riding the individual pursuit at the Sydney Olympics, and although I was still on the longlist, I took a step away from the team pursuit squad in order to give myself the best chance of winning a medal in the individual.

Everything was evolving rapidly. A new endurance coach, Simon Jones, had started to create waves around Manchester. I always got on well with Jonesy but he wasn't everyone's cup of tea. He was very active, hands-on, and the walking definition of a workaholic. His mind worked at a million miles per hour and there didn't seem to be an off switch. He was passionate and outspoken and he didn't mind upsetting people as long as we were always working towards the goal of riding faster. Although he could be a fiery character, he also had the ability to be totally detached and emotionless when it came to making hard decisions.

Our work became a lot more structured. By now there were so many riders – endurance athletes and sprinters – competing for track time that things were run a lot more rigidly. There was a pressure in training that hadn't been there before. If you were working on some technical aspect, you wanted to get it right in that session because there was no fat in the schedule. You couldn't hang on for an extra half-hour until you'd nailed it. Once your time was up, someone else would be on the track and you'd have to wait for another day. It meant there was a focus, sharpness and intensity about every session.

Apart from one or two flare-ups, I liked working for Jonesy, although I was probably a nightmare for him because I was so laid-back that most of what he said washed over me. Jonesy was animated and enthusiastic and too often he'd do his thinking out loud in front of the group. That was part of his problem – he probably had too many ideas and he was always trying to think about how he could sneak up round the back of a particular challenge instead of meeting it full on. A lot of athletes can't cope with a jumble of ideas; they just want to be told what is required of them. I didn't mind hearing Jonesy mulling over his ideas because I was able to filter out the good from the bad. And when Jonesy lost it, he really lost it. He had a temper on him and some people took it personally. I didn't, but I do remember saying to him, 'You're not going to be in this job long working at this intensity.'

Whatever people made of his methods, we made big strides forward in the eighteen months leading up to Sydney. Huge leaps, in fact, compared to the baby steps of the previous couple of years. Everything seemed to be slotting into place just in time.

During 1999, my confidence continued to build. I rode for Great Britain in the second PruTour stage race that May, and we prepared for that race really thoroughly. John Herety was the national road manager and I loved racing for him. He's got such a knack with bike riders. He knows how they tick and he has got a wealth of knowledge from his own racing career in Europe and years managing riders old and young. He would tell you if he didn't think you were pulling your weight, but he did it so even-handedly. He didn't just dish out a bollocking to show he was the boss, he did it when it was deserved, which is why riders listen to him. We did a training camp before the PruTour and we rode the course of every stage except the final day from Carlisle to Edinburgh. Ironically, that ended up being the one I won.

It was a horrible day, cold and rainy, and because the Dutch Rabobank team more or less had the overall lead in the bag, they were at the front of the bunch making sure no one dangerous got away. There was a lot of jumping around with riders attacking on the left and right of the road. One guy went, then another followed, and I got across to them and by the time I'd caught my breath and looked round, we had a nice gap.

I knew one of my companions – it was Stuart O'Grady, who had been a key part of the Aussie team pursuit squad before switching to the road. The previous year he'd won a stage and worn the yellow jersey in the Tour de France. He was a class act, and we'd raced against each other for years on the track so I knew he'd work hard to keep the break away. I didn't realize until late in the stage that the other guy was Pascal Lino, a Frenchman who had also worn the yellow jersey in the Tour. To be honest, if I had known who it was, I'd probably have crapped myself.

It was a funny stage – quite short, only about 87 miles – but the terrain was grippy and horrible. I knew it would be an ordeal back in the bunch. Twisting narrow roads that go up and down all day can be a nightmare to ride when you're in a big group. This was one of those days when it was probably easier to be up the road in a break of three.

Once we'd got a nice gap, the bunch let us go. Rabobank were happy because their man, Marc Wauters, was not in any danger of losing the race lead, and no one else wanted to put their backs into the chase because there was another stage in Edinburgh in the afternoon. I'd not raced with Lino, so I didn't know whether he was a good sprinter or not, so that worried me. I was confident O'Grady would wait for the sprint and became sure of it when he rolled past me at one point and said, 'Watch out for Lino, he will try to attack.'

Herety came alongside me in the car and his advice was simple and effective: 'Don't do any more than they are doing. Just do enough.'

The adrenaline was running, and being the least experienced rider, I could have slipped into the obvious trap of doing too much of the pace-setting on the front and gifting the win to one of the others. When we came into Princes Street in Edinburgh for the finish, I sprinted in the saddle – a legacy of my track background – and just got the better of O'Grady. It was, by far, my biggest win on the road and in its way a decent milestone.

By the time we got to Berlin for the World Championships in the autumn, there were only ten months to go until the Olympic Games. We didn't win anything that week but we were edging closer and, across the board, the team was gaining in strength.

Chris Hoy, Craig MacLean and Jason Queally got a silver medal in the team sprint (although it was called the Olympic sprint at the time, just to confuse everyone. They renamed it before Sydney because having an event called the Olympic Olympic sprint would have been daft.) We were fifth in the team pursuit, just 2.5 seconds slower than the bronze medallists, Russia, and although I was 11th in the individual pursuit, I was less than four seconds off fourth place, which would have meant a semi-final ride. For the first time I thought, 'I can do this. I can win a medal at the Olympics.'

So let me paint you a picture of domestic bliss. Two elite athletes in peak physical fitness, helping and supporting each other as they strive to be the best they can be.

A lot of the time it was like that, particularly when things were going well for both Vicki and me. When one of us was having a hard time, at least the other person knew what they were going through, but having so much pressure cooped up in a small house was difficult at times.

During the build-up to the Commonwealth Games, everything was fine because both of us were training well and achieving what we wanted to achieve. For the first time in my life, I was away from home and had a bit of money. We probably had more disposable income then than we have now we've got two children. I never once thought, 'We've got a week to go until the funding cheque goes into my account.' We both had a car and the fridge was always full.

We ate pasta with a jar of sauce, perhaps a bit of meat and some salad. We pepped it up with a pinch of mixed herbs and thought, 'Hey, we're doing well here. We're living the life.' We knew nothing of good parmesan cheese or balsamic vinegar, good coffee or fine wine. Looking back, we were probably only a couple of rungs above student life, but at the time it was brilliant. We were earning a living from the sports that fired us up. After the Commonwealth Games, we bought a little house together. It cost £56,000, which seemed a lot then.

As Sydney began to come into view, the differences between Vicki's lifestyle as a swimmer and mine as a cyclist began to cause some friction. Vicki would get up at 5.30 a.m. to go to the pool for a two-hour block of training. When she returned home at about 8.30, she'd wake me up and get back into bed and go back to sleep. I'd stay in bed another hour and then go training for a couple of hours, come back for lunch, and then she'd head to the pool for her second block. On a day-to-day basis, her training kicked mine into touch, and although there were times when I was working really hard, it was never the same relentless grind the swimmers had to cope with.

It is fair to say I wasn't the most sensitive person in the world. Vicki would say that for the first twenty-five years of my life, my mum had done everything for me, and now I expected her to take over, but that's not quite true. We just don't always notice the things that wind the other person up.

She thought I was the most laid-back person in the world until one afternoon when I was trying to set my bike up on the turbo trainer in our tiny kitchen. For some reason, it wasn't working and I was getting more and more frustrated. Vicki came in after training, starving and looking for something to eat in the way only a hungry athlete can do. I'd moved the kitchen table so it was blocking the fridge. She asked me to move it and that tipped me over the edge.

I picked up the bike, hurled it over the table and out into the back garden. Vicki stood there, arching her eyebrow as if to say, 'You're not always Mr Cool, are you now?'

It sounds really self-involved to say this, but unless you're an athlete, you don't know what it's like to have all those doubts and fears and uncertainties swirling round in your head. From the outside, it appears to be a wonderful, exciting life and of course a lot of the time it is, but when you're not going well and you shut the door behind you, it can be a lonely old place. Sometimes just knowing that Vicki appreciated how I felt was enough to get me through a rough patch.

As I've said, when we were both performing well, everything was great. When we were both going through a difficult time, we could at least empathize with each other. The worst times were when one person had come in from an amazing race or training session and the other one was down in the dumps. That was when things could be really awkward: one person bubbling and upbeat, the other down in the dumps.

In 1998, before the Commonwealth Games, everything was great because we were both in good form and winning medals. In the run-up to Sydney, I was going from strength to strength and Vicki was gradually falling out of love with swimming. I had a bounce in my step and she was so down she just wanted to climb under the duvet. It was harder for her, of course, and I probably wasn't supportive enough because I was in my own bubble, worrying about what I needed to do.

I couldn't believe how harsh the swimmers' regime was. It was like being in the army. The coaches were slave-drivers and every single session was conducted under the microscope. I'm not saying that cycling was a breeze, but in comparison I had it easy. I'd train in the morning, then ride over to Tim Buckle's house in Whaley Bridge and have a coffee. Tim raced for Great Britain and is one of my best friends, and hours would slip by as we chatted and laughed. Then the phone would ring and his girlfriend George would mouth, 'It's Vicki.' I'd mouth back, 'Tell her I'm not here,' before skedaddling out of the back door and riding home. I'd have completely forgotten I'd promised to have lunch ready for her.

'Imagine how good you could be if you had to work as hard as I do,' Vicki would say every now and then. She had a point, but cycling doesn't necessarily work like that. More in doesn't necessarily mean more out. It probably doesn't in swimming either, but the coaches would never have considered that possibility.

As Sydney approached, the clouds over Vicki's head got darker and darker. We were bickering and home wasn't the fun, relaxing place it had been. Which is why what comes next makes perfect sense.

# 8

# The Patron Saint of Nearly Men

I was quite relieved when Vicki flew off to Australia with the swimming squad for their pre-Olympic holding camp. I still had about a week before I was due to head there, so I was left by myself, rattling about in our house, trying not to overdo the last-minute training.

The tension at home had been getting worse the closer we got to the Games. Vicki had been having a really hard time all year. She had been diagnosed with anaemia, which explained her lack of form in the pool, and had been struggling to make the British team. I went to Sheffield to watch the Olympic trials, where she qualified for the 4x200-metre relay squad and was fastest in the 400-metre freestyle, although she hadn't reached the official qualifying time to guarantee selection. So she was on tenterhooks, worrying whether she would be picked for the individual event and fretting about her form.

Although I knew exactly what she was going through, I wasn't as much help as I could have been, because I was locked on to my own targets. I wasn't deliberately thoughtless, I was just in my own little world. And, of course, Vicki's training schedule had been so much more brutal than mine. Up at dawn, hours in the pool, all the while being analysed and assessed. Our cycling training had become more structured and it was hard at times. There were days when I was as exhausted as Vicki, but our programme wasn't designed to break me in the same way that the swimming training seemed to be. A lot of my work was done in races, which I got a kick out of. There wasn't the same variety for Vicki. It was length after length, the same chlorine-y smell, the same tiled pool wall to look at. Eventually that will crack anyone, but it did seem that there was already a big difference between what we were doing. Jonesy wanted to build us up and make us better by boosting our confidence. The swimming coaching was more a case of finding out who could hack it the longest. It was like the old saying, 'What doesn't break you, makes you stronger.'

One of the things I'd got used to was travelling, spending weeks away from home and coping with missing the people I loved. Our schedules meant we spent quite a lot of time apart. I'd be away racing and then get back, we'd have a day together, and then Vicki would be off somewhere.

We were used to it, but the Olympics was still going to be a strange experience. Vicki and I were going to the same place but we may as well have been a thousand miles apart.

I flew to the Gold Coast in Brisbane, where the British Olympic Association had set up the pre-Olympic camp at a smart hotel complex. We landed in the early morning and everything had been timetabled to help us get over the jetlag as quickly as possible. Usually, we'd arrive, go straight out on the bike for two or three hours, fall asleep in the afternoon, wake up in the evening, still on British time, and then endure a fidgety sleepless night. The next day I'd feel like I'd been tranquillized.

So the plan was to go to our rooms and unpack, have some

breakfast, then go to bed for a couple of hours in the late morning, train lightly in the late afternoon, stay up as long as possible and go to bed at ten or eleven at night. It was counter-intuitive to go to sleep so soon after arriving in Australia, but the coaches had consulted some sleep experts to find out the best way to adjust quickly. It worked a treat for me.

After I'd unpacked my stuff in my room, I headed down to breakfast. I turned the corner into the restaurant and practically walked into Vicki, who had just finished eating.

'Oh, hello, dear! How are you doing?'

It wasn't a huge surprise to see her because I knew she was there, but it was surreal to be so far from home, bump into the person I lived with and yet feel awkward. It was a bit like the awkwardness you have on a first date.

That was largely down to the fact that the swimming coaches treated their athletes like children and watched them like hawks. We were at the Olympic Games and Vicki couldn't afford to be seen hanging around with her boyfriend too much in case they thought she wasn't serious.

After about a week in Brisbane, I was due to fly to Melbourne with Jonny Clay to meet up with the rest of the squad and train on the new velodrome that had been built next to the Rod Laver tennis centre. From there, we'd head on to Sydney.

On my last night in Brisbane, I asked Vicki if she could get out of the hotel for the evening so we could go for a meal. She said she'd have to ask her coach and the head coach, Deryk Snelling, for permission.

Vicki wasn't too keen on the idea. It was too much hassle. She was asking permission to walk half a mile to the beach and eat in a restaurant with me instead of with the rest of the swimming squad at the hotel, but she may as well have been asking to hitch-hike to the moon.

'I don't want them to think I'm on holiday.'

'Oh go on, they can only say no.'

It was our last chance to spend any time together until the competition was over, but there was another reason I needed to get her out of the hotel for the evening. There was something I wanted to ask her.

Vicki rang and said she'd been given permission to go out, as long as she didn't drink and was back by ten.

As soon as she said that, my mouth went dry, because I had made my mind up that I was going to ask her to marry me. Now I know there's a perfect symmetry to events here – we met at the Atlanta Olympics and I was about to propose at the Sydney Olympics – but it wasn't as premeditated as it sounds. It just felt right. We'd had a pretty rough few months, but during those days at home alone, life felt very quiet, very empty and very dull without her. I knew I wanted to marry her.

Of course, I was woefully under-prepared. I hadn't asked her dad, or bought a ring. I hadn't even thought to get hold of a novelty ring, like you might get in a Christmas cracker, as a symbol of my love. Instead, I was going to pick my moment as we had dinner under the stars on the Gold Coast.

You might say that choosing a week before we were both due to arrive at the Olympic Games was not the most sensible time to make one of life's biggest decisions, but on the other hand, perhaps it was the perfect time?

We found a lovely restaurant with a beautiful outdoor terrace with twinkly lights all around the place and sat down. I could tell straight away Vicki wasn't in the best of moods. There wasn't a lot of sunshine and happiness for her in the swimming camp and the stress of having asked her coaches to let her go out for the evening was on her mind. She worried over what they would be saying about her. In fact, she was downright grumpy, but I was determined to get those four little words out. I just needed to pick my moment.

As the meal went on, there were plenty of opportunities to ask her but each time I steeled myself to speak, I'd wait too long, a waiter would suddenly appear and the moment would be gone.

I was thinking: 'I'll ask in a minute. I'll ask in a minute.'

Then, when I decided I couldn't put it off any longer and was about to just blurt it out, I heard a shout of: 'Hey, Vicki!' and suddenly a whole bunch of people were standing next to our table and Vicki was greeting them like long lost friends. It was a family Vicki had got to know during a previous training trip to the Gold Coast and, of course, they pulled up the table next to us and stayed for the night. I spent the rest of the evening mentally berating myself for not getting on with it.

Next morning, our bus for the airport was leaving at 11 a.m. but I was determined to see Vicki again before I left. I'd packed my stuff ready and was looking out for the swimmers as they came back from the pool. The clock was ticking on and time was running out.

I saw Vicki and said, 'My bus leaves in ten minutes, come up to my room.'

She replied: 'Oh yeah? That old one!'

Once we got upstairs, I asked Vicki to marry me. I didn't get down on one knee, I didn't make a fuss, I just asked the question. She said yes.

We had only a few minutes before I had to run to get on the bus.

I got on, apologizing for holding them up, and sat next to Jonny Clay.

'You're late.'

'I know, sorry.'

'You've asked Vicki to marry you, haven't you?'

Sometimes your teammates know more about you than you realize.

'Yeah, I have.'

'Congratulations, mate. You'd better win the Olympics so you can pay for a ring.'

I flew off to Melbourne feeling elated, at ease and ready to race.

My programme of events for the Sydney Olympics was the individual 4,000-metre pursuit, the points race, and the Madison, which I was going to ride with Brad Wiggins. Everyone talks about a time when they felt like they were in the form of their life, but that August I really was. My times were improving and I believed I could win medals in every one of my disciplines.

We'd improved so much as a squad that there were chances to win medals throughout the team, although there was hardly any pressure on us from outside the British Cycling Federation. No one was expecting us to do well: not the BBC nor the national press corps. The cyclists were still a bit of a curiosity. The improvements we'd made over the previous eighteen months hadn't exactly captured the imagination back home; we were far from being household names – well, not outside our own households. Our pre-Olympic press day had been very low-key. It was all over and done within about an hour and a half.

I knew I was in good shape and I was itching to get started. During one of my final sessions in Melbourne, I was riding so well and my times were so good that Jonesy walked on to the track and said: 'Stop, stop, stop . . . That's it. You've done enough. You're going so well we don't want to rub the point off your peak.' If the Olympics had started that afternoon, I'd have been ready.

Another indication that we were taking things more seriously was that when we arrived in Sydney, we did not go to the Olympic village. The BCF had rented two private houses for the riders to share so we could be away from the distractions of the village.

Because of the way Olympic places were allocated and restricted, I was officially nominated as reserve for the team sprint, just in case something happened to either Chris Hoy, Craig MacLean or Jason Queally, so I was staying with the sprinters, a few miles across town from where the rest of the endurance squad was based.

Living with Chris, Craig and Jason was an eye-opener. I'd been a sprinter so I knew all about how they prepared. So close to an event, it was all about rest. They'd go and do a handful of explosive sprint efforts at the track then spend the rest of the day on the sofa. Doug Dailey, an old-school road cyclist, used to call them 'sprinter types'. He didn't mean it in a disparaging way, but I was never convinced he thought of track sprinting as proper cycling. More than once I'd heard him joke to Chris, Craig or Jason, before they flew off to a training camp, 'Are you taking your bikes?'

Chris and Craig were pretty chilled out, but Jason took relaxation to another level. He was a former water polo player who had discovered cycling quite late. He was so laid-back he made me look edgy. He could spend hours on the sofa while the other two played a car-racing game on the PlayStation. I had to stop playing that video game after a few days because I could still see the little car going round the circuit when I closed my eyes, but they played it almost every waking hour.

We used to call the sprinters 'pie eaters' because they bulked up to give themselves the power they needed, rather than watch every calorie like the skinny roadies. When I opened their fridge, every shelf was packed with red meat. The cupboards were full of biscuits. Every night they'd make a late dash to the shop over the road just before it closed to make sure they were fully stocked up. It was like living with a pride of lions. When they weren't gorging on red meat they were asleep.

The individual pursuit qualification round was not only my first event but also the first event on the track cycling programme at the Dunc Gray velodrome. Although I had other events to come, everything had been building towards this moment. There was no gentle introduction to the Games; I had to be on my toes from the first moment because only the fastest four out of seventeen riders would qualify for the semi-finals. Finish fifth or lower and my competition would be over.

When it was my turn to get on the track, Brad McGee of Australia held the fastest time. After my ride would be two Germans, Jens Lehmann and Robert Bartko. I knew that if I was second to McGee when I crossed the line, I would be guaranteed a place in the semi-finals.

I never felt the same crippling nerves before an individual event that I experienced in the team pursuit or Madison. The thought of letting down other people tied my stomach in knots, but when I was the only person on the track, with only myself to worry about, a lot of that anxiety slipped away. I felt almost serene. I knew I was in the greatest form of my life and that I could qualify for the semi-finals. I just had to get on the track and ride to my schedule without falling into the obvious trap of setting out too hard.

Everything went perfectly. My start was good, my first kilometre was solid and then I settled into the groove. Towards the end of the second kilometre, the lactic acid starts to build up, but I was confident that I'd got my pacing strategy right and the clock was telling me I was doing a great time. I was up on

McGee and I knew that as long as I held it together I'd make the top four.

In the final kilometre, I had time to glance into the track centre at the area where the Australian team were sitting watching the action. I couldn't pick out the individual faces but I knew McGee was there and I knew they were all watching me. That gave me another little boost because it meant I'd made them take notice.

The clock stopped on 4-20.966 – the best individual pursuit time I'd ever done in competition – and more than a second quicker than McGee, the home-town boy.

When I stepped off the track and got on my static bike to warm down I said to Simon Jones, 'I told you I could do that!'

'Nice one . . . you've got to do it all again in about three hours.'

It sounds absolutely ridiculous now, but we hadn't thought about anything beyond the qualification round. Everything had been about the qualification ride and the importance of making the top four. Of course I knew there was a semi-final to come at some point, and I'm certain I had been told exactly what the schedule for the competition was, but I was so focused on getting that first ride out of the way, I didn't realize I would have to ride again that night.

Lehmann didn't manage to beat my time but Bartko did, by a couple of seconds, which wasn't a surprise because he was the best in the world at the time. He'd always been a bit aloof, but after the qualification round I went to the loo and I bumped into him as he came out. He said, 'Hey, Rob, congratulations. That was a great ride.'

So I was the second-quickest qualifier and would meet Lehmann in the semi-final. Lehmann was the old warrior – 32 years old and the man who had been caught by Chris Boardman in the Olympic final eight years earlier. He wasn't as strong as he had been but he was a wily old customer who could consistently knock out a good pursuit.

My weakness was backing up one strong ride with another, particularly if there were only two or three hours between efforts. Suddenly I had to reset my body and brain. There wasn't time to go back to the house and wind down, I had to somehow get myself ready for a semi-final ride which would decide whether I'd be racing for gold or bronze the next day. A girl from the British Olympic Association press office came up to me and said, 'Everyone wants to talk to you upstairs in the media centre.' I told her I was racing again soon so I'd have to speak to them after the next ride. Then I had a bite to eat with Peter Keen, before trying to find somewhere quiet to close my eyes for a while.

When I got back into the track centre, the kilometre time trial was going on and the velodrome was jumping. I was trying to warm up, trying to block it all out, but when Jason Queally got on the track I had to watch.

Jason set the fastest time and then we had to wait to see if the final three riders could beat him. When Australia's Shane Kelly was riding, I thought the crowd were going to blow the roof off the velodrome but then, when he failed to break Jason's time, it was like we were suddenly plunged into a vacuum. The place fell completely flat. Arnaud Tournant of France was last to ride and he couldn't beat Jason either. Suddenly we had an Olympic champion and it was chaos all around me as the team's staff celebrated with him.

I was trying to celebrate and warm up at the same time. My head was all over the place and I knew I had to distance myself from everything else that was going on, because I was due on the track in less than fifteen minutes.

A few minutes before our semi-final, I was sitting in my seat in the track centre, breathing deeply, waiting to be called up for my race against Lehmann. I saw Sandy carry my bike past me to take it up on to the track where he would fit the rear wheel into the starting gate that holds the bike upright and automatically releases when the gun goes.

Suddenly I remembered that my saddle had slipped with a couple of laps of my qualifying ride to go. The bolt had loosened and the nose of the saddle tilted down a bit. It wasn't enough to disrupt my ride but I definitely didn't want to race again with it like that. With all the drama of Jason's gold medal ride, I'd forgotten to tell Sandy Gilchrist, our mechanic. A wave of panic swept over me.

'My saddle, my saddle!'

'Calm down, we'll sort it,' said Steve Paulding.

By then it was too late. I could feel my heart rate racing again. There wasn't enough time to get my saddle exactly how I wanted it.

The gun went. I pushed on the pedals, got going and when I sat down, my saddle slipped again, tilting forwards by a few millimetres. That was it, my rhythm was upset and I was struggling to get it back. Against a rider like Lehmann, who was like a metronome, I was in trouble. I'd given everything in the qualification round and now, when I needed to produce it all again, the cupboard was bare. He beat me by seven seconds as I slipped to a 4-30 ride.

It was so frustrating. If I'd reproduced the performance I'd produced in the qualification round, I'd have beaten him and been in the final. As it was, I knew I'd be facing McGee for bronze the following night.

When I got off the track, the girl from the BOA was nowhere to be seen. Jason had won gold and I was no longer the story. I went back to the house and tried to get my mind straight. I saw

Jason later and it was as if nothing had happened. He celebrated his gold medal victory by chilling out on the sofa.

The next day, we tinkered about with the saddle so that it wouldn't slip. The design had a flaw in it which meant that even if the bolt was tightened up fully, it could still move, so Steve Paulding and Sandy Gilchrist bodged it so that it stayed firm.

The bronze medal race in a pursuit is all or nothing. Win and you get a medal, lose and you get nothing. At least in the gold medal final, if you're beaten you get a pretty decent consolation prize.

I knew McGee would be a tough opponent, especially in his home city, but I also knew that he always went out hard and tended to fade in the final stages. If I could match him going into the last kilometre, I knew I could overhaul him before the end.

Vicki was in the velodrome with her mum and dad. She didn't get selected for the 400-metre freestyle, so her parents sold their tickets for the pool and managed to get some for the track instead. Vicki got in with her athlete's pass. Knowing she was there gave me a real lift.

I started well and was up on McGee from the start. Every time I caught sight of the split times on the scoreboard, I could see I was ahead and I knew I hadn't over-cooked it. I was up but I was still on a schedule that was comfortable.

With three laps to go, I glanced across the track and said to myself, 'I've got you.'

But McGee didn't fade. In fact he was fighting back. I led him all the way to the penultimate lap and then he edged in front, with his home crowd roaring him on.

When we crossed the line, I was absolutely destroyed. I had ridden a personal best time – 4-19.618 – and he had beaten me by less than four-tenths of a second. It was a crushing, sickening blow. He later told me that if we'd been racing anywhere else in the world, I'd have beaten him, but because he was in front of his home crowd, he dug deeper than he ever had before.

Back at the house, Chris, Craig and Jason all had their silver medals from the team sprint. I was delighted for them, but wished I'd held on to the bronze I'd had one hand on.

I had a couple of days off before the points race, so I went to the Dunc Gray velodrome with Jonny Clay to watch the team pursuit qualification round. I watched as our team of Paul Manning, Chris Newton, Bryan Steel and Bradley Wiggins topped the leaderboard with a new Olympic record time (4-04.030). They'd averaged just over 59 kilometres per hour. Jonny and I turned to each other and said, 'Bloody hell. We can win this.' I was almost in tears.

Later in the session, they caught the Russians to set up a semi-final against Ukraine.

Back at the house, my mind was in turmoil. I picked up the phone and rang Jonesy.

'We can win this, but I need to be in that team. The way I am riding, I can make the difference. No one else could do a 4-19 in the individual pursuit at the moment but I did it yesterday. Put me in the team for the Ukraine race and we can go even faster.'

Despite not having been part of the team pursuit picture for months, I was throwing my hat into the ring. Jonesy's reaction was peculiar.

'This isn't because you can see a medal coming and you want in, is it?' he said. 'I don't want you in there just because you think there's a medal to be had.'

'Hold on a minute, that's not it at all. I can help us *win* this. We could be Olympic champions and I'm going well enough to improve this team.'

I can honestly say I wasn't just trying to piggyback on at the last minute. I genuinely thought I could improve the team. I was going fast – I'd proved it in the individual pursuit – and the team pursuit was my baby, it was what I'd done for years, so I was confident that slotting back into the line-up wouldn't be a problem. I thought they were mad not to consider it. I had no idea who they should leave out, that wasn't my call, and I didn't think about whether me chucking my name into the equation would cause any friction; I just thought we had a chance to win gold.

A bit later on, the phone rang. It was Jonesy.

'We've been thinking about it. We want you to ride the team pursuit quarter-final, but Jonny will take your place in the points race.'

'No way. I want to do the points race as well. I can get a medal in that as well.'

'Well, it's one or the other.'

Athletes can be pretty selfish at the best of times. Usually nothing else matters but the individual's needs. It's all me, me, me. I wanted to be in the team pursuit and keep my points race place, but I felt the team pursuit was the best chance of a gold medal, so I thought about it for a minute and agreed. The decision was made. Jonny and I would replace Bryan and Chris in the semi-final against Ukraine the next night and Jonny would take my place in the points race so I could stay relatively fresh for the Madison.

The Ukraine team we faced in that semi-final were strong, particularly at the start, and they got ahead of us. We stuck to our schedule, but they weren't coming back. By the time we began to fight back, it was too late. We lost, which meant any chance of winning a gold medal had gone. Instead, we would go into the bronze medal race.

But the crucial thing was that we'd set a new British record time of 4-02.387. Jonny and I had come into the team and we'd gone even faster. In fact, we were almost four seconds quicker than Germany, who beat France in the other semi-final, although admittedly the French were well out of it and the Germans took their foot off the gas in the closing stages. It was just our luck that the Ukrainians would do a four-minute ride, in world record time, to knock us into the bronze medal race.

There was only an hour between the semi-final and the medal races. I felt I'd done more than enough to keep my place in the team, but Jonesy and Paulding came to Jonny and me and said they were reverting to the original line-up for the bronze medal clash with France. While we couldn't take anything for granted, the French were much slower than us. We could have put the names in a hat and pulled out a quartet capable of beating them, but Paulding and Jonesy wanted Bryan and Chris back in.

I was livid.

'Aren't you even going to look at the splits?' I asked.

I wanted them to look at the times to work out which individual riders had been the quickest, but there wasn't time. They had made their minds up and they wanted to give the four of them as much time as they could to prepare.

By now I knew that neither Jonny nor I would get a medal, even if the lads beat the French and won bronze. The UCI had a rule that meant you only got a medal if you rode in the final, or failing that, in two of the rounds. Jonny and I had only done the semi-final, so we wouldn't qualify.

I lost my rag at Steve Paulding. Whether it was him making the decision or not, I don't know. I suspect everyone had a say – Steve, Jonesy, Doug and Peter Keen.

'So what about the points race then?' I asked.

'Jonny's doing that.'

I couldn't believe it. I'd given up my points race place to try to help the team pursuit squad win gold; now I was being left out of the medal race and had lost my place in one of my events.

It seemed things were going well for everyone else but me. Yvonne McGregor had won a bronze in the women's individual pursuit; now four of the team pursuiters had a bronze medal each. I'm not one to hold a grudge, or feel sorry for myself, but it was hard to sit in the track centre and watch the race between Great Britain and France. I wanted us to win, of course, but I felt I should have been on the track racing.

Then I watched the four of them step up on to the podium to receive their Olympic medals.

At the end of the night, Doug said, 'Get your head right for the Madison, we'll see what we can do about the medal situation.'

The Madison was the penultimate event on the track programme. Sixty kilometres, or 240 dizzying laps of the 250-metre track, with a sprint every twenty laps. My partner was Brad Wiggins.

Brad and I made a good Madison pair because we were both tall and we were both flexible riders. In the Madison, you need sprinting speed, endurance, a good tactical brain and a sixth sense. Both Brad and I could do a bit of everything, so we didn't have to be too obsessive about making sure one or the other of us was in the thick of the action at a particular time.

We didn't really have a pre-race team talk or much of a strategy, other than to make sure we got ourselves into a good position early on. To win a medal, we needed to score points, and the best way to do that was to get off to a strong start and put ourselves in the mix. It would be far better to score some points and make the other strong nations – Australia, Belgium and Italy – worry about us.

We won the first and third sprints and got third place in the fourth to open up a four-point lead over the Australian pair, Brett Aitken and Scott McGrory. At the halfway mark, the Aussies drew level with us and then they kicked on, with the home crowd cheering their every move.

After the penultimate sprint, with our legs beginning to tire, Aitken and McGrory had the gold medal sewn up. They were well clear of us on 26 points; we were in the silver medal position on 13. We knew we didn't have the strength to gain a lap. The Aussies would be on us like a shot and if we stretched ourselves so late in the race we risked losing what we had.

The Italians Marco Villa and Silvio Martinello also had 13 points, but we'd won more sprints than them so we were ahead on countback. The Belgians, Etienne de Wilde and Matthew Gilmore, were lurking in fourth on 12 points. It was getting very edgy.

Everything hinged on the final sprint, which offered double points. We knew we'd probably need to score something to cling on to a medal, and we also had to hope the Belgians and Italians didn't both get among the points.

The Olympic Madison is the most complicated, hectic and confusing event a bike rider can do. It's like having your brain put in a blender for an hour. When you're in the race, you can only see a fraction of the picture. All you have to go on is the leaderboard, which you try to get a glimpse of every lap to check where you are.

With so many riders on the track and so many people moving up and down, there's a constant danger of crashing. Typically, you survive near miss after near miss. I find it hard to watch a Madison race these days because experience tells me when a crash is going to happen. Every action has an equal and opposite reaction, as Newton (Isaac, not Chris) said. Sometimes I can watch a Madison and point to a part of the track and say, 'There's going to be a crash *there* on the next lap.' And there is, because you can see it brewing. It's possible to predict the chain of events that has been set in motion and then, boom, down they go.

When you're in the race, it's impossible to see the bigger picture. You're not planning, you're reacting and hoping for the best.

At the start of the last lap, I followed the Spanish rider Isaac Gálvez through a gap. I wanted to go into the final sprint ahead of the Belgians and Italians, to force them both to come past me. Gálvez had his head down and rode into one of the Austrian riders. I was so close to Gálvez I had nowhere to go, so when he went down, I hit the deck too.

My race was over but the rule was that if a rider crashed in the last kilometre, so the final four laps, you couldn't lose a lap. Because I was on the floor, we weren't able to score any points in the final sprint, but things could still go our way. We could still keep our silver medal.

I was lying on my side, in pain and gasping for breath, peering through the barriers, trying to see what was going on. McGrory, the Australian, knew they had won the race, so he was already celebrating as he entered the finishing straight. Gilmore won the final sprint for Belgium, lifting them to second place and bumping us down to third. Then Martinello pipped the celebrating McGrory for fourth place and the final two points on offer. That gave Italy the bronze medal and knocked us down another place to fourth. It was like one of those slow-motion moments in a film where the hero reaches out his hand in vain and says, 'Noooooooo!'

It was the final, painful twist of the knife. I couldn't believe it. Less than thirty seconds earlier, we'd had a silver medal. One crash and the ribbon was ripped from my hand.

I got to my feet and knew I had to get out of the velodrome.

Brad went one way, I went the other, each united by our own personal pain. I went down the tunnel under the track and saw a golf buggy in the corner. I sat on it and cried my eyes out. I just let it all flow until there was nothing left.

The week had been an emotional rollercoaster. Every time I was up, a sickening low followed. I'd missed a bronze medal in the individual pursuit by less than half a second. I was a bronze medallist in name only in the team pursuit, and we'd been robbed by misfortune in the Madison. I was the Olympic Games' plucky poster boy. Lady Luck's Nemesis. The Patron Saint of Nearly Men.

But I knew I didn't have it so bad. Vicki had come all the way to Sydney and didn't even get to compete.

The day after the Madison, Jonny and I were told we would get our team pursuit bronze medals after all. The BOA had got involved and a little ceremony was organized down at the quay in Sydney. We had a slap-up lunch and then stood on a little podium so Princess Anne could present us with our medals. It wasn't quite the same as joining the boys on the podium in the velodrome but I was just happy to get my medal.

After the track events, we moved into the Olympic village. My Games were not quite over because I had to start the men's road race. 'Have bike, will ride,' that's my motto. Another quirk of the way Olympic places were allocated meant that the British team for the men's road race had to be completed with one rider from the track squad (me) and one from the mountain bike squad (Nick Craig).

Our job in the road race was to try to do as much work as we could to support the team leader, Max Sciandri, who was a good shout for a medal. The race was 240 kilometres long, so there was no chance I'd get to the finish, or even close to it, but I was determined to help out where I could. After about a third of the race, I was moving up through the bunch when I took a corner too fast. My brand new tyres weren't the grippiest and I overshot the bend and hit the big water-filled barrier at the side of the road. I got up and rolled to the pits in the start–finish straight, bashed up and bleeding. Somehow it was the fitting end to my Games.

My roommate in the village was David Millar, who had worn the yellow jersey on his very first day at his very first Tour de France earlier that summer. He had been selected to ride the time trial, but it's not an exaggeration to say his head had fallen off somewhere between France and Sydney. I got the impression straight away that he was there for the village experience, as I had been in Atlanta. He was 23 years old and probably thought that Athens in four years would be his time.

But there was something a bit troubling about young Dave. One night, after the road race but before Dave's event, the time trial, I went out for a few beers and got back in the early hours. I was tiptoeing through our apartment, making sure I didn't wake him. He sat bolt upright, looked at the clock and said, 'Three hours' sleep, lovely.' He got up, got dressed and went out. I'd never seen anyone like that just a few days before a major event. He was a wreck.

In hindsight, it was probably the beginning of Millar's gradual unravelling, much of which I was about to witness.

Vicki had a hen-and-men do in Sydney, and Karen, Claire and the rest of the swimmers took her to a fancy jeweller's to choose an engagement ring. I actually got off quite lightly there because the bill wasn't too ridiculous. Afterwards Vicki and the swimmers went off to the Great Barrier Reef for a girls' holiday and I flew home club class with all the medallists.

Vicki and I got married in December, which is the perfect time for a party when so many of the guests are elite athletes.

One part of my life was settled, but another was about to change radically. I'd signed a two-year contract with one of the biggest professional teams in Europe, and wanted to give road racing a proper go. Before the Olympics, I had decided that Sydney would be my track swansong, but winning a bronze medal and coming so close to another couple made me think I could win in Athens. So I decided I would give it everything on the road for two years, but if I didn't get anywhere I would still have time to adjust to the track again in time for the 2004 Olympics.

But I was about to find out how deep the waters of professional road racing truly were.

# 9

# Millar Time

I first saw David Millar in 1995 when he was 18 and I was 22. We were at a race that was held on the motor racing circuit at Goodwood, near Chichester in Sussex. We didn't speak that day but I knew who he was. He was already rated as a very talented junior and I could see why. He pedalled the bike so smoothly and moved through the pack of riders with a grace that can't be taught.

Dave looked like a natural, so it wasn't a surprise when I heard he'd gone to Saint-Quentin in northern France at the start of 1996 to join one of the top amateur teams. During that year, he won a string of races and had the professional teams queuing up to sign him, even though he wasn't yet 20. He eventually joined a new, big-budget French team sponsored by a company called Cofidis, which loaned people money over the phone.

At the start, the team was run by Cyrille Guimard, a legendary team manager with a reputation for spotting and developing the best young talent. In the 1980s he nurtured Bernard Hinault, Laurent Fignon and Greg LeMond, all of them Tour de France champions.

Cofidis had signed Lance Armstrong, although the American would never actually race for them because he'd been diagnosed with cancer. The team eventually cancelled his contract. Millar's other teammates included a former world champion, Maurizio Fondriest of Italy, and the veteran Tony Rominger, a Swiss rider who'd won the Vuelta a España three times.

Dave went off to join the professional scene, a whirligig of races all over Europe, and I didn't see him again until the end of 1997, after his debut season as a pro. Tony Doyle, who was friends with Rominger, asked me if I'd like to train with Dave near his mum's home in Buckinghamshire a few times over the winter.

All I knew about Dave then was that his parents had separated when he was a teenager and that he'd chosen to go to Hong Kong with his dad, Gordon. He visited his mum, Avril, during the holidays and she was the one who had encouraged his interest in cycling. Although I was older than him, he was the more experienced on the bike. Outwardly, he appeared confident, but I always had the feeling that beneath the surface he was a lot more fragile than he let on. He was obviously a bright lad but he could be moody. One day he'd be chatty and all smiles, the next it was like the shutters had gone down. Sometimes he was happy to talk about life in France and what the pro races were like, but just as often it was the last thing he wanted to discuss. He had a similar attitude to the bike. In one way, we had a common relationship with cycling – he loved racing and saw training as a necessary evil, as I did. If he was in the mood, he could push himself to incredible depths and tolerate a lot of pain, but there were plenty of times when he'd want to head home after only an hour. You never really knew which Dave was going to turn up.

We met up a few times each winter and got on well, but I

wouldn't say we became particularly close. I'm not sure anyone was particularly close to Dave in those days. He was like the Littlest Hobo. He made superficial friendships easily but I got the feeling he could move on at any time.

My relationship with Dave became more significant in the summer of 2000. I was racing as a one-man band for a sponsor called Athletes 1, a sports law and management firm run by a guy called Mike Townley. The Sydney Olympics were just round the corner and, in my mind, I had decided that once they were over, I'd try to make a career on the road. I had no idea how I was going to go about that because I didn't really know what opportunities were out there for a rider like me. Compared to most road riders, I was still a big guy and would need to shed the kilograms to be able to cope in the hills.

I'd never dreamed of racing the Tour de France, so I didn't yearn to join a top pro team. I loved watching the highlights on Channel 4 but not once did I aspire to joining that world. For many years, I simply didn't think it was for me, but when the chance wafted past the end of my nose, I was immediately interested.

Dave had mentioned once or twice that there might be an opening for me at Cofidis. I didn't know much about the complex political workings of a pro team like Cofidis, but it seemed that he had managed to assert himself by virtue of his talent. By 2000, Dave was 23, and was seen as one of the most gifted and marketable young riders in the peloton, and he spoke French fluently, making him even more valuable to a team like Cofidis.

By now, Guimard had long gone, Armstrong had recovered from cancer and won his first Tour de France for the US Postal Service team, Fondriest and Rominger had retired and the

Cofidis team seemed to be engaged in an annual round of re-invention. Dave had been locked in a battle with the Belgian Frank Vandenbroucke to be regarded as the team's leading rider. Vandenbroucke was cycling's *enfant terrible*. He was outrageously talented but he was wayward and controversial. It seemed that Cofidis had lost patience with Vandenbroucke and had decided Dave was the man to become the team's figurehead. He was being trusted by the management to bring in someone as a sort of right-hand man.

I met Dave in the hotel bar the afternoon before the National Championships, which were being held near Solihull on the last Sunday in June. The Sydney Olympics were my main goal that summer, but Dave's objective was a lot closer. In six days' time, he would be making his Tour de France debut and he wanted to ride the world's biggest bike race in the British national champion's jersey.

We sat with a few other riders and had a chat in the bar. The conversation was a bit peculiar and I couldn't work out what he was trying to say. He seemed to be suggesting that there was a place for me at Cofidis without actually saying the words: 'There's a place for you at Cofidis.'

Dave and I would be in the same situation during the race – lone riders fending for ourselves – so it made sense for us to work together, or rather for me to work for him.

The race was eight laps of a very testing 16-mile circuit; 128 miles in all. The National Championships had been held on that course before and people seemed to think it was an easy one because there wasn't a particular climb to break up the field. Instead, it was a rolling circuit, up and down all the way, which made for an aggressive race. It was a true racer's course.

Dave and I came up with a loose plan, which was to make the race hard early on, sort the men from the boys and reduce the number of riders in contention. Then Dave could finish it off on the last lap. As we stood on the start line, I said to Dave, 'Can you sprint?'

He looked at me as if I was taking the piss. 'Yeah, yeah, yeah, of course I can sprint.'

What I meant was, did he fancy himself in a two-man sprint? Did he rate his chances from a small group of four to half a dozen? Or did he need to get away on his own to win? I was trying to gauge what sort of race he needed it to be but it came out wrong.

We stuck together at the start of the race and towards the end of the third lap, Dave accelerated hard. I was right behind, so I followed him. Dave was riding so strongly that most of the others were scared to go with him so early in the race. I followed his searing pace and after a minute or so looked around and found that we were away.

Once we were clear, I did a lot of the pace setting and a lap or so later, we were joined by eleven other riders. Then another twenty got across with two laps to go and all our earlier hard work threatened to be for nothing. We'd shaped the race once, only for the front group to swell out of hand again.

I knew the Solihull circuit would discover who had the weakest legs eventually, and going into the final lap we were down to nine again. On that final lap, Dave got clear with Jonny Clay and John Tanner, two of the toughest characters on the British racing scene at the time. I was quite happy to watch the gap open, confident that Dave would get the job done on the approach to the finish in Knowle High Street.

I swung round the final corner into the finishing straight about 40 seconds after the leaders, the last of the nine men who'd stayed away to the end, but well clear of the rest of the field. As I crossed the line, I saw Dave's bike lying down on the side of the road and for a moment assumed he'd dropped it there in a moment of mad celebration. Then I saw him, sitting on the pavement with his head in his hands.

'What happened?' I said.

'Third,' he replied, on the verge of tears.

'Fucking hell, I thought you said you could sprint?'

That went down like a lead balloon.

Dave quickly put the disappointment behind him. Six days later, he won the opening time trial of the Tour de France in Futuroscope, becoming only the fourth British rider to wear the yellow jersey, elevating himself to superstar status.

The move to Cofidis seemed to be on, although no one from the team actually contacted me. All the negotiations were done by Mike Townley by fax or email. In early August, a few weeks before I went to Australia for the Olympics, Cofidis asked me to go for a physiological test, to see if I was worth taking on. I flew to Charles de Gaulle airport near Paris, hired a car, drove across the plains of northern France to Amiens and checked into my hotel. At this stage, I had not even met any of the team's management, so I sat in my room and waited.

That evening, I got a call from Francis van Londersele, one of the team managers. He spoke no English and my understanding of French was very poor but by saying '*oui*' to everything, and after replaying the conversation in my head, I worked out that they'd be picking me up at *sept heures*, seven o'clock, the following morning.

I had no idea what to expect. I'd been told to bring my cycling shoes, pedals and some kit, so I assumed they'd have me hooked up to a static bike to put me through my paces. I was feeling pretty confident about that because the Olympics were only a few weeks away and I was bang in form. They'd also asked me to bring my training diary and that worried me because I didn't keep one.

Over dinner, I flicked through the blank pages and started to fill it in with the training sessions I thought I'd done. I couldn't remember much, so I just made it up, worrying all the time, 'What on earth are they going to think of me?'

The next morning, Van Londersele arrived and drove me to a sports science centre on the outskirts of town. He didn't say much on the way. We walked into a laboratory where a bike was hooked up to a computer. After a quick round of *bonjours*, I got changed into my kit.

When I got to the bike, I noticed straight away that the cleats on the bottom of my cycling shoes were not compatible with the pedals on the static bike.

Van Londersele shrugged his shoulders and threw his arms in the air in that typically French way that said this, and everything else that went wrong in the next couple of hours, was all my fault. 'Shimanooooo!' he said, dismissing my choice of cycling shoes as if I'd just tried to offer him a glass of Blue Nun with his steak.

Anticipating just this problem, I had brought my own pedals, but the Allen key bolt was a different size to the only Allen key they had in the place, so although we could take the original pedals off, we couldn't tighten mine up. After a lot of hurrumphing, a solution was found. They put some ancient old-style pedals with toeclips and straps on the static bike instead. They were like little rat traps and I could only just get the toes of my shoes into them. There was no way they could possibly judge me properly on this, I thought, but no one was in the mood for any more messing about, so I got on with the test.

A nurse came in with a box full of empty vials and took blood from my arm. I counted as she filled fifteen vials with my blood, labelled them and put them back in the box. I had no idea why they were taking so much blood; no one gave me a reason and that was the last I heard of it. I never found out what the samples were tested for and they never spoke to me about my blood values again.

Then I did a forty-minute test on the bike with half a leg's worth of blood missing. They put a mask over my mouth to measure the gases I was exhaling, which meant I couldn't drink, so they whacked a drip attached to a saline bag into my arm to prevent me becoming dehydrated. The whole test was a shambles. I was pedalling awkwardly, like a ballerina in football boots. All I could do was give it everything I had and hope for the best.

Afterwards they dropped me at my hotel and I drove back to the airport and went home. No one asked to see my training diary or even spoke to me about the possibility of joining the team. I wondered whether that was the last I'd hear from them.

Later on, someone told me that Cofidis had wanted to wait until the Olympic Games to see how I did against another of their riders, Philippe Gaumont, in the individual pursuit. I'm not sure if that's true, because after the qualification round (where I was second and Gaumont was fifth) I went over and introduced myself to him and he seemed to know I was joining Cofidis.

'Ah, *oui, oui*. You join us next season? When we have the first training camp, we'll have a party.'

When I met up with Dave in the Olympic village, he said Cofidis had agreed to take me but it wasn't until the following month that I finally signed my contract – a two-year deal worth €60,000 a year. Not too shabby, I thought, until I got my first payslip and saw that almost half of it had gone in tax. Having said that, it was still a lot more than I'd earned from cycling before.

I was about to become a proper professional with one of the top-ranked teams in the world. At the time, there were only four

British cyclists riding for the squads ranked in the UCI's elite division: Charly Wegelius was in his second year at Mapei in Italy, Jamie Burrow was at US Postal Service and Dave and I were with Cofidis. Then there was Jeremy Hunt at Big Mat and Roger Hammond at Collstrop–Palmans, which were two of the bigger teams in the UCI's second division.

When I told Peter Keen and the rest of the coaches at the British Cycling Federation where I was going, they weren't happy. They didn't want a member of their pursuit squad racing for a team in France. Chris Boardman was the only rider who had managed to successfully switch between the track and the road and back again, and that was because he was a supremely gifted rider. Us mere mortals were expected to stay at home and follow the plan. By joining Cofidis, I was effectively out of the track squad, although I was determined to keep the door open for a possible return at the start of 2003, which would give me eighteen months to fight my way back into the team for the Athens Olympics.

Vicki and I sat down that winter and decided that if I was going to do it, I would do it properly. I'd move to France, even if it meant being away from her, and give myself the best possible chance of being successful. Vicki was unsure whether she was going to stick at swimming, because Sydney had been such a painful experience, but she needed to get back in the pool before she knew how she felt.

In October, Mike Townley gave me my contract and I signed it on the bonnet of a car (oh, the glamour!) at the Grand Prix des Gentlemen, a fun amateur time trial event that pairs a younger cyclist with one of more advancing years to ride a fifteen-mile course in Surrey.

My first official engagement with Cofidis was at the end of

November 2000. I went to a hotel in Amiens to meet the team management and the rest of the riders. While I was there, I'd be measured for my new bike and clothing. There weren't any training sessions, so it was a chance to get to know people. I felt completely out of place the whole time I was there and my dad's words kept coming back to me: 'You never know, son, you might need to learn French if you're going to ride the Tour de France.'

I didn't understand much, so I just followed Dave around. One morning he put his head round the door and said, 'Put your kit on and come on, quickly.'

I'd just got up and hadn't done my hair, but I put my new Cofidis kit on and followed him down the corridor and into a room that had been transformed into a makeshift photographic studio. We were about to have our team photo taken. If you look at that team picture and wonder who the scruffy bloke at the back is, it's me.

I'm not sure what I was expecting from those few days, but I had assumed the team would feel a lot more professional and well drilled than it was. Everything was a bit haphazard. Cofidis was one of the biggest and best-funded teams in world cycling, with a budget that ran to about six million euros, but it seemed to be run like an amateur squad.

The management team was led by Alain Bondue. He'd won a silver medal in the pursuit at the Moscow Olympics in 1980 and was world professional pursuit champion in 1981, and again the following year in Leicester. I thought there might be some common ground between us because of that, but he rarely spoke to me. When he did he was pleasant enough but he left the day-to-day running of the squad to the other managers.

The other managers, or *directeurs sportifs*, were Van Londersele, who was cool and quite distant; Bernard Quilfen, who immediately struck me as warm and supportive and proved to be; and Alain Deloeuil, who, as far as I could see, just didn't take to me. I came to think of him as the poison dwarf.

One morning in Amiens, all the riders sat round waiting to be called in to talk to the management about their goals and programme for the coming season. When I went in, it was François Migraine, the owner of the Cofidis credit company, who chaired the meeting and did all the talking. At first, I assumed that the management had discussed everything beforehand and Migraine approved the plans and delivered the news to the riders. Pretty soon, I realized the extent to which the team was actually Migraine's baby.

He was paying for the team, so perhaps he was within his rights to call the shots, but it struck me as odd that he was so involved with the decision-making. It was like the chairman of a football club picking the team. Anyway, it didn't much matter who was making the decisions, because whoever it was, I wasn't involved in the discussions at any stage. I was a worker bee; it was my job to do as I was told.

One by one, I'd watched the other riders go in for their meeting and emerge either happy or pissed off with their race programme. Now I listened as Migraine rattled through the list of races I'd be doing. The Tour of the Mediterranean stage race in February, followed by the Trofeo Luis Puig and Tour of Valencia in Spain, then Paris–Nice in March, a string of other important stage races, before the Dauphiné Libéré in the French Alps in June and then, if all went to plan, the Tour de France.

When I came out and told Dave, he laughed.

'You're on the A team with me, Rob.'

Before I'd even started the season, my race programme had been tweaked half a dozen times with races added and taken away, but the general idea was that I'd be by Dave's side right the way through to July and, if I did enough to impress the bosses, I'd go to the Tour with him.

It didn't take long to realize that Cofidis was a very dysfunctional family. The first training camp was in Calpe, southern Spain, in early December. I'd trained my nuts off for three weeks beforehand because I was terrified of getting dropped by my new teammates. We were split into groups depending on which races we were supposed to be targeting. I was in Dave's group, with the other riders who were in the frame for a Tour de France place. We were training at a fairly even tempo, logging the kilometres without digging ourselves into a deep hole. Meanwhile, the Classics group, who were aiming to be in peak form for the tough one-day races in March and April, were absolutely burying themselves on the climbs.

Every day, our group would get back and we'd shower and be ready for lunch just as the Classics guys got back. By the time the Belgians – Nico Mattan, Peter Farazijn, Jo Planckaert and Chris Peers – and the other Classics specialists walked into the hotel, they were practically on their knees. Yet when we compared average speeds for their ride and ours, there wasn't a lot of difference, it was just that they were staying out longer and battering each other on the climbs.

That was the way they worked. That was the way generations of riders had worked, and they thought it was the best way to prepare for the toughest races. We now know that such a one-dimensional training programme only gets you so far. For years I had trained in a similar way myself. Early on, I'd raced against myself; a few years later, I'd suffered on Tony Doyle's wheel as he hammered me into the ground, but the Great Britain coaching techniques had evolved and training programmes became tailored more specifically. I was learning that it was much more effective to chip away, building up steadily and allowing the body to soak up the work than it was bludgeoning away until there was nothing left to give.

My French was limited but I knew this was not a very progressive environment. There wasn't a lot of dynamism or a free exchange of ideas. The managers were set in their ways. They'd each worked the same races for years and were well into the groove. There probably hadn't been any new ideas thrown around for decades. It was a very traditional world. Professional cycling worked the way professional cycling worked and there was no questioning it.

Having come from a British Cycling set-up that had placed the needs of the athletes first and structured everything towards specific goals, seeing how Cofidis worked was a shock. I'd expected them to run a slick operation but it was a shambles a lot of the time. There was no attention to detail. Right from the start, I could see ways to improve the way they worked, but I was a nobody, so it wasn't my place to suggest anything.

There were a few cliques among the riders. The Belgians spoke good English and they were pretty welcoming, but the French seemed to want to make it as hard as possible for me to settle in. They weren't being malicious, but the culture meant I had to earn my place. They never spoke English and if I pronounced something incorrectly they'd scrunch up their faces and say, '*Quoi? Quoi?*' ('What? What?'), as if they didn't have a clue what I was on about. It was only halfway through the season, when they started dropping in the odd English phrase, that I thought, 'You bastards.' Successive generations of British or Australian riders will tell you the same thing. The French take a while to warm to *les étrangers*.

Once Vicki decided to stop swimming, she enrolled in a course at the London school of massage to become a qualified masseur and physical therapist. My plan was to go to my first race, the Tour of the Mediterranean, and then stay with Dave in Biarritz while I looked for a little place of my own. I planned to throw myself into the season.

But, like a lot of things at Cofidis, the plans weren't worth the paper they weren't written on.

# 10

# First Day at Big School

14 February 2001. St Valentine's Day. The perfect day for a massacre. My first day as a professional cyclist in Europe; and nine years to the day since I'd packed in my job at Gales brewery.

Early spring races like the Tour of the Mediterranean are supposed to be a way to ease into the season, a chance to get into the groove of the racing and test how effective the winter's training has been. Sure, they are important and plenty of guys want to win, but these races are like pre-season friendlies compared to the Champions League of the Classics and major tours.

The opening stage of the Tour of the Med is starting in Antibes this year and heading towards Mont Faron, on a steep road that rises from the coast at Toulon up through the woods for about 5.5 kilometres until the sea is 500 metres below you. The stage is only 140 kilometres long and it will take even the slowest riders about three and a half hours to complete. This looks like one of those easy stages they're always telling you about, the perfect place to blow away the cobwebs and get my feet under the table.

Mont Faron is still a long way off. We've been racing just under an hour but already we've covered almost 50 kilometres. For the third time in five minutes I'm apologizing in two languages for bumping into someone. 'Sorry. *Désolé.*' My French is coming on. I've learned a whole bunch of swear words this morning.

I'm down at the back of the peloton; the long, thin rope of riders has slipped through my palms until I'm right at the end of it, bouncing around, feeling the full whiplash effect. I'm stuck in a knot of riders that has flared out at the back of the line. Way up in front of me I can just about see the head of the snake. There are more than a hundred riders ahead of me, all in single file, before it gets to us desperate few who are trying in vain to move up the line.

I can see where I want to be – slotted comfortably in the first third of the field – I just can't get there. As soon as I reach the front of our little knot of riders and try to go past a couple of the men at the back of the line, I have to ride in the wind, unprotected from their slipstream. Immediately it causes my heart rate to rise and my breathing to gallop out of control. So I ease off ever so slightly and in the blink of an eye the half a dozen riders it's taken two minutes to scrabble past swamp round me and I'm at the back of the knot again. I feel like the odd sock in a washing machine full of clothes. I just hope everyone else back here feels the same.

I glance across at some poor sod a few metres to our left. He's riding out of the slipstream, trying to make his own way forwards, but he's getting nowhere. Far better to get nowhere while I've at least got a bit of shelter, I think.

Because I've taken my eyes off the road I bump wheels again, almost causing a crash. Another shout, more swearing.

'Sorry. *Désolé.*'

I daren't look back because the last thing I want to know is that I'm last man.

Up ahead, I can see that the road will soon start to rise and, for a moment, I feel a slight sense of relief. The hill will slow them down a bit, surely. But as the riders at the front reach the slope, they shift up a gear, rather than down, increasing the resistance, not lessening it, trying to leverage some more power to carry them up the hill. One by one they get out of the saddle and sprint up the slope. The pace doesn't slow much but the intensity of the effort multiplies. Now the whole bunch is in single file and I can see a hundred and fifty arses all wiggling from side to side as everyone rides out of the saddle. In the amateur races, things typically eased up on the hills. Here, they go harder.

Christ.

I crane my neck to see who's at the front setting this insane pace, but I can't tell. It's just a blur of coloured jerseys. I bump into someone else. Another reprimand.

'Sorry. *Désolé.*'

I've been a pro for about an hour and I want to yell out: 'Is it always like this?' Then, as the pressure begins to tell, the gaps start to open. Only a few inches to start with, but then it's six inches, soon a foot, and then the wind exploits the gap and starts blowing the rider who's lost contact backwards. Some guys have the strength to ride round the fallen few and fill in those gaps, but I can't take that risk. My legs are screaming and my lungs are burning. If I increase my effort now I might just go pop. But I know I can't just swing out of the line and give up either. I have to hang on.

As I'm starting to despair, I hear a car horn. I look round and it's a Cofidis car, driven by our team manager Deloeuil. He beeps again and gestures at me to fall in.

Behind the car, one of my teammates, a Frenchman called Jean-Michel Tessier, is riding just a few inches from the bumper, taking full advantage of the draught. Behind him is Dmitriy Fofonov, a Kazakh, and one of our team's protected riders this week. Fofonov had punctured and is taking a tow back up to the bunch. You're not supposed to ride behind the cars as blatantly as this, but the race judges usually turn a blind eye for puncture or crash victims, as long as they don't take the piss.

I jump in behind Fofonov and although it's still bloody hard work, we are at least moving forwards, past the line of riders. We steal a couple of dozen places and then slip back into the group, where the suffering resumes.

This is harder than any road race I've done before. A thought goes through my head. If this is the Tour of the Med, what the hell is the Tour de France like?

Over the winter, I lost count of the number of people who said, 'It doesn't matter who you are, how old you are, or what you've done, your first year as a pro will be a baptism of fire.'

I'd bumped into Micky Morrison in Calpe and he said, 'You're going to get your head kicked in,' with a little too much relish.

I tried to convince myself I might be the exception to the rule, because I was 28, an Olympic medallist, and I'd ridden enough international stage races to believe I could skip the painful initiation. I had tens of thousands of miles in the bank – hundreds of thousands, probably – I wasn't some wet-behind-the-ears 22-year-old. I thrived when the pain started to bite and I knew I could dish it out too.

OK, so I wasn't a dreamer. I knew I wasn't going to turn up and win the biggest races, but I thought I'd be able to hold my own; I thought I'd do a little more than make up the numbers.

I'd been thinking of the Tour of the Med as a relatively gentle introduction, but the way Bondue, Van Londersele and Quilfen had stressed to me that they weren't expecting too much from me in my first year had been nagging at me. It made me fear I was in for a kicking.

We'd arrived at Antibes that morning in our Cofidis team camper van. I was excited but also nervous. It's a cliché to say it was like my first day at school, and it's probably not true either, because I never looked forward to school, whereas this was something I'd been looking forward to all winter. I couldn't wait to get stuck in and do my bit for the team. But it felt like that first day at big school, when everyone else looked so much more assured and seemed to know what they were doing and where they were going.

The camper van parked up in the car park and I pulled back the curtain and saw the crowd of spectators who had gathered to watch us, the riders, get ready for the race. And I was one of them. Bring it on.

As the start of the race got closer, I expected some sort of team talk. I thought we'd be briefed about the course and the weather. I thought we'd have some sort of tactical battle plan – such as to protect our leaders Fofonov and David Moncoutié – particularly as Mont Faron would shape the rest of the race – but there was nothing. Deloeuil just clapped his hands and said: '*Allons-y*.' 'Let's go.' That was it.

On the way towards the start line, I rolled alongside Dave.

'Is there anything you want me to do in the race?'

'Just get to the finish, Rob.'

As I hugged the gutter, trying to stay out of the gritty, stony verge where the edge of the tarmac had started to crack and break, while also watching out for drains or grates that might cause me to swerve or crash, I decided there was nothing for it but to call on my experience to block out the suffering. None of the things here were that unfamiliar. I was a good bike-handler

– I could survive the chaos of a Madison – I was used to riding in the red zone on the track and I could manage the pain. I just wasn't used to being right at the back.

I didn't know the route, or how far there was to go, or when the next hill was coming, so I just fixed my eyes on the tyre of the guy in front, switched my brain off and pedalled. At times I was sprinting – head down, arse up – to make sure I didn't let a gap open.

It was miserable, but I knew that negative thoughts wouldn't help. This wasn't bike racing as I knew it, because I was trapped. I couldn't go forwards, because I wasn't strong enough, and I daren't go backwards. Tactically, I held a hand full of twos and threes of different suits. I had no cards to play. I was just trying to survive, knowing that if Fofonov or Moncoutié punctured, I'd be fucked one way or another, either because I'd have to give them my wheel, or because I'd blow up trying to pace them back up to the bunch.

Eventually we reached the bottom of Mont Faron, this climb I had heard about but didn't know. It was often included in the route for Paris–Nice, one of the most prestigious stage races of the early season, and the list of winners there was impressive.

It was steep, which was a blessing in disguise, because at least it shattered the bunch into pieces, and for the first time I could ride at my own pace. Because I was a racer, my instinct was to bury myself on that climb. I was riding as hard in 80th place as I would have in pursuit of a victory back at home. I looked down the cliffside and I could see Dave and Jez Hunt, three hairpins behind me, just rolling along, chatting, while I was turning myself inside out.

At the finish, I slumped in my seat in the camper van. My eyes were stinging and everything ached. Dave came in ten minutes afterwards, looking as fresh as a daisy.

'Good training,' he chirped.

The camper van's engine started and we headed to our hotel for the night. Deloeuil said, 'Well done,' but no more. I didn't feel I deserved more. I didn't feel like I'd contributed to the race at all. I'd just been there, one of the suffering many.

The next day, and for the four days after that, we did the same thing, zigzagging across the south of France towards Béziers and Carcassonne and back to Marseille. We rode through some of the most beautiful countryside in France but I didn't take in a single thing. The only sights I saw were the bicycle tyre and backside of the guy in front of me. Although it was hard, horribly so at times, I loved it.

When we reached Marseille at the end of the race, the idea was for me to go to Biarritz with Dave. He had been a bit aloof during the Tour of the Med but as I still didn't know him that well, I wasn't sure whether that was unusual or not. Perhaps he'd just had his race face on. That afternoon, he told me there was a change of plan. Dave had been on holiday in Australia after the Olympics and while he was there, he'd met a girl called Shari in Noosa, which is a party town for the rich kids.

Dave said, 'You can stay for a couple of days, but then Shari is coming over, so you'll have to find a place of your own.'

Suddenly I felt like a bit of baggage, rather than Dave's training partner and wing man.

The next day, a fax turned up at Dave's place. It was addressed to me, from the Cofidis bosses, and it was yet another revision of my race programme. This time Paris–Nice, the Dauphiné Libéré and the other major stage races were missing.

# 11

# Rob Ezz

It amazed me how quickly the job of a professional cyclist began to feel like just that. A job. After the Tour of the Med, I did two races in Spain then shelved my plans to find a place in France, headed home to Vicki and commuted to the races from England.

At home, I'd train and wait for the fax to whirr into life. My race programme was never anything other than fluid and the fax would churn out a piece of paper with the news that I had to go to Belgium or northern France for some one-day race or other.

I couldn't fault Cofidis for the way they organized all our travel to the races. Flights were booked and they'd pick me up from the airport, just as they did for all the riders; it was just when I arrived at the races that things tended to fall apart.

At the end of March, the fax summoned me to Belgium for a series of three one-day races I'd never heard of. I had to look the last one up on the internet just now – the Omloop Wase Scheldeboorden, held in a town called Kruibeke, not far from Antwerp in eastern Flanders. It wasn't an important race – none of our big hitters were there – but it was still early days and I was flushed with enthusiasm, so I was happy to go and get stuck in.

My French was still rusty, so I didn't pick up much of the team talk, but I later pieced together the gist of it. Cofidis had injury and illness in the camp and were struggling to cobble together an eight-man roster for the spring Classics: 'Whoever does well today will be going to De Panne, Flanders and Roubaix.'

The first half of April is defined by the cobbled Classics. The Tour of Flanders and Paris–Roubaix are two of the hardest races of the season. They are 260-kilometre-long epics that cover the harsh, unforgiving landscapes of western Belgium and north-eastern France, where the farms are linked by ancient cobbled tracks. The Tour of Flanders criss-crosses the region and takes in almost twenty steep climbs, many of them cobbled too. Paris–Roubaix is flatter but it's nicknamed the Hell of the North, and for good reason. The cobbles there are so uneven that you can lose a front wheel in the craters that lurk in the gaps. The Three Days of De Panne is a warm-up race for the other two, with a couple of long stages to get the riders ready for what's to come. It's a bit like eating a three-course meal before a couple of banquets.

The Tour of Flanders and Paris–Roubaix are prestigious events, two of the five biggest one-day races known collectively as the 'monuments', and I assumed any rider would want to be a part of them.

I discovered at the Omloop Wase Scheldeboorden that not everyone did. After we'd been through the feed zone, where we'd snatch bags of food and a fresh bottle of drink from the *soigneur*, a break of about fifteen riders eased clear. I was right at the front of the bunch with a couple of teammates either side of me as the gap began to grow. They looked at me and then at each other and put the brakes on so that they slipped backwards through the bunch. I pushed on and rode across to the break – the only Cofidis rider to make it – and eventually I finished ninth.

It wasn't a victory, or even a podium position, but I'd ridden well enough to be heading to De Panne on the Belgian coast to join up with the rest of the cobbled Classics specialists. It was the equivalent of putting my hand up in class and volunteering for some extra-hard homework. My two teammates hadn't fancied having their heads kicked in at the Tour of Flanders and Paris–Roubaix.

After the race, Alain Deloeuil told me I'd be staying in Belgium for another fortnight to do the Classics, so I had to ring Vicki to tell her I wasn't coming home.

The downside of riding the Classics was that it meant a couple of weeks with Deloeuil, my dreaded *directeur sportif.* As I said earlier, in my opinion he didn't take to me; he had his own favourites and he had a mean streak to him. He was very old school. He was only interested in your results and whether you finished a race or not. If you rode at the back all day but finished with the bunch he'd say, 'Good, good.' But if you worked hard for your teammates, dropping back to fetch water bottles and clothes for them from the team car, closing gaps, or sheltering someone from the wind, but didn't actually finish the race, it didn't register.

He could be temperamental; he took credit for the good results and blamed everyone else for the bad ones. In one race quite early on, Jo Planckaert won a bunch sprint for third or fourth place and Deloeuil was all over him. 'You see, I said you could do it. It's just about your confidence.' The next day Planckaert didn't do so well, and as far as Deloeuil was concerned it was a disaster.

The riders called him 'Schnoy'. I have no idea why, but it was clearly derogatory because they didn't say it to him directly. He just had one of those miserable faces, like the cartoon character Droopy.

In the Three Days of De Panne, I tried to be a help to the

team, but that wasn't easy the way we rode, all scattered through the bunch with one over here, another over there. We weren't a unit, we were a collection of individuals who happened to be wearing the same jersey. Not knowing the roads put me at a serious disadvantage. The Belgians and the other specialists who did these races every year knew each turn. They knew where every traffic island and speed bump was. For me it was like Wacky Races – exhilarating, exhausting, terrifying, but fun.

I was just doing the best I could and Deloeuil wasn't complaining, so it must have been enough.

A few days before the granddaddy of them all, Paris–Roubaix, I went down to the car park outside the hotel and walked over to the trucks where the mechanics were working. The week between the Tour of Flanders and Paris–Roubaix is one of their busiest of the year, especially if the weather is bad. The Belgian mud slips off the fields and on to the roads and coats every millimetre of every bike, working its way into every tiny gap. In the rain, the brake blocks can get ground down to almost nothing and need replacing every day. Cables and chains have to be replaced, everything needs to be washed and greased and checked. Usually the mechanics are out there late at night, working under floodlights. No wonder they get grumpy, because hardly anyone thanks them.

Paris–Roubaix is the only race where the riders have specially customized bikes to cope with the terrible cobbles. The Cofidis team had aluminium bikes that were designed for cyclo-cross, which is basically a combination of cycling and cross-country running that the Belgians are good at. These bikes had brakes with extra clearance so they didn't get clogged up with mud. The mechanics put on an extra layer of handlebar tape to give a bit more protection against the jarring from the cobbles.

I counted the bikes leaning up against the truck. There were seven, with one more clamped in the stand that the mechanic was working on. I knew this was the bike I'd be riding, even though I could tell from several paces away it was far too small – at least three centimetres too small.

'Where's my bike?' I asked, with a fake air of innocence, because I knew this was it.

The mechanic tapped the bike he was working on.

I noticed from the sticker on the top tube that this was Francis Moreau's bike from the year before. I knew Moreau was quite tall, but I was a bit taller. I was a late call-up to the Classics team and there hadn't been time to get a frame in the right size, so this was the best they could do, but it was like asking a footballer with size ten feet to play a cup final in size eight boots.

I picked up the mechanic's tape measure (they never like you touching their stuff) and with my best impression of Gallic distaste, I measured the length of the bike from the tip of the saddle to the handlebars.

'It's too short,' I said. 'Way too short.'

The mechanic undid the bolt that held the saddle in place, whacked it hard with his palm so it slid back on the rails as far as possible, tightened the bolt up, took the tape measure from me, measured it and said, '*Voilà*.'

'You're joking, aren't you? I'm about to ride 260 kilometres on someone else's bike?'

The mechanic shrugged. 'Ahh, it's better for the cobbles this way. More comfortable.' To his credit he didn't say what he was thinking, which was probably, '260 kilometres? You won't make 260 kilometres.'

If he had said that, he probably would have had a point. I knew I wasn't going to win Paris–Roubaix – I knew I probably wouldn't make it to the finish at the velodrome – but I was fastidious about my bike. I knew what every measurement should be and I wanted it to be just so. I thought that was being professional, and if I was a big-name rider, they'd probably have seen it that way. But because I was one of the small fry in the team, I was just being a pain in the arse.

I rode the bike for a couple of days, determined to make the best of a bad job, but at the start of Paris–Roubaix, as we rolled through the streets of Compiègne, still in the neutralized zone, I decided the saddle was a smidge too high, so I dropped back to the team car to get it sorted.

Minor mechanical adjustments like this are carried out on the move, with the mechanic leaning out of the window of the car. He loosened the bolt and the whole saddle fell right down to the frame and he had no way of knowing where it should be, apart from trial and error.

I went back to the team car about five times in the first 15 kilometres, trying to get it adjusted. In the end, we got it sorted, which was a good thing too because Deloeuil's already thin patience had worn out.

'I don't want to see you back at this car again,' he said, as I rode up to the back of the bunch.

Paris–Roubaix was a brutal experience that day, but I was so excited to be part of it. The rain made the cobbles muddy and by the time we'd completed the first of twenty-six sections of *pavé*, we were covered from head to toe in a thin film of grey-brown sludge.

The roads were slippery and dangerous and, because of the rain, some sections were under water. I reached the Arenberg Forest, the famous section of cobbles that cuts a tree-lined avenue through the woods, and saw a body in one of our jerseys by the side of the road. He was halfway under one of the crowd barriers, so he'd obviously gone down hard. I later found out it was Philippe Gaumont, and that he'd broken his femur.

After Arenberg, the race shattered into bits. I was in a small group battling to stay upright on the cobbles but losing ground to the leaders. I pressed on for about 30 kilometres after I'd eaten my last bit of food. One of my water bottles had bounced out on the cobbles, the other was empty and I hadn't had a drink for almost an hour. I was soaking wet, but the inside of my mouth was bone dry. At one point, I was riding with the Russian Viatcheslav Ekimov. We were creeping along but we passed some poor lad who was going even more slowly. The way his bike bounced off the cobbles made him look like a drunk staggering home after closing time.

With about 40 kilometres to go, I saw a Cofidis team car, pulled over and got in. That was my race done. There was nothing to be gained from going on to the finish. I was still an hour away. As we went on down the route I saw Vicki and her parents standing by the side of the road. They'd come out to see me but had positioned themselves an optimistically long way down the route.

When we reached Roubaix, I had a shower, got changed and then Vicki drove us back to Calais, through the tunnel on the train, and then back north and home. It was nearly midnight when we got home to see a fax that told me I was booked on a flight from Manchester to Milan in two days' time. I'd be racing the five-day Settimana Lombarda stage race in northern Italy. I was absolutely exhausted. I'd been on the road for almost three weeks, battering myself on the cobbles; now I had to do a stage race with skinny Italian climbers.

There was a little note from Bondue explaining that Cofidis were so short of bodies, they just needed me to start (each team needed a minimum of six riders), and I could pull out and come home after the first day if I felt like it.

In Italy, I felt surprisingly good on the first day, but the fatigue began to tell when we got into the hills. The third stage was hilly all day and I was getting spat out of the back of the bunch every time we got to the climbs, then killing myself to get back on. After about half a dozen instances of this, the constant yo-yoing caused the invisible string that binds the peloton together to snap. I swung to the side of the road and waited for the second team car.

When Van Londersele saw me, he didn't say anything, just shook his head in disgust at the feeble *rosbif* who'd climbed off his bike. He wouldn't let me fly out the next day, as Bondue had promised; instead I had to wait until the race finished. So I spent a pointless couple of days hanging around in Italy when I could have been at home. I didn't want Van Londersele thinking I was a shirker, so I rang Bondue to ask him whether he knew I'd just done three weeks racing in Belgium and that I'd been asked to fill in at the last minute? Bondue said Van Londersele knew what I'd been doing, but I wasn't convinced.

I'd been a professional for less than three months and had learned that riders like me, a lot further down the food chain than the stars, were fodder. We filled in the gaps when there was no one else. We rode until we were empty and then waited for the fax or phone call. It was like being a junior doctor, per-manently on call. The race programme was written only in light pencil. Everything was subject to change. If even Dave was un-able to get his programme set in stone, what chance did I have?

It was hard to train for a specific event when you didn't know what that event might be. In fact, the constant uncertainty made it hard to train full stop. I'd go out for a hard five-hour training ride at home and come back to the news that I was getting a late flight to France and would be racing in two days' time. Some-times things were as short-notice as that.

I quite quickly worked out that if there was a specific race I didn't want to do, the best way to get out of it was to volunteer for it. The Cofidis bosses didn't like thinking they were doing you a favour or that you might be enjoying yourself.

From the outside, being a member of the Cofidis team must've looked amazing. For a lot of keen amateur cyclists, being a professional seemed like the dream job. Getting paid to ride a bike, having the best equipment and travelling round Europe in the glamorous bubble that was the pro peloton certainly looked brilliant. Don't get me wrong, I enjoyed my time racing as a pro in Europe, but it wasn't all it's cracked up to be.

A couple of weeks after Paris–Roubaix, I went to my local bike shop, Will Wright's in Heaton Chapel, Stockport, and the guys there asked me how I got on.

'I climbed off at the second feed.'

'Where was that?'

'Forty k from the finish.'

I could tell from the looks on their faces that they simply couldn't understand why I'd get so close to the end of a race like that and not bother to do the final 25 miles.

They asked how I'd done at the other races, the Three Days of De Panne, Ghent–Wevelgem and the Tour of Flanders. I told them I hadn't finished any of them, that I'd done my job for the leaders, I'd fetched the bottles and done the donkey work and called it a day, as a lot of the other *domestiques*, or helpers, did.

Although they knew their cycling, they didn't get it; they didn't understand what it was really like, and I wasn't able to explain it to them. All of a sudden, I understood why Dave could be so monosyllabic when I'd asked him about life as a pro in France. I decided that when I met keen cyclists or fans, I didn't want to be the moody sod who spoiled the illusion of the dream job. The life wasn't a woe-is-me slog, either; it's just that, in my first few months at Cofidis, I'd learned that the Great Britain set-up at Manchester was better organized and more innovative. The needs of the riders were at the centre of everything they did, whereas at Cofidis it felt like we were an inconvenience some of the time; or at least riders of my status were.

The fax would go, I'd immediately scan to the bottom of the page to see who the *directeur sportif* was. If it was Alain Deloeuil, my stomach would sink and I'd have the same horrible sick feeling that ruined my summer holiday when I knew I was moving into Mr Peake's class. I'd spend a day travelling, race in an event I didn't know, without a clearly defined role, then travel home. It wasn't what I'd imagined it would be, but that first year was still a fantastic experience.

Everyone assumed that, as a pro, you had a stash of top-of-the-range bikes in the garage at home, but during my first year at Cofidis I was given one bike. I had to train on it and take it to races. After our first training camp, before the start of the season, I went out into the car park and borrowed the mechanics' hose to wash down my bike before carefully packing it away in a bag like I'd always done. The other guys were taking the piss out of me because they just threw theirs in a bag and then when they turned up at their next race, they expected the mechanics to spend an hour putting it right.

There was a truck crammed full of the best equipment – carbon-fibre wheels, the lightest saddles and handlebars – but when I went and asked for a better pair of wheels I got a shake of the head. 'Not for you, Rob, this is for the Tour.' They saved all the best stuff for the Tour.

I kept my bike in good working order but I deliberately scuffed up the frame. People would ask, 'Is that your training bike, then?' and I'd say 'No, I did the Tour of Flanders on this.' A lot of club riders back home had better bikes than the one I was riding.

There were lots of things about the culture at Cofidis that were strange. Everyone had a variation of the same nickname: Fifi, Noo-noo, Cha-cha, Putt-putt. Except me, I was Rob Ezz, which is how the French pronounced Hayles. I probably got on better with the mechanics and *soigneurs* than I did with most of the riders, because they were more on my wavelength.

When I'd met Philippe Gaumont in the track centre at Sydney, he'd told me we'd have a party at our first get-together. I thought he was joking but when we met up at the hotel in Amiens, I found out what he meant. There was no training to do, so in the evenings we had a meal and went out for a few beers. That night I realized some of the riders had a habit of taking sleeping tablets – Stilnox – when they drank.

Gaumont had a reputation. He later wrote a book in which he talked about his doping. When the Cofidis team was under investigation in 2004, after I'd left, Dave called Gaumont a nutter, which he was, in all fairness. He was a bizarre character. He'd wander round the hotel in his trademark silk underpants and spend time on the sunbed at training camps.

He was always on at me about my ride in Sydney, where I had beaten him.

'What did you take for that? . . . What do the British team do?'

I told him we didn't do anything, but he wouldn't have it. He couldn't believe you could get results without help, and that suspicion went throughout the team. At Cofidis, they thought everyone else was at it, which given the reality of cycling at the time probably wasn't unreasonable. There was paranoia everywhere.

'Did you see him on the climb? *Pas normale.*'

That was the culture they had and it didn't matter how many times I told them I wasn't doing anything. They just chuckled and said, 'Ah, you Brits.'

At times, the obsession with Stilnox was in danger of becoming a problem, but the management either turned a blind eye or were too weak to get a grip. I noticed it the first time we had a few drinks at the get-to-know-you camp in Amiens. Gaumont ordered the champagne and passed round the sleeping tablets. Because the pills made you drowsy, they reacted with the booze and made the riders giggle like kids.

That night in Amiens, I stuck to the beers and ended up chatting to David Moncoutié, one of the team's most talented riders. After I'd gone to bed, I could hear the others running up and down the corridors, still giggling. It was like we had mice in the plumbing.

Sleeping tablets aren't banned and when you're spending every night in a different hotel, surrounded by unfamiliar sounds and in a strange bed, some riders found them useful. I did use them very occasionally myself to make sure I got a good night's rest. They really worked. I'd wake up and immediately feel fresh and alert, rather than sluggish and dull.

Later on, the Cofidis management instructed the doctors to keep a tighter rein on who got the tablets. Our Estonian sprinter, Janek Tombak, was one of the riders who used to take Stilnox to help him sleep. When I roomed with him, he'd get the doctor to give him one tablet, then ask me to go and get 'my' tablet and give it to him. I didn't object to doing this, but the doctor got wise to it because they knew I'd not taken it much before. I could sleep for England. I went to the doc and, suspecting that I was going to give it to someone else, he made me take the pill with a glass of water. I kept it under my tongue and gave it to Tombak. 'Sorry it's a bit wet.'

Another time, I was counting out some amino acid tablets, which help neutralize the build-up of lactic acid, with a caffeine tablet. Caffeine was permitted up to certain limits. Tombak saw the pill and, pointing to the caffeine tablet, asked what it was.

'Oh, it's a sleeping tablet. Like Stilnox,' I said, just joking.

With that, he grabbed it and necked it.

That night, I could hear him tossing and turning in bed, and in the morning he was a wreck. He'd barely had a wink's sleep having taken the equivalent of a cafetière of coffee so late in the day. Tombak had been in the break the previous day and, because he'd run out of drink and didn't have a team car up with him, he took a bottle from the Mapei team car that was following the leaders.

'I tell you, there was something in that Mapei bottle, I'm sure of it.'

And so the cycle of suspicion went on. I daren't tell him what had really happened.

# 12

# Crash and Burn

I didn't spend a lot of time in Biarritz during the first year because I preferred to commute home. Whenever Shari was there, Dave was almost unreachable anyway. She was a pretty, blonde, Aussie girl who'd come to Europe on holiday. She had no real understanding of what Dave's life was like. She just wanted to enjoy the vibe in Biarritz, go out every night and make the most of it. Dave, being Dave, didn't take much persuading.

Dave was one of the best riders to race with when he was on form, because he was decisive and rode like a leader. He would take control of a situation and tell people what he wanted them to do. Training was the opposite. Sometimes he just couldn't be arsed. If I needed to go out for a good ride, he'd say, 'Come on, Rob, lighten up. Let's go and get a coffee.' But if he needed to cram in some work, he'd go out and smash himself into the ground. Basically, it was always on his terms, and I was expected to train the way he did.

After being the golden boy on his Tour de France debut the previous year, the 2001 Tour had been a disaster for Dave. He crashed in the prologue time trial in Dunkirk, then struggled on at the back of the bunch for ten days before pulling out in the

Alps. Later in the summer, he won the Tour of Denmark and then led the Vuelta a España for a few days, before being beaten to the gold medal in the World Championships time trial by Jan Ullrich.

At the end of the year, I told Alain Bondue that Vicki and I would be moving to Biarritz, as we had originally planned. He seemed pleased about that because he was worried about Dave and the kind of life he was living; although it could just as easily have been that he was worried about how much money Cofidis had invested in Dave doing well.

We were planning to pack up our life in Stockport to head for the south-west coast of France, but I had been feeling ill. I'd booked myself to see British Cycling's doctor Roger Palfreeman in Manchester to have a blood test to check nothing was wrong. Vicki and I had been staying with my parents in Horndean. Because the doc said the blood had to be taken in the morning, we set off really early.

Big mistake.

I'd done the first stint of driving and we stopped for a coffee at the services just before we got on the M40. Vicki got in the driving seat and I settled in to have a sleep. The slip road was short and, as she accelerated up to speed, the truck that was in the inside lane flashed her to let us out onto the motorway. She felt the back end of the car, the BMW 3 we'd only had a few weeks, swerve, and she over-corrected it, sending us spinning across the carriageway until we were in the outside lane, at 90 degrees.

I was in the passenger seat and I took the full impact of the truck that hit us. I was knocked unconscious. I remember waking up and feeling the pain.

As luck would have it, a nurse had been driving on the opposite side of the motorway and she pulled over and then climbed over the central reservation to help. The next thing I knew, the fire brigade were cutting the roof off the car and I was helicoptered to hospital in Oxford.

I had a triple fracture of the pelvis, fractured vertebrae, two broken ribs and a big bang to the head. Fortunately Vicki was less badly hurt, although she suffered whiplash for months.

It was also a stroke of good fortune that the pelvic specialist was at the hospital that day, because the standard treatment would have been to plat and pin my pelvis back together, which could have been the end of my cycling career there and then. At the hospital, Vicki said to anyone who would listen: 'He's a cyclist.' That saved me, and I was told later that car crashes that bad can be fatal, so we got away lightly.

Once I had recovered from my injuries at the start of spring 2002, we packed more or less everything we owned into the car for our new life in France. I'd bought an Audi A6 estate especially for the journey. But I only had a year left on my contract, I was 29, and I hadn't set the world on fire the previous season; so we set off knowing that it would probably be a short adventure and that we'd be heading home again at the end of the year.

The Commonwealth Games were to be held in Manchester that summer, practically on my doorstep, and I was keen to ride. Doug Dailey said the decision had been made to offer me a place in the scratch race, providing I committed myself to the track training again. I told Doug that would be a tough sell to Cofidis, who were paying my wages, and, besides, I wasn't prepared to dedicate months to the track if all I was being offered was the scratch race. I'd prefer to get back into the team pursuit squad. There was a bit of a stand-off and neither they nor I were going to be flexible about it, so I resigned myself to missing the Commie Games.

Vicki and I found a great little apartment for a reasonable rent and settled into life in Biarritz. Dave's relationship with Shari had been on and off and she was back in Australia. Dave was just as flighty as ever. Our friendship was based on a very clear hierarchy. Everything was on his terms. If he wanted to train hard, we trained hard; if he wanted to party hard, we went out and stayed out late into the night.

I was relaxed enough to accept that this was how it was, and I suppose I was a bit wary of upsetting him by speaking out of turn. He had got me the place in the team and I was there for him. That was the deal. What wasn't part of the deal was me telling him to wind his neck in or knuckle down, not that he'd have listened.

Vicki worried about Dave and she tried to help him. Here was this 25-year-old lad, with all the talent in the world and a salary that added up to hundreds of thousands of euros, but at times he was like a little lost boy. The bills piled up on the table at his place and went unpaid for weeks on end. He'd come back from a race to a laundry basket full of dirty clothes and a fridge of mouldy food. Vicki's instinct was to look after him, mother him a bit, but as she wasn't a shy, doormat type, she wouldn't just go round after him sorting out his life. She wanted him to take control. She offered to go through all his bills with him and sort them out. Dave would agree but put it off and then bury his head in the sand. I would get cross with him but I never really pulled him up on it. Vicki would tell him when he was behaving like a dick, and he would accept it because she was right.

The problem was, it seemed to me, that Cofidis didn't see their riders – even their most prized and expensive assets – as anything worth protecting. As far as the management were concerned, their job ended once the rider had been dropped off at the airport after a race. They were expected to train, and live like professionals.

I'll always remember the time when Dave won a stage race in northern France, the Tour of Picardie, which although a small event was quite an important one for us because it took place on the doorstep of the Cofidis HQ. He'd been to the anti-doping control to wee in the jar and he was standing on the pavement waiting for the Cofidis camper van to pick him up. He looked like an orphan or a drowned rat, skinny, still in his racing jersey and shorts, with a jacket thrown over his shoulders, and a half-full bottle of champagne in one hand (he'd drunk half of it so he could provide a urine sample) and the winner's bouquet of flowers in the other. He was half-cut because he'd done a hard four-hour race and the champagne he'd necked had gone straight to his head. He got in the camper, which didn't have a shower on board, unlike today's hotels on wheels that the top teams have. All he could do was have a quick wash-down with a flannel and get changed into a tracksuit. On the plane back home he said to me, 'If only people knew what it was really like sometimes.'

Having said all that, Dave could be his own worst enemy too. I lost count of the number of times we got off a flight at Biarritz airport after a race and we'd just walk straight out of the airport and head straight into town. Instead of waiting for the bags, he'd want to go and get a beer, so our Cofidis luggage and bike bags would go round and round on the carousel. The staff there knew him so well that they'd either wait for us to collect them the next day or put them in a taxi and send them to his house, where he'd pay the driver for his trouble.

Biarritz was fantastic, but it was probably the last place Dave needed to be at the time. He was the boy about town, he knew all the bars, and the bartenders all knew him. He was popular and had a lot of friends, but there were a lot of hangers-on too, people who wanted to be seen out with the cool pro cyclist. And Dave would often pick up the bill. Vicki and I used to joke – although it wasn't really funny – that Dave got rid of 50-euro notes like he was spreading them round Biarritz with a leaf-blower.

His sister, Fran, came down and Vicki told her what was going on. 'Between us, let's make sure we split the bill tonight. Make sure he doesn't put down his credit card and pay for everyone.' You could tell who the hangers-on were that night because they were the ones who looked grumpy at having to pay their way.

The thing about Dave was that he was great company. He could be funny and generous and kind, but he could also be a monster. Cofidis built him up, made him into a monster, and the more he was pandered to, the worse he got.

Cracks were beginning to show in August 2002. As Dave had won the Tour of Denmark the previous year, Cofidis were going to get a big wedge of money as long as Dave turned up and rode again. One of Vicki's friends, the swimmer Claire Huddart, was staying with us, so a couple of nights before Dave and I were supposed to fly to Copenhagen, we arranged to go out for a meal. I say that like it was a rare or special occurrence, but it wasn't. In the whole time we lived in Biarritz, Vicki and I cooked for ourselves only a handful of nights. There were so many good restaurants in Biarritz, we ate out all the time.

We'd arranged to meet Dave at a restaurant in town. When we arrived, he was there with a load of other cyclists who had just been round the corner in San Sebastián for the Classic there. Most of them would be flying to Denmark in a couple of days too. Bobby Julich, Stuart O'Grady, Matt White and Kevin Livingston were there, and so was Lance Armstrong, although he wasn't slumming it in Denmark, he was off on his private jet for a lucrative exhibition race somewhere. When we got a table outside the restaurant, Lance sat in the corner with his hat pulled down over his eyes, texting on his phone all night.

After we'd eaten, they decided to kick on to the infamous

Blue Cargo that was the centre of our life in Biarritz. It was a restaurant where they cleared away the tables at the end of the evening and it became a bar and nightclub on the beach.

Bobby asked, 'Are you coming?'

Vicki replied, 'No, he's got to race in a couple of days. Haven't you?'

Bobby said, 'Hey, man, it's not the Tour de France, you know.'

The next lunchtime, we found Dave in another bar with O'Grady. They were absolutely smashed. I'm pretty sure they can't have been to bed and they were a mess.

I left them to it and met up with them at the airport the next morning. Dave stunk of booze. He wasn't hungover, he was probably still drunk. We'd checked our bags in and Dave ran to the toilet. Then he came out and said to the staff, *'Annulé, annulé.* I'm not going. Take my bags off.'

He rang the Cofidis doctor, Jean-Jacques Menuet, and told him he was ill. Jean-Jacques knew what Dave was like, but of all the people at Cofidis, he was one of the kindest and most understanding. He didn't want to bust Dave's balls about it.

Dave stood there, swaying slightly, and Vicki said, 'You're an idiot, you know that?'

He just stood there like a naughty schoolboy: 'Yeah.'

Vicki drove him home and I got on the flight to Paris, and waited for my connection to Copenhagen. While I was waiting at Paris airport, I turned on my phone and there were missed calls from Vicki and from Deloeuil.

Deloeuil was fuming. He wanted to make sure I was on the flight because if I went AWOL too, Cofidis would have too few riders to be allowed to start the race. Deloeuil wasn't daft, he knew what had happened, but I couldn't admit to him that Dave had been on the lash for three days, so I said, 'He's sick, honestly, he's sick.'

When I got to Copenhagen, I waited for my bag to come through. Nothing. Back in Biarritz, the ground crew had taken everything with a Cofidis logo on it off the plane. A professional cyclist learns very quickly – usually the hard way – to take their cycling shoes and one set of kit in their hand luggage. My bags chased me round Denmark for half the week and eventually turned up two days from the end of the race.

There was a bit of a mutiny among the swannies, the *soigneurs*, whose job it was to massage the riders, make the food for the races and do the laundry. They were having a right to-do, saying their workload was too much, so they'd decided that instead of doing the laundry every day, they'd do the washing every other day.

On the second morning of the race, I asked where my kit was and Philippe, one of our *soigneurs*, who looked like Uncle Fester, said, 'Haven't you heard? We're only doing washing every other day.'

'Haven't you heard? My bags got lost and I've only got one set of kit.'

They quickly washed my kit and I had to tie it to the roof rack of the team car so that it dried out on the drive to the start of the stage. At times, I couldn't help but curse the name Dave Millar, and this was one of those times.

I didn't win a race in either of my first two seasons with Cofidis. After the car crash at the end of my first year, I missed a lot of training and, by the time I was back in action, I was six kilos lighter. Jean-Jacques, the team doctor, reckoned, 'You'll be flying on the climbs now.' As it turned out, I still couldn't climb, and now I didn't have the grunt to stay in the wheels on the flat either. So the first half of the second year was a struggle, and I'd more or less accepted that Cofidis would let me go at the end of the season.

The closest I came to winning a race for Cofidis was at the

**Above:** Our team pursuit squad was stronger than ever at Athens 2004, with Paul Manning and Steve Cummings alongside me and Brad, plus Chris Newton and Steely in reserve.

Telling Graeme Brown what happened **(left)**. The Aussies were too good for us in the end, but me, Paul, Steve and Brad could still show off our silver medals **(below)** – one step higher than in Sydney.

**Left:** Brad had won gold in the individual pursuit, but now I was slinging him straight into my second shot at a medal, in the Madison.

**Left:** Another Madison, another crash. At least this one wasn't fatal to my chances, unlike in Sydney four years earlier.

**Left:** Giving my all on the last lap, chasing Switzerland's Franco Marvulli and with O'Grady holding me down the bottom of the banking.

**Below:** Brad tells me we won bronze. I look a bit shocked.

**Left and below:** Celebrating a third Olympic medal with a future Knight of the Realm and Tour de France winner. I might forgive his practical jokes now.

**Bottom:** Rejoicing in the moment with my wife Vicki and my dad John. We'd come a long way from the track at Portsmouth.

ATHENS 2004

**Above:** The World Championships in Los Angeles in 2005 brought gold at last for Great Britain's team pursuiters – our first ever in that event.

**Left and above:** On the final night of the championships it was a stripy jumper for both me and Cav in the Madison. You could hardly notice the age difference.

**Left:** The morning after. Double world champion. Twice the hangover.

**Above:** Showing off the rainbow bands at a Revolution meeting back home in Manchester.

**Left:** Then I joined a women's team. This was above Abergavenny in 2008.

**Left:** 2008 brought another great honour, as I became national road race champion. What is it with me and winning in the pouring rain?

Shattered after the race **(below left)**, then spraying the old champagne in another GB jersey **(below right)**. A teenage Peter Kennaugh (right) took the silver and Dean Downing bronze.

**Bottom:** All smiles with Shane Sutton and Dave Brailsford. That hadn't been the case earlier in the year.

**Above:** By now British cycling was dominant, with a new generation coming through in my slipstream. Here I celebrate a World Cup team pursuit gold medal in Manchester with Steven Burke, Ed Clancy and Geraint Thomas.

**Left:** Come in, number 135… The National Hill-Climb Championship in October 2011. My final race, and I loved every minute of every one.

**Left:** The Secret Squirrel: testing in the wind tunnel at Southampton has taken days of my life, but all in a good cause!

**Above:** A new career: my first ever interview for Eurosport, with Rod Ellingworth before the London Olympics road race test event.

**Left:** I do like to dress up (for charity, I assure you: this was for a Children in Need meeting in Manchester). You should see my Rihanna.

**Below:** Vicki and me above our home in Hayfield with our children Madeleine and Fergus. This is the life.

Tour of Sweden in that second year. It was the second stage, to a place called Motala. It was pouring with rain and my job was to try to steer Janek Tombak, our designated sprinter, into position for the finish. With about five kilometres to go, Tombak crashed as they all skidded in the wet. There wasn't any point in stopping and waiting for him so close to the finish, because we'd never get back in touch with the bunch, and even if we did, we wouldn't have a hope of getting back up to the front, so I just kept going.

I followed my nose and called up the old racer's instinct that had been dormant for the past eighteen months. A few hundred metres from the line, I was at the front, with daylight ahead of me. Everything around me seemed to slow down; it was like I imagine an out-of-body experience to be, and I thought, 'I've got this. I'm going to win.'

Then I noticed the shadow coming alongside me, and a Dutch guy called Steven de Jongh pipped me on the line. So close.

The Tour of Sweden wasn't a big race, but I was buzzing after racing at the pointy end. I rang Dave after the stage and he happened to be with Bondue.

'We've just been talking about you, and whether Cofidis should keep you on,' he said.

Off the back of that one result, a second place in a stage of the Tour of Sweden, Cofidis gave me another year.

When I told British Cycling I was staying with Cofidis for 2003, they more or less told me it would affect my chances of making the team for the Athens Olympics. They didn't think I was committed enough to the track, and Peter Keen summoned me to Manchester for a meeting.

At the meeting were Keen, Dave Brailsford, who was now running the elite programme, and Simon Jones. They thought I wanted to have my cake and eat it. I wanted a pro contract and a salary one year, then a pass back into the team pursuit the next.

But it wasn't about money at all: it was going to the Olympics and winning a gold medal that motivated me. I felt that racing at a high level on the road, getting the hard yards in, could benefit me. I also believed I could slot back in and add something to the team pursuit.

Someone said, 'You can't pick up the team pursuit just like that after two years away.' But I felt I could do exactly that, because the team pursuit was what I'd done for years and years.

They said that I needed to ride the World Track Championships in Stuttgart in early August to have any chance of being in the frame for Athens the following year. That was fine, I said, Cofidis would let me have the time.

Then they said I'd need to ride a World Cup meeting in Moscow in mid-February. This was more problematic, because it was right at the start of the road season, and Cofidis were bound to need me to fill one of their rosters somewhere. I tried to argue that flying all the way to Moscow to ride a scratch race and a Madison, with Chris Newton, who hated the Madison at the best of times, was pointless, but they said it was that or else I was out. I think they were testing my commitment.

Keen said he wanted to see me on the track, going through some drills with the team pursuiters. He thought I'd gone to France, raced on the road, and forgotten what it was all about.

He stood at the top of the track as we went round and got ourselves up to speed. He had his arms folded, watching for the details. The first changeover came and I flew up the banking in a smooth arc and settled neatly in the slipstream of the last rider in the chain. It was a textbook change. Next time I looked up to where Keen had been standing. He'd turned his back and was walking away. It was like that moment in the movies. He'd seen enough.

The opposition to me riding for a pro team on the road was strange because, a few years later, it became the blueprint for track success. By 2007 British Cycling were falling over themselves to fix up their endurance track riders with pro teams, so they could get that hard, deep, consistent workload that racing on the road gives you.

The 2002 season ended at the Tour of Poland with the worst crash of my career. I don't remember anything about it other than lying on the ground watching the pool of blood flood towards the drain in the gutter. They took me to hospital by helicopter. Bernard Quilfen, our kindly uncle of a team manager, brought the rest of the lads to see me before they flew home from the race. It was good to see them but I noticed no one was making eye contact with me. They wouldn't look at me. As they shuffled out of the room, I heard Tombak say something. I caught the word 'Frankenstein', but he wasn't saying it in a jokey way.

I dragged myself out of bed and hauled the frame with the drip attached to it across to where there was a mirror on the wall. I looked at the swollen bag of meat my face now resembled. My cheeks were scraped and puffed up, my forehead was battered, and I had scabs on both eyelids. It was a kaleidoscope of deep red, purples and blacks. My chest was badly bruised too. I started to cry, because I didn't recognize myself.

A few days later, when I was well enough to go home, I had to get a taxi to the airport. Everyone was staring at me. On the plane, the woman who was sitting next to me pressed the bell, called the stewardess, and asked to be reseated. I wanted to say, 'It's OK, love, it's not catching.'

Bondue had called Vicki to warn her I was in a bad way. She met me at the airport and she'd used make-up to paint a black eye and some stitches on her face to try to make me feel better. When she saw me, she burst into tears at the shock. I really was in a state.

*

I started my final year at Cofidis in good form because I'd been training for the track, but the trip to Moscow made the wheels fall off. A week eating cereal and Pot Noodles didn't help my road form. After that, I was little more than a peripheral figure. I wasn't too concerned though, because I now had the Stuttgart World Championships to build towards, and Athens was around the corner.

Increasingly, the world at Cofidis looked flaky and bizarre. It was all about appearances. If we looked good from the outside, everyone seemed happy – even if the reality was a shambles. The team acquired a brand new, medium-sized team bus for the smaller races. It wasn't as big as the main bus that went to the big races, but it was far better than the camper van. Cha-cha, the guy who drove the camper, was really proud of it, so there was a race between the riders to christen the toilet. Tombak beat me by about two minutes and Cha-cha went absolutely mental that someone had defecated in his brand new toilet.

The problem was, Cha-cha's driving licence only permitted him to drive this bus when it was empty; he wasn't allowed to take passengers. So we still had to travel between the hotels and the races squashed into team cars while Cha-cha drove this swanky bus to the start, and we'd all climb out of the cars and sit on it for forty-five minutes before the start.

Fifi, the *soigneur* who looked like Uncle Fester, drove one of the other camper vans, and he had a little party trick that summed up the team. He'd get it up to about 80 k.p.h. on a straight bit of *autoroute* and the riders would all be sat in the back, clapping and chanting, 'Fifi, Fifi, Fifi.' Then he'd leave the steering wheel, run the length of the camper van, touch the back wall and get back in the driver's seat before we veered off the road.

That was Cofidis in a nutshell – bowling along the motorway without anyone at the wheel.

# 13

# Biarritz

Life in Biarritz was good. In fact, it was the thing that kept me going during that final year with Cofidis. We knew it wouldn't last for ever, that we'd be going back to England at the end of the season, and I knew, at 29, that I was never going to become a star of road cycling, so we were determined to make the most of it. It was a means to an end and Biarritz became a year-long warm-weather training camp for Athens, punctuated by the fax machine telling me to go to Sarthe or Picardie or Belgium or Italy, depending on where Cofidis needed a body to pull on a jersey and fill a place.

The rest of the time, we threw ourselves into life in Biarritz. I'd sent the Audi back to the UK and had bought my ideal car – a Renault 5 GT turbo. I know what you're thinking, whose dream car is a Renault 5? All I can say is that ever since I was a child I'd wanted one and now we were in France it was the perfect car to have. The Renault 5 was made for the tight streets of Biarritz, where motorists drove around like they were in bumper cars and parked any old how. You could do a great photographic exhibition of the quirky, carefree parking in Biarritz.

Vicki and I got heavily into surfing and bought boards. Our friend Lauren McCrossan and her husband Gabe Davies, the big wave surfing champion, would come and visit. I probably spent as much time surfing as I did training that year. I was living the dream. The sun shone, we ate outdoors, we spent time at the beach, we surfed.

I dreaded going to the races with Cofidis because my mind had already shifted to the track and the Stuttgart World Championships, but still the fax would upset my plans.

At the start of February, I got a late call-up for the Étoile de Bessèges, a little week-long stage race in the south of France, because Janek Tombak was ill. I turned up at the hotel just in time for dinner the night before the first stage. As I sat down, Jo Planckaert asked, 'What are you doing here?' My name was not on the list of riders that had been sent round to everyone. I explained that Tombak was ill, and that I was taking his place.

'When did they tell you you were coming?' asked Planckaert.

'This morning.'

'Oh, that's dangerous. Imagine if you'd done a bit of prep?'

I didn't do the sort of prep he was referring to.

I rode really well that week. I got sixth on one stage when we were trying to set the sprint up for Robert Sassone. On one of the other stages, I was climbing with the second group – I was only just hanging in but I was still there and going well. When Gaumont got on the bus, he saw I was already there ahead of him and wondered, 'How can Rob Ezz do that on the climbs? It's not right.'

Their mentality never changed. If you were going well, you must have been on the gear.

I wasn't daft. I knew that doping went on. I heard the gossip on the bus about who was doing what, but a lot of the time it felt like they were convincing themselves that everyone who'd finished ahead of them was on something.

At the training camp at the start of the year, we'd had a big meal, the whole team of twenty-five riders at one long table. When I got down to the dining room there was only one place left, opposite Gaumont, who was sitting there like a medieval king. He was a nutter, but he was funny to be around.

'Ah, Rob, you have the honour of sitting in front of me,' he said. 'Let me tell you, Rob, if you finish your career with half the results I have got, you'll have had a very fine career.'

This was the one time I stood up for myself with Gaumont in front of the other riders (probably because I knew it was the start of my last year and I wouldn't be spending much time with him). 'Philippe, if I'd have done half the gear you've done, I'd have twice the results you've got.'

Fair play to him, he did laugh.

The atmosphere in the Cofidis camp was becoming increasingly strained and Dave was even more erratic than usual. At that training camp there was a long and rancorous discussion about the way the bonus system was structured in the team. Dave's gripe was that Cofidis rewarded riders who gathered UCI points rather than dedicated themselves to the good of the team. So, if Dave needed a teammate to help, he couldn't rely on many people, because they were thinking of themselves. It was more valuable to the riders to get a top-ten place of their own, score some UCI points and increase their salary, than it was to help Dave or another of the leaders to win. I was just observing the row because I was on a fixed salary, so it barely applied to me, but the lack of leadership by the management was pulling the team apart.

It's easy to look back now and recognize the signs that Dave was deeply unhappy at the time, and it's possible to work out why that was, considering what was to happen to him. But at the time, I just thought he was burning the candle at both ends.

One night when Vicki was away, working with the British table tennis team, we went out and I had a couple of glasses of champagne and a Stilnox. The rest of the evening was a blur, but when I woke up in the morning and went into the kitchen, there was an exhaust pipe on the table. The screws that had held it in place were all laid out neatly in a line, pointing up, with a spanner and screwdriver next to them. Also there were a pair of sun visors for a Renault 5 and then it dawned on me that I'd been round Biarritz trying the car doors (most people left their cars unlocked) and I'd liberated the visors from one of them. I have no idea why I'd removed the exhaust from a Ford Escort, as it wouldn't have fitted my car. I didn't touch Stilnox after that, because I wasn't in control of what I was doing. Well, judging by the way I'd laid everything out so perfectly on the table, I was actually completely in control, but not in a good way.

Away from the races, Dave was becoming difficult to talk to, and I suppose I wasn't much of a friend, because the signs I did notice, I ignored; although I didn't know at the time what he was into. He bought a house in Biarritz that he sunk a lot of money into. It was beautiful, but it was a wreck, and he had great plans to do it up. Perhaps he was trying to lay down some roots, perhaps he was trying to give himself something else to think about, or perhaps he needed something to show for his large salary, I don't know.

But he was certainly a name and a face in Biarritz. He knew everyone in the town and sometimes that came in handy. We had a friend called Laurent, who had been a special in the police and was now working as a security guard, and we were down in a bar at la Côte des Basque with another couple of friends, Xavier and Didier, who later ended up buying Dave's house when he had to sell it. They had this brand new fifty-inch plasma TV and we were listening to Sade on it – very French. Dave said, 'I'll go and get my Underworld DVD.'

So he headed off in his Subaru, which didn't have a corner left on it, thanks to Biarritz's driving and parking culture.

Half an hour later, he still hadn't returned, even though his place was only five minutes up the hill. Laurent and I were getting a bit worried, so we went to find him.

His car wasn't at his apartment, but a police van was outside and the door was open, so we went in. I stuck my head through the beads that hung in the doorway to the lounge and there was Dave and three gendarmes, all drinking a glass of red wine.

'Everything OK?'

'Yes, wait in the kitchen,' he said.

We later found out that Dave had flown into a tight corner and crashed into a building, knocking himself out for a moment or two. It was actually fortunate, because if he'd crashed a few metres further along the road, he could have gone over the sea wall and on to the rocks below. He'd done a runner, then came to his senses and returned to the car to find the police there with a flat-bed truck ready to take it away. Because the police knew Dave, they went back to his apartment with him.

After we'd been waiting in the kitchen about twenty minutes, the three policemen left. Dave opened his cupboard and gave them each a bottle of red wine and a brand new pair of Oakley sunglasses.

'That's how you deal with things round here,' he said, after they'd gone.

I thought it was a bit fucked up but it was how a lot of things worked. If I got a parking ticket, I could take it to the local bike shop, which sold the MBK bikes that our Cofidis team rode, and somehow the fine would get cancelled by a guy at the council.

Dave's extremes of behaviour became more noticeable. Before the Tour, he switched himself on and became incredibly dedicated for three weeks, like a student cramming for an exam. I used to joke, 'You like a six-week stage race, don't you.' He locked himself in this boot-camp mentality. That was obviously his way of handling it.

It seemed like he had a lot of disrespect for cycling and cyclists. He did it because he was good at it, but he acted like he thought bike riders were stupid. He hated himself, and you could see it in the way he trained and lived. He either put himself through the mill on the bike or he blitzed himself down at the bar getting pissed. And because he was trying to get in shape for the Tour, he wasn't eating. He'd rather have his calories in a glass.

'How are you going?' I'd ask.

'I'm a kilo and a half over.'

'No, but how are you going?'

'I'm a kilo and a half over.'

It wasn't a healthy life and he had no one to support him. The signs were all there, but I didn't do enough to help. To tell the truth, I didn't know what I could do.

That summer in Biarritz was roasting hot. I set the turbo trainer up outside the apartment and did punishing interval sessions in the sunshine and watched the Tour de France on television. Then I went to the World Championships in Stuttgart and did well enough in the team pursuit to prove I deserved a place at the Olympics. Brad Wiggins, Paul Manning, Bryan Steel and I won the silver medal, although our time of 4-00.629 was more than three seconds slower than the Aussies. We had a big gap to close.

There was no leaving party with Cofidis, no fond farewells. I'd been selected for some race in France but hadn't had confirmation of my flight time, so I rang my teammate Hayden Roulston to ask if he knew.

'You're not down for it.'

'What do you mean, I'm not down? This is supposed to be my last race.'

A few days earlier, I'd seen Alain Bondue by chance near our place in Biarritz. I stopped at the traffic lights and a white Opel estate pulled up alongside me. At the wheel was Bondue. My heart stopped for a moment, because I thought I had the surfboard strapped to the roof of the car. Even though I was only scheduled to do one more race, the management still had that strange hold over me. He wound down the window and said, 'How you doing? I'll phone you.'

I never heard from him again.

A week later, I got a letter saying thanks for everything and good luck for the rest of my career, and that was it.

We still had several weeks to run on the lease at the apartment and we were determined to stay and milk the last days of the summer.

When the time came to leave, I spent two days packing the car – a process of Jenga and Tetris combined, as I crammed all our stuff into the tiny Renault 5. We had the surf boards and Vicki's bike on the roof, about sixty bottles of red and a few Sauternes. We drove up through France and when we went over the ramp on the ferry, the bottom of the car was almost scraping on the floor.

That was it, my life as a professional in Europe was over; time to get back on track. I'd headed to Biarritz in an Audi A6 estate and I was returning home in a Renault 5. That summed it up, really, but I couldn't have been happier because I'd seen it for myself. I'd ridden Paris–Roubaix three times, the Tour of Flanders twice, and I'd been in the lead-out train sprinting shoulder to shoulder with Mario Cipollini. The first year had been great, the second year OK and, although I hated the racing in the third year, there were few better places in the world to live than Biarritz.

We bought a house in the Peak District and I rejoined the track squad. Dave was a world champion – he'd won the time trial at the World Road Championships in Hamilton, Canada, the previous autumn – and now he was going to see if he could slot into the team pursuit squad. The way he pedalled so smoothly, he could probably have done it.

But things were unravelling at Cofidis. Bob Madejak, the Polish *soigneur*, and one of their former riders, another Pole called Marek Rutkiewicz, were arrested and banned drugs were found. Some of the Cofidis riders returning from their training camp in Spain were met by police at Charles de Gaulle airport. A couple of months later things had escalated so much that François Migraine pulled the team from all their races, so Dave was unable to ride the track World Cup in Manchester. Dave said it was nothing to do with him, and I believed him.

In June 2004, I returned to Biarritz with the British pursuit squad for a training camp. I hadn't seen Dave for a few months, so I sent him a couple of texts asking if he wanted to meet up. No reply.

The Tour de France was only a couple of weeks away, so I thought perhaps he was locked into one of his boot camps, but I also thought: 'You miserable bastard. We're down here, two minutes up the road from you, and you can't even be bothered to answer a text.'

One day we'd been training and Jonesy pulled me to one side. 'Dave's been arrested.'

'Dave who?'

'Millar.'

'Fuck. Why?'

When Dave got out of custody, he rang me. I said, 'Are you all right? What's going on?'

He sounded relieved. His voice was flat but not tense. 'Yeah, yeah, it's going to be all right. I told them everything.'

'What do you mean everything?'

'Everything. About the EPO, everything.'

Dave's sister, Fran, flew down to Biarritz and I went to meet her and Dave at a bar down by the beach. I walked in and hugged him and he burst into tears. It was the first time I'd seen him like that. The veneer of confidence had been stripped away and the vulnerable boy underneath was all that was left. He was a mess, but in an odd way he was ready for what was going to happen next.

Dave had been with Dave Brailsford, British Cycling's new head honcho, when he got arrested. They'd been having a meal at the Blue Cargo when the police came in. After that came hours of questioning – the nice/nasty routine. Dave told me he had watched while the police searched his apartment, knowing that he had kept an EPO syringe in a hollowed-out book.

Then he told me that his phones had been tapped and, although he was nothing to do with the operation involving the Poles, they'd pieced together what he'd done. The police had records of all his calls and texts and were asking him, 'Who's Rob? Who is this Rob? Tell us who Rob is.'

All our conversations had been brief and banal. 'What time are we meeting?' 'See you at the bar.' 'See you at 8.' 'Where are we going tonight?'

But seen through the eyes of the drugs squad, they could have looked incriminating. If the police had wanted to question me, I was only down the road.

*

I remember after I'd been at Cofidis a few months, having my arse handed to me on a plate most days, I went back to England and rode some local race and I heard someone say, 'Rob's on the juice now.'

I thought, 'You cheeky bastards. Do you know where I've been racing the past few weeks?'

Racing at a higher level, only just managing to cope, changes your perception of effort. So going back to racing at home felt easier than it ever had, and obviously looked that way to others, who jumped to the wrong conclusions.

It would have been very easy to get involved in that world. It was all around me. Bob Madejak had been my *soigneur* at plenty of races. A couple of times, while he was massaging my legs, he would ask (in his strong Polish accent), 'What do you want, Rob? I can get you what you want. Hormone? EPO?' I used to say, 'No, you're all right, Bob,' and laugh to humour him and change the subject.

There was one rider I shared a room with at a race in France. We were racing the next day in Belgium before coming back to France and he didn't want to take his suitcase across the border. It didn't take a genius to work out why.

Unlike my teammates, I always had the option of going back home to the track squad and the Premier Calendar races. I didn't have the same stark choice that some of the others had. In that way, I felt very fortunate.

# 14

# In Pursuit of Victory

As much as we loved our two years in Biarritz, moving home wasn't difficult, although we chose to move to the village of Hayfield in the Peak District rather than back to Stockport. Settling back into the regime at Manchester velodrome was seamless too. As soon as I settled into position on my pursuit bike, I felt comfortable. It was like sliding my feet into a familiar pair of slippers.

I quickly embraced the routine of riding to the velodrome, spending all day with the lads, working hard, and then riding home. It was the closest thing to a nine-to-five I'd had since I'd been at Gales brewery, and it was a world away from the disorganization and free-form existence at Cofidis.

Things had moved on a lot at British Cycling since I'd last been involved with the squad on a day-to-day basis. Under Dave Brailsford, the number of support staff had grown. For a start there were more coaches. Dr Steve Peters, a psychiatrist, came in as a sort of mechanic for the mind. We had a nutritionist, more physiotherapists, and performance analysts – people to video the races and training sessions so we could study every pedal stroke to see what we were doing right and where we were going wrong. Everything was moving on. There was the birth of the Secret Squirrel Club, led by Chris Boardman and Matt Parker, to look at every aspect of bike, equipment and clothing design to see if there was a legal way to make the tiniest improvement. We had some fantastic state-of-the-art track bikes designed by a former Greek sprinter and engineer called Dimitris Katsanis, which were developed and built by the UK Sports Institute. The era of 'marginal gain' was well underway.

Everything we did was studied to see if we could do better. Generally speaking, mistakes were only made once. An example: at the World Championships in Stuttgart in 2003, Bryan Steel was put on the wrong gear for the team pursuit final against Australia. The mechanic put the wrong chainring on his bike and he was under-geared, which meant that we were basically racing with three men. After that, Ernie Feargrieve, the head mechanic, devised a colour-coding system and a protocol to check and double-check every gear ratio before every race. It sounds so simple, perhaps unnecessarily so, but the simplest mistakes are also the most avoidable. The first major impact Brailsford made was to look at everything we did and tighten up on all the little details. He encouraged others to do the same. Brailsford's motto was that he wanted us to leave no stone unturned in the quest to go faster. He also encouraged the free exchange of ideas. A good idea was a good idea no matter who suggested it, and everyone was welcome to speak up if they thought they had one.

The Olympic Games were the focus of everything we did. All our training built towards that. The 2004 World Championships were going to be held in Melbourne at the end of May, just ten weeks before the Olympics in Athens. Being so close together, I knew I couldn't be in peak condition for both, so the Worlds were a stepping stone to the Games. Neither Brad

Wiggins nor Brad McGee were riding the individual pursuit in Melbourne, so I thought I had a good chance of winning my first world title.

I reached the final, where I was up against Sergi Escobar of Spain. He had too much for me in the last kilometre, but I had to be happy with the silver medal because it was my best result in an individual event. The time wasn't too shabby either; in fact, it was world class. That result convinced me that I could win a world title in the individual pursuit one day. Turning in a 4-20 pursuit so close to the Olympics, knowing there would be more to come, boosted my confidence.

The team pursuit was looking good too. We were beaten by the Australians in the final, just as we had been in Stuttgart the year before, but we were well clear of the rest.

From Melbourne, we went to Biarritz for our final road-based training camp, then, before heading to Athens, we spent a couple of weeks at Celtic Manor in south Wales, fine-tuning things on the track at Newport. We had found that it was very hard to get into the zone in Manchester, because so many riders lived nearby. Although we checked into a hotel as a squad, the temptation to pop home now and then was too great for some of the riders, so we found it worked better if we got away from everything that was familiar and felt like home.

There are worse places to stay than Celtic Manor, that's for sure. The food was incredible, so it was a shame I was in the middle of a ten-week diet designed to get my weight down. I was concerned about the effect the heat in Athens would have, particularly in an hour-long Madison race, so I wanted to be as lean as possible. Paul Manning started the diet first, cutting out all processed foods and anything with added sugar. The diet was designed by our nutritionist Nigel Mitchell and it was very simple. But it meant that I could only shop in two of the aisles at the supermarket – fruit and veg, and fresh meat. When you look at the packets, it's startling how many foods have sugar added to them.

I'd never really been concerned about what I ate before. Food was fuel for the engine, especially in my sprinting days. When I trained hard, I ate more and there was no problem with that because I didn't put weight on. But the time when I could load up on pastries and chocolate was over for a while. My diet was stripped back so it was simple and plain. I even cut out fruit juice – unless it was squeezed directly from the fruit – because sugar is often added. I ate a lot of vegetables, avoided any processed meats or cheese, and drank water.

I can't pretend it wasn't hard at times, particularly for a chocoholic like me, but because Paul was doing it too we were able to stick to it. The only temptation was when I saw the spread of cakes and desserts on offer after dinner at Celtic Manor. One night I stood transfixed by a tart with a thick layer of chocolate on top. A swirl of cream had been expertly flared into a neat pattern with the tip of a knife or a cocktail stick in a chef-y way. It looked divine. I broke off a little piece of the chocolate and put it in my mouth. It was like an explosion of sweetness, the rush of sugar I'd been missing for weeks. I know that in the grand scheme of things, cutting out chocolate for a few weeks is hardly the greatest sacrifice, but it was surprising just how much of a buzz I got from such a small taste.

As a result of the diet, I shed a lot of excess weight and I felt sharper, lighter and leaner than ever before. My training had been planned to the day and, for the first time, I had a full taper down to the competition. Basically the body responds best if it is rested before the races. Training in the week before the Olympics isn't going to improve things any further – in fact, it could be detrimental – so once all the training was in the bank, it was a case of tapering down, letting the body absorb all the work it had done and repair itself so it was fresh for the Games. The only work we'd do would be light rides to turn the legs over and keep the muscles loose or short efforts to maintain the top end power and speed.

But when we arrived in Athens, I was concerned that my form wasn't going to come good in time. Three days before the start of the individual pursuit competition, everything still felt like a struggle when I had hoped to be pinging round the track.

In comparison, Brad Wiggins was flying. We weren't riding over the full four-kilometre distance but he got up on the track and was knocking out times that would put him six or seven seconds ahead of me over the full individual pursuit distance. He made it look so easy, and I thought then that the gold medal in the individual pursuit was his to lose.

As race day approached, I gradually started to feel that my form was improving, but I still went to bed the night before the individual pursuit qualifying round just hoping that it would be all right on the night.

There were a few changes to the way the competition was structured that meant it would be a different challenge to the one I'd faced in Sydney four years earlier. Back then, the fastest four riders in the qualifying round faced each other in the semi-finals and the winners advanced to the gold medal final. That meant that the emphasis was on posting a fast time in qualifying, because if you missed the top four, that was it, game over.

This time, the top eight in the qualifying round would go through to the first round, which made it a little less daunting. Instead the first round became the most important ride. The fastest qualifier would race the eighth fastest, with second against seventh, third against sixth and fourth against fifth. The winners of each first-round heat would go through to race for the medals but the crucial thing to remember was that instead of there being semi-finals, the two fastest first-round heat winners would race for gold and the two slower heat winners would race for bronze. So, not only did I have to make sure I won my heat, but I had to do it in one of the two fastest winning times.

So, although the qualification round was still important, because it determined the strength of my opponent, it was the first-round match that everything hinged on. That race had to be won, or else the chance of a medal disappeared. And if I won it, I had to hope I was one of the two fastest.

Despite my anxieties, I knew I had enough in me to finish in the top eight, so I approached the qualification round in a relatively relaxed frame of mind. I say relaxed, but I mean that in the context of the Olympic Games. It's probably more accurate to say I wasn't taut like piano wire.

Everything came together at just the right moment. I settled into the groove quickly and posted a personal best time of 4–17.930, which was the fourth fastest time behind Wiggins, who had broken the Olympic record, Sergi Escobar, the new world champion, and Brad McGee, who had pipped me to bronze in Sydney.

Once the qualifying round was over, there were only a couple of hours in which to wind down and then warm up for the first-round match. That would be win or bust.

My opponent was Volodymyr Dyudya of Ukraine. He was no slouch. He'd been only two-tenths of a second slower than me in the qualification round, so I knew this would be a real head-to-head showdown.

Pursuiting is at its best when there are two evenly matched competitors on the track together. My strategy was clear in my mind. I wanted to start well and put him on the back foot, while holding a little bit back just in case I needed to turn the screw in the final kilometre. My hope was that by getting ahead of him early on he'd try to keep pace and leave himself short at the end. The pursuit is a test of judgement as well as strength. Make a mess of your scheduling, or fail to stick to the plan, and things can quickly get out of control.

I hoped that if I won the match, the time would look after itself and I'd qualify for the race for gold or silver. I couldn't be cagey with a rider like Dyudya, because if I gave him any encouragement he could cause an upset.

I rode a very strong race and was on top from the start. Dyudya was down but he was never truly out, until the last three laps when the fight slipped out of him. Once I knew the match was won, I emptied the tank in search of a good time. I crossed the line in 4-19.559, which I thought gave me a very good chance of making the final.

Now I had to watch the remaining three heats and hope that my time stood as one of the fastest two.

Brad Wiggins was up against the Frenchman Fabien Sanchez in the fourth and final first-round heat. I knew that Brad would probably get close to catching Sanchez and would certainly post one of the two quickest times. That meant everything hinged on the other two heats.

I was convinced that the final would be between Brad Wiggins and me. The other two first-round heats were between Brad McGee and Germany's Robert Bartko and between Sergi Escobar and Luke Roberts of Australia. McGee was going well but I thought he might be outside my time. Everyone knew Bartko was struggling with his form and probably wouldn't have a chance. I was certain that McGee and Escobar would win their heats, but I was confident that my time would be good enough. It would be close, but I fancied my chances.

I got straight on my road bike to warm down but kept an eye on what was happening on the track.

McGee got the upper hand on Bartko very early, which was bad news for me. In a pursuit match like that, McGee had the ideal scenario unfolding in front of him. He had the advantage of having a big guy like Bartko dangling in front of him. The perfect carrot to chase. And, of course, the closer he got to catching Bartko's back wheel, the more benefit he got from being in the slipstream. Even when the gap between two riders on the track is 50 or 60 metres, there is still a slipstream effect. Bartko's broad shoulders were pushing the air out of the way, creating a little invisible tunnel for McGee to ride through behind him.

McGee's time was incredibly fast – 4-17.918, bumping me down to second place with two heats still to go, and Wiggins certain to go quicker than me unless he had a mishap. Take nothing away from McGee: he rode extremely well, but he definitely had an advantage.

Escobar won his heat, but went slower than me, which left Wiggins. It was a formality. Brad knocked out a world-class ride, faster than the rest of us, to set up a final against McGee. That meant I'd be facing Escobar for bronze the following day.

I was crushed. I was convinced that I was on course for a final against Brad Wiggins. I felt I'd got my strategy absolutely spot on. My weakness was always backing up a strong first ride with another one a matter of hours later, but I'd done just that. I felt a little bit robbed by circumstances. It wasn't McGee's fault, because that's how pursuit racing is. If you have someone to chase, you chase them, and it helps you get a faster time. I just wished I'd had a slightly below-par Bartko on the track with me, because if the roles had been reversed, I know I'd have been in the gold medal final.

If I am honest with myself, I think I lost the bronze medal

there and then. That night I was riding my bike back from dinner and I bumped into Claire Huddart, Vicki's friend who was working with the British swimming team. She asked how it had gone and I told her I was racing against Escobar for bronze the next day.

'What do you reckon?' she asked.

'Well, he is the world champion.'

It's highly likely I didn't give myself the best chance. Don't get me wrong, I went out there and gave it everything I had, but my mind wasn't quite right. I'd put everything into the first-round ride, hoping that it would get me into the final, which would guarantee me at least a silver medal. Now I had to scrap against Escobar, one of those metronomic pursuiters who could bang out two or three rides all within a second or two of each other.

I fought hard, but didn't have it. Escobar replicated his time from the qualifying round, more or less, whereas I slipped back five seconds to a 4-22. Bronze slipped away from my grasp again.

In the Olympic Games, there's very little time to dwell on defeats or feel sorry for yourself. Next up was the team pursuit. We knew we were at least the second best squad in the world and that if the competition went to form we should reach the final to face Australia. Our squad was stronger than ever. We had Wiggins, Steve Cummings, Paul Manning, Chris Newton, Bryan Steel and me – six men who had been working together so long that we knew everyone's strengths, weaknesses and individual nuances. We were completely interchangeable too. The coaches could have picked four names at random and been confident of a good time.

Unlike in Sydney, we knew in advance that no matter who rode in which round, everyone would get a medal if they stepped on the track at some point. That relaxed everyone because there could not be a repeat of the medal fiasco four years earlier. It meant there wasn't the underlying tension in the camp. It also helped that the strategy and team selection had been decided in advance. Brad and I would be rested for the qualifying round. Then Brad would come in for Steely in the first round and, if we made it, I'd come in for Newton for the final.

After the disappointment of a quarter-final exit on home soil in the 2000 Sydney Olympics, the Australians had developed into the best team pursuit squad the world had ever seen. They had raised the bar (or perhaps lowered it, is more appropriate) when they became the first squad to break the four-minute barrier on our track in Manchester at the Commie Games in 2002. Then they lowered the world record to 3-57.185 in the World Championship final against us in Stuttgart in 2003. They had a really well-oiled fastest four of Graeme Brown, Brett Lancaster, McGee and Roberts, with a couple of handy reserves who could step in for barely any reduction in speed.

They topped the leaderboard in qualifying with a time of 4-00.613. Our boys – Cummings, Manning, Newton and Steel – were second, and although the three-second gap between the two squads looked a little daunting, we still had Brad Wiggins and me in reserve.

In the knock-out round we faced France. Brad stepped in and they caught the French, becoming the first British team pursuit squad to break four minutes. In the very next heat the Aussies rocked up, caught the Lithuanians, and broke their own world record with a time of 3-56.610.

We were the second quickest of the four first-round winners by quite some margin, so we knew it was us against Australia in the final. The Ashes on bikes.

The day of the final passed in a sort of fog. Nothing felt quite real. All morning I had this surreal, almost out-of-body experience, punctuated every so often by a stab of reality and a sick feeling in my stomach.

We got to the velodrome about three hours before the final. I walked up into the track centre, as I had done so many times before, and the noise and the heat made me want to stop and turn back. I pushed on and stood in the track centre. It was strange feeling like I had to make an effort to get used to the atmosphere, even though it was an atmosphere I was incredibly familiar with. The adrenaline was pumping. We still had hours to go before the race, so I knew it was far too soon to start getting worked up. If I let the adrenaline flow now, I'd be spent before I even got on the bike.

I fled to the sanctuary of the cabin below the velodrome, where we could relax until it was time to start our warm-up, but it was just as noisy down there. Loudspeakers hung from the ceiling so the riders and staff could hear the announcements from the velodrome. The roar of the crowd and the excitable voice of the commentator were filling my brain. It was doing my head in be-cause I couldn't push it to the background, so I reached up and yanked the wires out of the wall so the two loudspeakers nearest me fell silent. That offered me a little bit of calm.

The build-up to the biggest race of your career is a funny thing. One minute I couldn't wait to get on the track. I just wanted to get on with it. Actually, I wanted to get it over with. The clock seemed like it had stopped. Then a wave of doubt would wash over me and I wanted to run away. I half-wished something would happen so that the race would be cancelled. Perhaps a giant hole could open up in the middle of the track. The clock seemed to be on fast forward.

And so it went on. A battle between fight and flight was taking place in my mind.

The nerves were always worse before a team event. Personal

failure I could just about cope with. I knew it was only sport. The world would go on turning, no matter who won the bike race. But the thought of making a mistake and letting down my teammates terrified me. I didn't want to be the one to ruin some-one else's chance.

I closed my eyes and tried to take my brain to a safe, secure place, using a few techniques Steve Peters had taught me. I be-gan to visualize the perfect ride: getting away to a powerful start before settling on to my teammate's wheel perfectly. Then I went through the first changeover in my mind, picturing myself swinging neatly up the banking, easing off the gas gently and slotting neatly at the back of the line in one smooth move.

Executed with precision, the team pursuit is a beautiful thing to watch. There's a pleasing symmetry to it as the four riders speed round the track in a neat formation. Without a word the lead rider swoops up and down the banking with the grace of a bird of prey. The gaps between each rider remain pleasingly uniform, as if they've been arranged by hand. It all looks so effortless.

Appearances can be deceptive. I can assure you that when you're on the inside it's anything but effortless. It can be purga-tory in there, riding so close to the limit that you know it could unravel at any moment.

The opening kilometre is a test of patience. All the adrenaline in the build-up to the race is telling you to stamp hard on the pedals. But four kilometres is too far to go flat out so the pace must be judged. It can feel like you're going too slowly at the start. One part of the brain is yelling at you to 'go, go, go'; the other part is urging caution: 'Stick to the schedule.'

The second kilometre is when the pain begins to pop up all over. The effort required to hold the body in the aerodynamic tuck position while riding at 60 kilometres per hour is considerable. The calves, the shoulders, the small of the back are all under pressure.

The third kilometre is the worst. That's the point of no return in pursuiting terms. That's when I want to lift my head, relax the diaphragm and take a deep lungful of air, but I can't.

The final thousand metres is purgatory – pure, unsophisticated pain management.

And all the while, the team on the opposite side of the track are trying to turn the screw. It's a battle of wills, sort of like a tug-of-war on wheels. Once you're on the back foot it is very hard to come back. If you get the opposition on the floor, you kick them while they're down.

No one needed telling that we were up against it in the final. The Aussies had broken the world record the previous day. We needed to step up, as well as hope that they had an off day.

My head was wobbling before I even got on the bike, because Jonesy's strategy was that we would 'gear up' for the final in order to go faster. That was one way of 'stepping up'. It meant that we'd ride a slightly bigger gear than the one the team had used in the earlier rounds, the theory being that the bigger gear would take us a little bit further with each revolution of the pedals and therefore put us on schedule for a faster time. On paper, it made sense, and Brad, Steve and Paul had bought into the idea.

When I talk about a bigger gear or a smaller gear, we're only talking about tiny differences. On the bigger gear, the bike would travel only a few inches further with each full turn of the pedals. But over four minutes – or hopefully three minutes and 56 seconds – it could be the difference.

But I wasn't so sure. I felt we should stick with the smaller gear because it would give us a bit of flexibility. We wouldn't need to put as much effort into getting up to speed and it would enable us to squeeze a bit more out of the tank at the end of the race if we were in with a chance of beating them.

Gearing up was a bit of a shit-or-bust idea – great if it worked, but a recipe for disaster if it didn't.

I thought we needed to save our legs a bit on the smaller gear, try to match them early on and then give ourselves somewhere to go towards the end. Riding the bigger gear would be more of a battering-ram approach. The team had ridden within themselves on the lower gear in the earlier rounds, so my argument was we should pedal quicker on the smaller gear and we'd go faster. Simple!

On the evening of the final, the velodrome was blustery. Although there was a roof at Athens, the sides were open, so there was always a draught. The wind was up, which made me even more sure we needed to go with a smaller gear.

We sat side by side in the special chairs bought from the Canadian fire-fighting service, waiting to be called up to the start line. The chairs had water chambers on either side with iced water in them. As we sat there, the blood in our arms was cooled, helping to keep our core temperatures low in the furnace-like velodrome and reducing the chances of overheating in the race. I expect a few people laughed at us for that but it was an example of a marginal gain.

When I got on the bike, the reality of what I was about to do hit me. Suddenly I wanted to be anywhere else but there. This was the final of the Olympic Games. It might be the only time in my life that I got to experience this. It might be the only time I had a chance to win a gold medal. And it was bloody terrifying.

The race passed in a blur. The Aussies were in control in the first kilometre and we were playing catch-up. They were formidable, and although we gave it absolutely everything we had, it was not enough. The Aussies were too good for us.

Believe me, when you cross the line, defeated, in an Olympic final, the last thing you think is, 'Oh well, at least we got silver.' I was absolutely gutted.

By the time I went to the podium for the medal ceremony, the sting of disappointment had subsided a little bit and, yes, it was an Olympic silver medal. I wasn't going to chuck it in the back of a drawer at home and forget about it.

With the Madison still to come, I wondered how my partner was going to hold up. He was in great form and he already had a gold medal in the individual pursuit and a silver from the team pursuit. Just before the competition, he'd had a phone call from his wife, Cath, telling him she was pregnant. So I wondered how much he had left to give. I thought perhaps it would all hit him at some point and his head would roll off his shoulders and into the track centre.

I needn't have worried. He, like me, felt we had a score to settle with the Madison.

We knew that the style of the track at Athens would make it a sprinters' race, so we had to be among the points early on.

The velodrome was scorching hot and the air was dry. From the first lap, my tongue stuck to the roof of my mouth. I zipped my skinsuit down in an attempt to stay cool.

I was on my favoured gear (92.6 inches for those of you interested in that kind of thing). I was also feeling fantastic, I was going so fast early on I was the quickest rider on the track in the early sprints. We were scoring well in the sprints, getting a few points here and there, but, as the race went on, some of the other teams started to gain a lap.

The Aussies, Stuart O'Grady and Graeme Brown, were going well. At the start, O'Grady was carrying Brownie, who was creeping, but when he started to come round, they were formidable. Switzerland had Franco Marvulli and Bruno Risi, two stars of the Six-Day circuit; the Germans Robert Bartko and Guido Fulst were also strong.

We were fighting on two fronts. Firstly, we were making sure we kept scoring points, and, secondly, we were biding our time before putting in the effort to gain a lap.

With around eighty of the 240 laps to go, there was a minor disaster. One of the French riders swung up the banking and I went forward to undertake him, but he came back down and swiped my front wheel away from me. I skidded down the banking, taking the Dutch lad Robert Slippens with me. I couldn't believe it. Another Olympic Madison, another crash. As I said afterwards, 'The British public must think I'm a right idiot.'

Luckily, this one was far enough from the finish that I could get back in the race without us losing ground.

I took my spare bike for a few laps while the mechanic gave my race bike a quick check over. As soon as I got back on the bike, I realized that the crash had caused the cleat on the sole of my shoe to slip, which meant that when I clipped into the pedal, my foot was wonky, with my heel pointing outwards, instead of my natural position.

I had to do another twenty kilometres with a crooked foot. If it had been any race but the Olympic final, I'd have stopped to get it sorted, because that sort of thing can cause an injury, particularly to the knee, but I had no choice but to block it out and get on with it.

The Aussies had a good tally of points and were one of six teams that had gained a lap on the rest of the field. Switzerland, Germany, Spain, New Zealand and Ukraine were also up on us and the laps were counting down, so we knew we couldn't delay our move much longer.

Brad put in a bit of an acceleration just before he threw me in and I pressed on. It was a hard scrap, but we joined up with the back of the bunch with one sprint remaining.

Now we were on the same lap as the other leaders, we had jumped up to second place. The Aussies were going to win, unless someone else gained a lap, which was looking increasingly unlikely.

So it was all going to come down to the final sprint again. We knew we'd have to score to keep hold of a medal. With the first four teams over the line taking points, we got ourselves into a great position.

On the last lap, I was on Marvulli's wheel, knowing I had to outsprint him to keep the silver medal. O'Grady came alongside me, holding me down the bottom of the banking so I couldn't draw level with the Swiss guy. I was rapidly running out of legs and this was the last thing I needed. The Aussies had the gold medal in their pockets no matter what happened, so it was annoying that O'Grady was up there blocking me. Perhaps he was still smarting because I'd beat him at the PruTour!

I now wasn't going to beat Marvulli, but I had to hang on ahead of the Ukrainians or else we were going to get shunted down to fourth place at the death again.

I came out of the sprinters' lane, moving up the track and forcing him to stall a bit to ensure I held on to the points. If it had been a Keirin or a sprint race, I'd have been disqualified for that move, but in the Madison it's more of a free for all. I had to stop him getting past me and I did it.

These days a bronze medal would be seen as a bit of a disappointment in the British team, but to us it felt like a victory. Brad and I got off our bikes and hugged. He now had the full set – gold, silver and bronze – and to us it felt like justice had been done. This was the bronze medal we should have had four years before.

I was sitting down in the track centre, enjoying the moment, when someone told me the Germans had put in an appeal. I wasn't sure exactly what their beef was. I think they were claiming that the points we'd scored when we gained a lap shouldn't have been given to us but should have been given to the riders at the front of the bunch – one of those complex situations in Madison races the jury has to decide on. Frankly, I didn't care what the problem was; I just knew there was a problem.

In the space of a few minutes, I'd gone through the full range of emotions. The elation of winning, to the uncertainty of not knowing, and the possibility of having the bronze medals wrenched from our grasp. I sat with my head in my hands. Brad hurled his towel down and stormed out of the velodrome.

We waited for what seemed like ages, although it was probably only a few minutes, before the head judge ruled in our favour.

As my heart rate returned to something like normal, I took a deep breath. It seemed like nothing at the Olympic Games could ever be straightforward for me.

# 15

# The Pot of Gold

The rainbow jersey was close enough to touch, but it remained just out of my reach. Silver in the team pursuit, silver in the individual pursuit. I'd seen some of my teammates go to World Championships and come home with a gold medal and a jersey and I wanted one of each too.

But I sensed I was beginning to run out of time. At the start of 2005, I was 32 years old, and although the thought of calling it a day had yet to cross my mind, I knew I couldn't go on for ever. In cycling, the clock is always ticking. At some point the bell curve reaches its peak and, once you are over the top, there's no way of knowing how quickly gravity will carry you on the descent towards retirement.

I believed I still had room for improvement. I wasn't yet in the phase of my career where everything becomes about managing the decline.

Every athlete wants to be able to say they were world champion. The first championships after the Olympic Games, in Los Angeles, offered me a great opportunity to do that because

Brad Wiggins and Brad McGee, who contested the Olympic individual pursuit final, weren't going to be there.

The velodrome at Carson, just south of downtown LA, had a reputation for being a slow one. For the uninitiated, one 250-metre velodrome probably looks identical to the next, but when you are racing, you realize there can be dozens of different factors that influence the performance. The LA track was sluggish for two main reasons – the angle of the banking and the length of the straights. Without getting too technical, and causing everyone to glaze over, the angle of the bend meant that as I entered it, I felt encouraged to accelerate. The track almost goads the rider into going hard. But then, as you exit the bend and the banking levels out, the effect is almost like having a parachute on your back. The track starts coming back at you and the long straight means there's no time for recovery and a long way to go before getting the slingshot effect from the turn into the banking at the other end of the track.

Before the qualifying round for the 4,000-metre individual pursuit, Jonesy said, 'We're going to change your gear and back you off a bit.' That meant my bike was fitted with a slightly smaller gear so that I wouldn't be tempted to bully my way through the corners.

Whether changing my gearing so late in the day threw me, I don't know, but I warmed up poorly and when I started my qualification ride I couldn't get into the right rhythm. Instead, I set out on my original schedule but with the new gearing, and the result was disastrous.

I went out too hard. The guy on the opposite side of the track, riding in my heat, was Fabien Sanchez, a Frenchman I should have beaten quite easily. After a strong opening two kilometres, things began to unravel. Sanchez was coming back at me, which panicked me into digging deeper into the hole. At that point, my legs fell off. Before the three-kilometre mark, I knew I'd made a hash of it, and a glance at the scoreboard confirmed that I was well outside the top four places that would fight it out for the medals. The individual pursuit is an unforgiving discipline, particularly at the World Championships, where you have to set one of the two fastest times to reach the gold medal final.

I eased off for the last three laps of the track, saving myself for my other two events. I finished 14th of 21 competitors – my worst result in the individual pursuit at a World Championships since I had pulled my foot out of the pedal in Perth eight years earlier. Afterwards, there were no excuses; it was a poor ride, particularly considering the form I was in.

That night, the team pursuit squad got together and we revised our strategy so that we wouldn't get caught out by the track. There were five of us – Steve Cummings, Paul Manning and Chris Newton, who had been in Athens – plus a 20-year-old called Ed Clancy, who was a product of the British Cycling academy run by Rod Ellingworth.

The plan was for Clancy to ride the qualification round, to give me a bit of extra recovery time before I stepped in for the final. We talked about the need to treat the track with respect and to be careful going into the corners. The rider leading into the bends had to resist that temptation to step on the gas, because he would stretch the line and possibly create a concertina effect that would make it difficult to maintain a smooth rhythm.

Watching the qualifying round was nerve-racking because it was completely out of my control. I knew the lads had enough to qualify in the top two, but that it might be close. The Aussies had put a young team out, as often happens at the start of a new four-year Olympic cycle, so the Dutch were now our biggest threat. We topped the leaderboard to set up a final against the Netherlands, who were just under a second slower. I was confident that I could help the team go faster in the final, and for most observers we were probably the favourites to win gold, not that that means anything before you've stepped on to the track.

The team pursuit has long been considered the blue-riband event on the track. It's a complex event that rewards speed, endurance, discipline, organizational skills and strength in depth. It was also the foundation that underpinned the development of the entire British Cycling track squad. The endurance coaches thought that if we could crack the team pursuit, we could dominate the world.

For five years we'd been creeping up on a gold medal, taking baby steps towards the title. The journey we'd begun back in Berlin in 1999 was almost complete. Back then, the Germans had been the top dogs – they won gold at the Sydney Olympics and held the world record. Just as the British team overhauled an ageing and fading German squad, the Ukrainians popped up to win the world title in 2001. Then came the Aussies, who kept getting faster and faster, winning gold and breaking the world record in Athens, as the Germans had done before them.

It seemed like there was a glass ceiling preventing us from winning gold. I'd been in the silver-medal-winning team in Stuttgart in 2003 and in Melbourne and Athens the following year, beaten each time by the Australians. Now the Australians had failed to qualify for the final, we knew we had a glorious opportunity in front of us, no disrespect to the Dutch.

The final was as businesslike a ride as I can remember. We got up and we got the job done. We were narrowly up at the end of the first kilometre and continued to turn the screw. With four laps to go, we were well up on the Dutch – two and a half seconds is a big gap to close in a kilometre – so we knew we had done it. For the last four laps I was thinking so clearly, 'Whatever you do, don't crash.'

We came round the final bend and fanned out across the track to take the line. We were world champions.

Chris Hoy, Jason Queally and Jamie Staff had already won the team sprint and Vicky Pendleton won her first world title that night in the sprint, so the mood in the camp was sky-high. For me, though, there was no time for celebration because I still had the Madison to come on the last night of the championships.

The plan had been for me to ride the Madison with Geraint Thomas, who was one of the first products of Rod's boot camp. He was still only 18, but he was a talented lad and he knew how the Madison worked, so I was looking forward to showing him the ropes in a major competition. But a few weeks before the World Championships, Geraint crashed while riding to the velodrome for the Sydney World Cup meeting. He hit a piece of metal in the road and went down heavily, rupturing his spleen.

It meant I would be riding with another kid from the British Cycling academy, a 19-year-old called Mark Cavendish. There wasn't really any other choice. I don't think Paul Manning had ever done a Madison race; I'd ridden with Chris Newton a few times, but he didn't really like it. The Madison is an acquired taste. You have to want to do it and you have to go into it whole-heartedly; any hint of caution can lead to disaster. Teaching the academy lads how to ride the Madison had been part of Rod's strategy. They were versed in it, so when Rod told me Cav would be fine, that was good enough for me.

I didn't really know any of the academy lads that well, even though we often trained at the same time. We used to watch with a bit of a smile as Rod made them work their nuts off. I felt sorry for them because he pushed them to the verge of tears sometimes. If we were doing four start efforts on the track, Rod had the academy boys doing eight. He wasn't just driving them hard for the sake of it, he was laying the foundations for their careers, knowing that some wouldn't make it but that those who did would have proved they were bloody good and had half a chance of achieving something.

For the old hands like me, Chris Newton, Paul Manning, Steve Cummings and even Brad Wiggins, to an extent, we were more or less as good as we were going to be. We were training to maximize our performance in competitions now, whereas the kids were being pushed to see where their limits were. Seeing them suffer made us feel better about ourselves too. 'This might be hurting but look at those poor bastards.'

I didn't know Cav but I knew of him. He was the lad who used to pull into the car park at the velodrome at 60 miles per hour, skidding sideways in his Vauxhall Corsa. A gold Vauxhall Corsa with the word 'Goldfinger' spelled out across the top of the rear window. I say 60 but I don't think that car could have reached that speed, especially with the rest of the academy lads crammed in the back. They could have been any group of teenagers tearing round town.

Cav was the wannabe scouser from the Isle of Man – he had that cockiness and self-confidence that you associate with people from Liverpool. He was an alpha male, always right, never wrong, and he had this edge to him. People either loved him or hated him, even then.

I also knew that he was possessed by a bike racer's spirit. The stories had already gone round the velodrome about this lad who barely registered when he was hooked up to the bike in the lab but who had a killer instinct in the races.

That week in Los Angeles, Cav was this ball of energy with a buzz cut. Nothing about the way he behaved led you to believe he was making his World Championship debut. I was in the velodrome to see how my new Madison partner got on in the scratch race. There was no pressure on him from the coaches; they told him to go out and enjoy himself, get a feel for the track and the level of competition and soak up the experience.

Immediately, the way this lad raced in a field of experienced track riders caught the eye. He ducked and dived, made the right decision more often than not, and put himself in with a great chance of winning. On the last lap, he got himself on the front of the bunch a bit too early. He had a good line but he'd given himself a bit too much to do and they came past him in the home straight. He finished fourth, behind the Danish rider Alex Rasmussen, New Zealand's Greg Henderson and Belgium's Matt Gilmore – all of them good Madison riders.

I watched Cav come off the track and sling his bike down. It was like he'd walked straight off the page of the *Ladybird Book of Body Language*. He was absolutely gutted. It was as if he'd been denied his birthright. I'd not seen a young British rider act like this before. This was his first World Championships, remember. He had seen some of his teammates win their rainbow jerseys and he expected to win one too. I thought to myself, 'You'll do for me.'

On the morning of the Madison final, we did our own thing. I was 32, he was 19, so we probably didn't have a lot in common even then. I always consider myself to be younger than everyone else around me, even if I'm not. I'm the boy who never grew up. But knowing that Cav was more than twelve years younger than me was surreal. I'd started racing a bike before he was born.

We didn't sit down and plan the race, we were just going to have a go and see what happened. For him, it was a learning exercise and I was the teacher, the newly crowned team pursuit world champion. As we sat in the changing rooms beneath the track just before it was time to go out, I tapped him on the back and said, 'Come on then, let's go and get you a stripy jumper too.'

He giggled, but there was also a look in his eye. He'd come to LA for a stripy jumper, not for the experience.

It was madness to think we could win. We'd never ridden a Madison together before, we barely knew each other's racing styles and we hadn't even practised a hand-sling. The first one we did was about two and a half laps into the race.

No one else fancied us either. I was an Olympic bronze medallist and a well-known face on the Six-Day scene, but no one had heard of Cavendish. To win the World Championship Madison you needed two strong riders, not one and a passenger, which is how they would have seen it.

Our plan, if you can call it that, was to ignore the sprints and to try to pick the right moment in the race to lap the field. It would need an all-or-nothing effort, and it would probably fail, but we knew we couldn't match the Dutch duo of Robert Slippens and Danny Stam, or the Belgians Matthew Gilmore and Iljo Keisse, in a sprinting shoot-out. They'd keep picking up the points and we'd waste our energy trying to keep up with their scoring power.

We weren't the only nation that would try to gain a lap. That tactic was an Argentinian speciality and Juan Esteban Curuchet and Walter Pérez were pretty good at it. They were, after all, the defending champions. The previous day, figuring that we'd be spectators in the race, the Belgians, Dutch and Germans all approached me to ask if we'd help chase if the Argies went on the attack. They were trying to rope in a bit of assistance, but I told them we would be doing our own thing.

The start of the race was horrific. The pace was high and I felt awful. My legs felt spongy and dull. There was no zing at all, as if the euphoria of winning the team pursuit had sucked the life out of them. Early on, I wasn't schooling Cav; he was keeping us in contention at the front.

Just as we suspected, it was a sprinters' race: Slippens and Stam versus Gilmore and Keisse. If we'd had to sprint, we wouldn't have got anywhere near them. Early on, I looked down at Jonesy, who was standing track-side, and shook my head as if to say, 'Uh-uh, nothing's happening here.'

But while I felt flat, Cav was flying. He was racing with the enthusiasm of a junior, although he wouldn't have lasted long among the Six-Day veterans by diving down the banking and coming up the inside of our opponents. The etiquette is to go the long way round, rather than undertake, but the World Championship Madison isn't an exhibition race, it's a shit-fight, and he was so skilful on his bike he got away with it every time.

Although I felt terrible, I was trying to encourage Cav every time we changed over. 'That's good.' 'Nice one.' Always positive messages. There's no time to communicate any more than that during the seconds it takes for one rider to hand-sling the other into the action, so we had to rely on intuition and bike-racing instinct. Cav was confirming what I'd seen in the scratch race the previous day: he could read the race; he could see the danger coming and avoid it.

On LA's dead track, it was developing into a slog. The sprinters were battling among themselves, but the longer the race went on, the more threat the diesel engines posed. It wasn't a slow race, it was incredibly fast, but the pace was very even, which meant there were few opportunities to attack. Instead, it was a test of nerve and timing. Put your effort in at the wrong moment and the medals would be gone.

Around two-thirds of the way through the race, the Argentinians attacked, as we knew they would. They were so strong that they had the rest of the field gasping, but they never quite managed to gain the lap they needed because the Germans chased them down.

The Six-Day mafia was alive and well. Robert Bartko had won the individual pursuit at the start of the week, so they were happy to help Belgium and the Netherlands control the race.

But Curuchet and Pérez were stubbornly strong and they took an awful lot of catching. By the time they were back in the bunch, the Germans were finished, and it looked like the Dutch and Belgians could continue trading blows in the sprints.

And then the Yanks went. I was about halfway down the line of riders when I saw it and I knew it was time to react. When everyone is on their knees, you have to take advantage. Colby Pearce launched the attack, then threw his teammate Marty Nothstein in. I chased and, just as I reached Nothstein's back wheel, his coach signalled to him to swing up the track. I have no idea what they were thinking and I wasn't going to wait to find out. I powered underneath him and kept on going. I didn't want the Americans coming with me because they had scored a point, and if we finished together, they'd beat us to the gold medal.

This was it. We were committed to an all-out effort now. We'd either lap the field and set up a victory, or we'd crash and burn trying. There was no option but to give it everything.

It took us just under twelve laps to gain the 200 or so metres we needed to rejoin the back of the bunch. That's pretty standard. There's a limited window of opportunity. If you don't do it in twelve laps, you're going to blow up. So we dug in for our three kilometres of pain, swapping over every couple of laps, and closing the gap, centimetre by centimetre.

We reached the back of the field with thirty-six laps to go, knowing that if anyone else was going to join us, they'd have to do it pretty damn quickly. All we had to do was hang on to the bunch until the finish. It didn't matter who won the last two sprints, as long as we remained a lap up on the field, we'd win.

I say that like it was a formality. It wasn't. There was still plenty of fight in the rest of the riders and Cav was on his knees by then, bless him. We were just about keeping it together.

Every time I threw Cav back into the race, I flew up the banking and tried to take several deep breaths to get as much air into my lungs as I could before it was my turn again. Each thirty-second breather had less effect than the last. The needle just about ducked into the black before it went flying into the red again. We were both running on empty by the end. Cav dug so deep in the last ten laps and a couple of times we slid so far back down the bunch that we were in danger of letting our advantage slip.

With about three laps to go, I held Cav's hand a split second longer during the change and said, 'Well done, son, you're a world champion.' I felt his hand go limp. Afterwards, he said he couldn't take it in, and refused to believe it until we'd actually crossed the line.

I was in the race at the end and I had time to celebrate as I came round the bend into the home straight. As I crossed the line, I let out a pure caveman roar. The feeling was so different to winning the team pursuit a couple of days before. That had been a feeling of relief, that we'd won a race we were hot favourites for, and that I'd finally won the world title I had been fighting for all these years. This was a completely different feeling, the thrill of a totally unexpected victory.

When I came to a halt, Brailsford got me off my bike and bear-hugged me. There was real emotion because it was such an unexpected win. I then looked up in the stand and saw Vicki, my brother-in-law, Scott, and his fiancée, Claire.

After the jersey presentation, I said to Cav, 'See, I told you we'd get you a stripy jumper.'

In that moment we established a bond. I had helped him win his first world title but he had also helped me win my second. He'd been so committed to the job where plenty of other riders would have wilted in the final third of that race. At the end, it was just guts and a collective will to win that got us there. If we'd been in the lab doing a max test, he'd have given up five minutes before the end, and I'd perhaps have lasted another couple of minutes. But because there was a finish line to reach and a rainbow jersey to win, he pushed on further than he probably thought possible.

After we'd been presented with our jerseys and medals, we had to compose ourselves for an interview with the BBC's Jill Douglas. Cav, the 19-year-old debutant, was the story, of course, and I had no problem with that.

'How does it feel?' Jill asked.

'I've been waiting so long for this,' he said.

It was his second event at the senior World Championships and he says, 'I've been waiting so long.' There's an insight into his character right there.

I looked at him and shook my head. 'Try waiting twelve years,' I thought.

That night we had to find a bar that would let us in, because half our team weren't 21. We found a place just south of Santa Monica and partied. Scott got Chris Hoy on the tequilas. We had to call the LAPD out because he went missing (my brother-in-law, not Chris Hoy). They found him clutching a bottle of tequila. Scott's an ex-rugby player, a big lad and an even bigger drinker, or at least he was then.

I drank so much I spent half the night throwing up. The next morning, I was in pieces. Me, Vicki, Scott and Claire were going on a road trip up the Pacific Coast Highway past Big Sur, and then all the way to San Francisco. I sat in the back of the hire car as we headed out of LA. I missed it all because I was so hungover.

Around mid-morning we stopped at a diner and ordered a big stack of pancakes with maple syrup, and a pot of coffee. The sun was shining and across the road from the diner was a Porsche dealership with a parking lot full of beautiful old classic 911s.

My hangover had eased a bit, but as I sat there, I could feel the tears run silently down my cheeks.

'Are we really on holiday?' I asked.

My work ethic might not have been as strong as some others' – you couldn't have called me a workaholic – but it felt like I'd been cycling non-stop for years. Since 1996, I suppose I had, as road season gave way to Six-Day season, and the Olympic cycles ebbed and flowed from Atlanta to Sydney to Athens. Everything had built to this point. I was now a double world champion. I had the rainbow jersey, the stripes and the medals, and no one could take them away. Life was pretty much perfect. We had a fantastic week's holiday driving up to Monterey and Santa Cruz and then San Francisco.

One night Scott and I were sitting outside our apartment block under the stars, drinking a few beers. A shooting star blazed across the sky and he said, 'Make a wish.'

A few minutes later, in the apartment opposite, the light went on and this woman stripped off and got in the shower. She couldn't see us because it was dark outside, but we had a full view of her.

Scott turned to me and said, 'Bloody hell, Rob, what did you wish for? Two gold medals in a week not enough for you?'

# 16

# Winding Down

The Great Britain cycling team was never a holiday camp, but there were always practical jokes and pranks to lighten the mood and ease the tension. What do you expect if you lock a bunch of highly strung, twentysomething athletes in a hotel for days at a time? It can get pretty boring.

It was usually pretty innocent stuff, but the tit-for-tat retaliations would eventually get out of hand and a truce would be called.

The oldies were the best ones. We'd take someone's bike, let the tyres down, then fill them with water using a track pump. We'd hang someone's bike over the edge of the hotel-room balcony by the handlebars, or hide house bricks in someone's rucksack. And a lot of fun could be had if you spotted a dead bird or rodent by the roadside during a training ride.

Sandy Gilchrist, one of the mechanics, and Simon Jones were always pranking each other. At a World Cup meeting in Moscow, Sandy took a boiled egg from the breakfast buffet to put in Jonesy's rucksack. As he unzipped the bag, he discovered the dead bird he'd put in there at the previous round of the World Cup.

Another favourite was to dismantle someone's room and pile everything in the bathroom. We'd raid the mechanic's toolbox for spanners and screwdrivers and unscrew the legs of the bed, strip all the sheets, take apart the table and chairs and stack everything neatly in the bathroom, so when they opened the door they were met with a completely empty bedroom.

The management weren't exempt either. On a stage race in France one time, I got the key to John Herety's room, unscrewed the side of the bath and turned the water off, then screwed the side panel back in place. John went down to reception to complain that no water was coming out of the taps. In the meantime, I unscrewed the panel again and turned the water back on, so when the receptionist came up to investigate, he thought John was either mad or wasting his time.

Once or twice, our stupidity nearly got us in trouble. At the 1996 Tour of Langkawi in Malaysia, our room was eighteen storeys up. We got the wastepaper bin, filled it with water and waited on the balcony for an unlucky victim to wander across the quadrant way below. Poor Sandy Gilchrist didn't know what had hit him. We tipped the water over the edge and as it went down it seemed to disappear. We thought it must have vaporized in the heat. Then, as if out of nowhere, it hit him, knocking him flat on his face.

The Aussies always took things a bit too far. At the Commie Games in 1998, we would hear the booms echo round the athletes' village as they dropped bin liners full of water over the side of a high balcony. They worked out that if they used two bags the noise would be even louder. Then one of their sprinters dropped a TV over the edge. It all stopped after that.

Brad Wiggins loved to dish it out but he couldn't take it back. He didn't like it if the joke was on him. He could be a nightmare at the Six-Day races, where we had to share a small track-side cabin. While I was up on the track, he'd be down there, doing goodness knows what.

At the Berlin Six he hid my spare shoes in our piss bucket and when I came off the track I almost peed on them. He put a handful of chamois cream and crushed-up digestive biscuits in the seat of my shorts. I couldn't get all of it out so I had to race for half an hour with gritty bollocks. Another time, I was having a wash-down with a flannel in our cabin, stark-bollock naked, trying to freshen up between stints on the track, and he whipped the curtain back to give the crowd a good view. He used to piss himself laughing but he was never quite so jovial if the tables were turned.

The spirit in the team at Los Angeles was better than I'd ever known it. Winning world titles helped, of course, but for the first time it felt like we had the beginning of a fully integrated squad. There was no longer such a split between the sprinters and endurance riders. Vicky Pendleton won her first world title and although the women's team was only two riders strong (Emma Davies was the other) we were all united.

The party after the championships was the night when everyone came together to celebrate. Early in the evening there had been an incident that became known as Ketchup-gate. Jonesy and Chris Hoy flicked ketchup at each other, then a bit more, then some more, until it got completely out of hand when Jonesy covered Chris in sauce. Not that there was an ounce of malice in it, but that probably spelled the beginning of the end for Jonesy.

Our life in the Peak District was great. We made the village of Hayfield home and the area became a bit of a base for the cyclists. Brad and Cath Wiggins lived just over the hill from us for a while, Dave Brailsford wasn't too far away, my friend Nick Craig, the mountain biker, lived 300 yards away. And, of course, there was Mike and Pat Taylor, two people who had helped dozens of young British riders over the years. Mike used to be the Great Britain junior team coach and he'd taken scores of riders to race in Europe. Their door was always open to cyclists and Pat would have the kettle on and the cake sliced before you'd even sat down in the kitchen. They are two people who have given so much without expecting anything in return, because they loved the sport.

Sometime in 2005, Dave Millar moved to the village. After being arrested by the French police and confessing to using EPO, Dave had lost everything. The huge house he'd been doing up in Biarritz had to be sold, he owed the French a stack of tax and, of course, he'd lost his salary at Cofidis when he started his two-year suspension from cycling. The life he had constructed had collapsed until there was almost nothing left. He'd spent about six months living at his sister Fran's flat in London. Most of the time he was completely pissed, just drinking night after night away.

I'd not seen too much of him in that time but I'd heard he was not in a good way. Brailsford and others at British Cycling were worried about him. Dave went to see Steve Peters, who told him that he had to surround himself with people who wanted to spend time with him because of the person he was, not because he was happy to spend every night on the lash pretending to be the life and soul of every party.

Dave moved up to Hayfield and got himself a little flat and a battered-up second-hand car. He got away from the bars and clubs of London and got back on his bike. Even though he was banned from the sport, he still hoped to come back, clean. He was a completely different character compared to the one we had known in Biarritz. It's not that he was nasty or unpleasant to be around, but he was unpredictable. At times there had been flashes of the smart, bright, joyful Dave, but too often the self-centred one got in the way.

In Hayfield, stripped of his money and his status as one of the top professional cyclists, we saw the normal Dave. He was funny, humble, kind and sensitive. In the two years we lived in Biarritz, he came to our apartment twice, partly because we were on the outskirts of town, so it made more sense for us to go to him. In Hayfield, it was like he was our lodger, and we were happy to have him.

The back door would go and we'd hear him open the fridge and have a nose in. It was like a role reversal and Vicki and I were more than happy to help him get his life back on track. Getting busted and admitting to everything was a disaster for his career in the short term but for him, as a person, as a human being, it was the best thing that could have happened. Dave wasn't cut out for living a lie. Looking back, he was hating his life and punishing himself. It would have destroyed him in the end.

Previously he had done cycling because he was good at it, but he almost resented it. He resented that it was hard work and took a lot of his time and forced him to live a certain life. He viewed the professional sport with contempt, I think.

But once it was all taken away from him, he realized that he loved riding a bike. He loved the physical feeling of well-being it gave him, and he enjoyed pushing himself until it hurt. He discovered that, actually, he did want cycling to be his life.

During his time in Hayfield, we trained together a bit, or he'd go with Nick Craig, but just as often he'd go off on his own. He did a lot of huge training rides: five, six, seven hours in the hills of the Peak District. It's tough countryside round here and he was pushing himself so hard. Sometimes I thought he was going to finish himself off with the amount he was training, but I soon realized how serious he was about a comeback. And then, when he finally got a chance to compete again, it turned out that his first race back would be the 2006 Tour de France. Typical Dave, he never does anything half-heartedly.

Although there were some bleak days for him, I'm sure, the opportunity to re-boot his life turned out well for him. He met a wonderful woman, Nicole, who lived in Henley, near where Dave's mum lived, and then moved up to Hayfield to work for a business owned by our next-door neighbour. Getting together with Nicole was the final piece of the jigsaw for Dave.

When Dave returned to racing, he became a spokesman for anti-doping. He joined the Garmin team and when he won a stage of the 2012 Tour de France, he said, 'We must not forget that I'm an ex-doper.' He's no longer hiding anything, he's open about his past and clear about his present. As a result, he's happier in his skin, and I am happy for him.

Talk about impeccable timing. Vicki was pregnant and due to give birth a couple of months before the 2006 Commonwealth Games in Melbourne. I'd be around for the birth but then I'd miss the disrupted nights for a few weeks. I didn't plan it like that, honestly. Madeleine was born on 23 January 2006, two days after my 33rd birthday.

The Commonwealth Games were always an us-and-them battle between the British riders and the Aussies, even though we were broken up into our separate nations: England, Scotland, Wales, Northern Ireland and so on.

I got a silver medal in the individual pursuit. Paul Manning beat me in a very close final. There was only a couple of hundredths of a second in it. Steve Cummings won the bronze medal, so three-quarters of the England team pursuit squad had won a medal in the individual.

It was sweet to beat the Aussies in their own back yard. They'll say they had a young team out, which is a fair point, but a win is a win. There's no room on the medal to engrave the names and ages of your opponents!

My third event was the 20-kilometre scratch race. Technically, I was racing for England and Cav was racing for the Isle of Man, but the reality was that we were racing together.

When five riders, including Cav, lapped the field early on, the pattern of the race was clear. In that move were Cav, an Australian, Ashley Hutchinson, Canada's Zach Bell, Scotland's Jimmy McCallum and the Kiwi Timothy Gudsell.

The rest of the race was spent trying to make sure no one else gained a lap so that the finish would be contested by those five. And, of course, the other Aussie and Kiwi riders in the race would then work to help lead out their men for the sprint finish. Cav, being the lone Isle of Man rider, had no one to help him, officially.

So it was obvious I was going to lead him out. If the Aussies and Kiwis couldn't work out thirty laps from the finish what was going to happen, they didn't deserve to win the bike race. What were we going to do? Leave Cav on his own?

Cav got on my wheel in the closing laps and I wound it up and gave him the perfect lead-out. He came out of my slipstream and finished it off. It was the Isle of Man's first Commonwealth Games gold medal for forty years.

When I came off the track, Brailsford and Shane Sutton were celebrating, but Dave said to me, 'Don't go down there,' meaning don't walk past the Aussie camp, where their performance director Shayne Bannan and coach Neil Stephens were spitting feathers. They were livid that a 'rival' nation had given Cav a hand, but all week they'd seen Shane Sutton swapping T-shirts according to which riders were on the track. One minute he was wearing an England top, the next minute a Wales one. Cav was a British Cycling rider; I was a British Cycling rider.

I went and sat down, well away from the Aussies. Willi Tarran, an experienced race organizer and judge, was the head of the jury. He came over, a smile on his face, and placed his hands on my shoulders. 'Lovely ride, Rob, but I'm going to have to disqualify you.'

I smiled back. 'Oh well, that's a shame. I was only sprinting for sixth place.'

Bannan had a go at Brailsford shortly after that and Dave replied, adding fuel to the fire: 'That's the first time I've seen a chink in your armour, Shayne.'

I later heard that it took the ex-track and field athlete, now working as a commentator, Steve Cram, to explain the situation on the BBC. 'They're good mates, they won the world title together for Great Britain last year, what do you expect to happen?'

In late 2006, we went to Perth for a six-week training camp. Having Maddie at home made these trips harder, but with the Beijing Olympics less than eighteen months away, these camps were not just important, they were compulsory. The sprinters had always spent the run-up to Christmas in Perth, and now the endurance squad joined them. There were the established team pursuit riders (me, Chris Newton, Paul Manning and Steve Cummings) and all the kids (Cav, Ed Clancy, Andy Tennant, Ross Sander and Geraint Thomas) for weeks of really intensive work. We had two performance analysts there and four cameras set up round the track to record everything. We did a mixture of training on the road, specific sessions working on technique on the track, and then time in the 'classroom' watching the videos the performance analysts had prepared. It was hardcore. We were staying at the Swan Valley golf course hotel, which was a beautiful place to be, although there was absolutely nothing to do.

After three or four weeks, we began to go stir crazy. Steve Cummings, who had previously rivalled me as the most laid-back character in the team, had been turned into a monster by British Cycling's constant questioning of everything we did. He'd begun to ask questions. 'Why are we doing this?' 'Why are we doing that?'

It was driving me nuts. Even Paul Manning was getting the hump with him and Paul is as calm and collected as they come. In the end, I flipped and turned on Steve: 'Look, just shut up and do it, will you?'

It wasn't really anything to do with Steve. My attitude was that we needed to do as we were told. The real problem was that I was halfway round the world, away from Vicki and my new baby, stuck in a featureless golf hotel with nothing to do. It was the Aussie summer so it was boiling hot, and we were working hard on the bike every day. One Sunday night, me, Steve and Ross Edgar, one of the sprinters, went into town for a few beers and to make up. Just getting out of that environment for a few hours did us the world of good.

The day we left the hotel, we drove a few minutes down the main road in the opposite direction to the track and we passed this shopping mall with lively looking coffee shops and restaurants. I couldn't believe it had been on our doorstep all the time and we'd not known.

On the way back from Perth, we stopped off at the Moscow World Cup where we fielded two squads in the team pursuit. Ed, G (Geraint), Paul Manning and Chris Newton rode as a team sponsored by Recycling.co.uk, while I rode with the kids in a Great Britain line-up. They won the gold medal, we finished fifth.

I arrived back home shortly before Christmas and was surprised how much Maddie had grown in six weeks.

In the spring of 2007, the World Championships were held in
Palma, Mallorca, and for the Great Britain team it marked a
watershed moment. It was the first time we truly dominated the
world, winning seven gold medals and topping the medal table
by miles. But while the rest of the squad celebrated, I was feeling
miserable.

For the first time in almost fifteen years, I had been dropped
from the team pursuit. I finished seventh in the qualifying round
for the individual pursuit, in a time of 4-25, and missed out on a
ride for the medals. I knew I wasn't going well but it was still a
real blow to the ego to be left out. I asked to see Dave and Shane
Sutton, British Cycling's Aussie bulldog, to talk about what I
needed to do to keep my chances of making the squad for the
Beijing Games on track.

As we sat down, Shane said, in typically abrasive style, 'Whatever happens here today isn't going to get you back in the team
for this week. That decision's been made.'

I knew that was how they worked. They talked a lot about
how every decision they made was focused on the athletes, but
what that really meant was making every decision focused on the
athletes that were riding. If you weren't in the team, you weren't
even in the room.

A depressing week was rounded off with a poor performance
in the Madison. Brad had won the individual and team pursuit
world titles and was starting to tire, but I was stuck to the boards.
I came off the track and felt terrible, almost paralysed. I couldn't
move properly. It was far worse than just being tired after a bike
race.

When I arrived home, I opened the garden gate and saw

Maddie's little ball lying on the grass. That moment put everything in perspective. Bike racing had been my life. It was still a huge part of my life, but there was now more to it than that.

The day after getting back from Mallorca, I had an appointment with a new dentist, who gave me a full X-ray. She said, 'I'm ever so sorry but you've got an abscess.' I could have hugged her there and then. 'Don't be sorry,' I said. 'It's good news.' I was relieved to have a reason for my poor form on the bike.

I had some root canal work done and the effect was incredible, like coming round after a bang on the head. It went a long way to explaining why I'd felt so terrible on the track.

Since leaving the Cofidis team, I'd been pretty self-sufficient. I'd ridden one season with the Recycling.co.uk team but after that I looked after myself, riding as a one-man band again, like in the old days.

Meanwhile, other members of the team pursuit squad had been riding for a small Belgian team called Landbouwkrediet, which was sponsored by a bank. Steve Cummings had been there first, then Paul Manning and Ed Clancy joined up. There was an arrangement between the managers of the team and British Cycling. The riders qualified for funding, which meant they were already paid, so they were effectively free riders for the Belgian team. In exchange, they were given flexibility with their racing programmes, so that they could concentrate on the track when they needed to. It was a win–win situation.

During 2007, Shane was on at me to join Ed and Paul at Landbouwkrediet for the following year: 'If you want to make the Olympics, you need to be on a pro team,' he said.

It was a complete change in attitude compared to five years earlier when they weren't keen on me being at Cofidis and said I needed to be back in Manchester with the track squad. Anyway, they'd come round to the idea that a heavy load of road racing at certain times gave a solid base to build track speed upon.

But I wasn't keen on going to Belgium. I didn't want to spend any more time away from Vicki and Maddie, and I knew we couldn't really afford it. I was getting British Cycling funding, plus bits of sponsorship money I had managed to attract. If I went to Landbouwkrediet, I'd have to give up my personal sponsors and survive on the funding cheque. With a child to support, that wouldn't be easy.

I also thought there was something unprofessional about giving a Belgian team a 'free' rider which, in turn, was taking a place from a Belgian rider. I didn't think it was right. Earning a living as a rider at that level is hard enough without a foreigner turning up and doing the job for free.

But Shane went on and on about it, so Vicki and I talked it over and we agreed we'd make it work one way or another if it meant giving me the best chance of making the team for Beijing. Once I'd made up my mind, I went to see Dave at the velodrome and told him I'd go to Belgium.

He said, 'Actually, we don't think it would be right for you to go there.'

He slid a proposal across the table which had my photo and CV on it. He'd given it to Halfords, the car and bike parts re-tailer, as part of a document pitching for sponsorship.

Halfords had agreed to sponsor a British women's team, led by Nicole Cooke, but they wanted a presence in the men's races too. So Brailsford had suggested me and Tom Southam. It was being presented to me as a done deal and, to be fair, it looked like a good arrangement. I liked Tom and his style of racing and I knew we could have a ball.

The team launch for the media was held at London Zoo,

bizarrely. I made a joke along the lines of, 'You know things are going badly when the only team that'll take you is a women's team.' I know Dave cringed a bit when I said that, but it was a joke at my own expense, not at Nicole or the girls'.

The winter before the Olympics wasn't the smoothest. I travelled round the globe competing in the World Cups, trying to help us score the points we needed to qualify for a place for the Madison at the Beijing Olympics, although I could see which way the wind was blowing. Brad and Cav were now emerging as the A-team for the Madison. I was out on the fringes of the team pursuit squad, which left the individual pursuit as my most likely route to the Games. I needed a decent result at the Worlds to force my way back in.

# 17

# Blood on the Track

26 March 2008. The morning of the opening day of the World Track Championships in Manchester. The Olympic Games were five months away and I knew I needed a good result and performance in the individual pursuit to keep alive my flickering hopes of making it to Beijing. I believed I could do it. I was certain my form would come good at the right time, but I also knew that the men who were picking the team probably needed convincing.

I'm woken early by a knock on the door of my room in the Holiday Inn. The UCI's blood testers had arrived and the Great Britain and Netherlands teams had been selected to have their haematocrit levels checked. This was routine stuff. I'd been tested before, dozens of times. Being tested is part of the job for an elite cyclist.

First, I need to give a bit of background to explain why these blood tests were routine in cycling. I am not a haematologist, or a scientist, but most cyclists had at least a basic grasp of the reasons that led to the haematocrit rule being introduced.

Haematocrit testing had long been one of the UCI's tools in the fight against doping. EPO, or erythropoietin, is said to have been first used by professional cyclists in the very early 1990s, and by the middle of the decade its abuse was out of hand. Erythropoietin is a hormone produced by the kidneys that prompts the body to produce fresh red blood cells. Red blood cells are important because they transport oxygen round the body, to make the muscles work. Cyclists, and other athletes no doubt, were using EPO to artificially boost the production of red blood cells to make their bodies more efficient at processing oxygen and, therefore, faster and more durable.

The problem for the authorities was that a test to detect the illegal use of EPO had not yet been developed, so in the 1990s cyclists were able to boost the number of red blood cells to dangerous levels.

The haematocrit level is expressed as a percentage of red blood cells in the blood. So, a haematocrit of 48 per cent means that in every 100 millilitres of blood there are 48 millilitres of red blood cells. A normal adult man's haematocrit percentage is somewhere in the mid-40s, although there are exceptions.

Haematocrit levels can fluctuate too. Time spent at altitude can increase the level, as can dehydration, illness or inactivity. Hard physical work and fatigue generally leads to a decrease in haematocrit levels. In the 1990s, riders were using EPO to keep their haematocrit levels high during the three-week stage races when their levels should have dropped over time because of the stress of racing so hard for so long. Even during a day, haematocrit levels may not stay constant.

To prevent riders from taking ridiculous risks with their health, the UCI introduced a haematocrit ceiling in 1997. Riders had to keep their levels below 50 per cent. If they were over, they were withdrawn from racing for two weeks and, as long as their levels were below the limit after a fortnight, they'd be allowed to race again. As there was not a verified test to detect

EPO use until just before the Sydney Olympics in 2000, this was the only way the authorities could curb the drug's use. But once the EPO test was ratified, the haematocrit checks remained in place. Riders were suspended or disciplined or, in the words of the UCI, they were 'rested' for the good of their health.

So, on this morning in Manchester, I answer the knock on the door and I'm asked to go to a room where the UCI's doctors have set up ready to do the tests. I ran up the stairs to the room, eager to get the test over and done with so I could go and have breakfast. There were already about a dozen people in the room but, as I was closest to the doctor doing the tests, I happened to go first. Then I went down to have my breakfast. There was not a flicker of worry because I hadn't taken EPO. I hadn't doped.

A bit later that morning, another knock on the door. It's Dave Brailsford. There's a look of concern on his face. The sort of look he has on his face when he knows he has to deal with something ugly.

'Have you got a moment? I need to speak to you.'

'Sure, come in.'

Steven Burke, my young teammate whom I'm rooming with, is lying on his bed.

'Not here,' says Brailsford. 'Come to my room.'

We walk down the corridor, through reception, past a TV crew, and down to Brailsford's room. He sits on the edge of the bed, I take the chair next to the desk.

'What is it, Dave?'

He's matter-of-fact. 'You've failed the haematocrit test.'

With those five words, my world begins to collapse. My mind is full of questions. 'How? Why? What the hell is going on?'

Brailsford has some questions too.

'Have you been up to something?'

'No! Absolutely not! I swear.'

'Because if you've been up to something, I need to know. I've got to go and meet the press later. I'll have to go on the BBC.'

'I haven't taken anything, Dave. I haven't done anything.'

Dave asks the same question a different way. 'If you haven't done anything, we'll stand behind you. And if you have, we can't support you, but we're not going to throw you to the lions either. But I need you to be honest.'

'I am being honest.' By now, I'm in tears. 'I haven't done anything. And if I had, I wouldn't bring the ship down with me. I haven't, I promise you.'

Brailsford told me my haematocrit level had been recorded at 50.3 per cent, which meant I was 0.3 per cent over the limit.

The thoughts came thick and fast. I knew a lot of people would make their minds up as soon as they heard the news. Failing a haematocrit test may not have been a doping offence, but to the general public it meant one thing. Drugs.

And I knew how it looked. Here was a 35-year-old rider who needed a good result to secure his place at the Olympics.

But I also knew I hadn't taken EPO.

We had to go across town to the Marriott hotel, where the UCI officials were based, so I could do a urine test. This one would detect whether I'd taken EPO. I knew the test would come back negative because I hadn't done anything.

My blood was also screened to make sure there weren't any cells in there that suggested I'd manipulated my blood another way. A high quantity of young cells, for example, would suggest blood manipulation. I knew neither test would show anything suspicious because I hadn't done anything. But although I wasn't concerned about the tests, I was worried that no matter what I did to prove I hadn't done anything, I knew there would be those who had already made up their minds.

Dave drove me across the city and I phoned Vicki and told her what had happened. The first thing she said was: 'Have you done anything?'

I said, 'No.'

'Because if you have—'

'I swear, Vic, I haven't done anything.'

Vicki was still at home with her parents and my parents, getting ready to head to the velodrome to watch me race. I told her I'd be home in a couple of hours.

When I hung up, Dave asked me again. 'Rob, if you've done something, they will find out. Don't be one of the ones who denies it all the way and then has to confess at the end. That'll be much worse. If you've done anything, now is the time to admit it.'

'Dave, I can't admit to something I haven't done.'

After I'd given my sample to the UCI's doctor, I drove home. I knew by now that all my teammates would know and that the news would be on the radio. No matter how they explained it, I knew some people would just interpret it as, 'Olympic cyclist fails drug test.'

On my way back, the phone rang. It was BBC Five Live radio, requesting an interview. They wanted to come to the house. I said I'd talk to them because I knew I had nothing to hide. But, equally, I didn't have any answers either.

I spoke to British Cycling's doctor, Roger Palfreeman, to try to find out what had happened. He explained that haematocrit levels are known to rise during a period of rest, not because there's an increase in the number of red blood cells, but because resting causes plasma volumes to decrease. So the same number of red cells, when expressed as a percentage, can lead to a higher figure.

During the week leading up to the World Championships, I had been resting. As I mentioned before, this period of rest right before a major goal is known as 'the taper'. The theory is that the training work has all been put in the bank and the body needs to rest so it is fresh for the races.

I volunteered to undergo testing every other day during my two weeks out of competition to prove there was nothing funny going on with my blood values.

Being so close to the limit, just 0.3 per cent over 50, people assumed I'd miscalculated or something. Others asked why I hadn't known what my haematocrit level was. They thought that every cyclist would know what their number was, but it wasn't like we were tested on a daily basis by British Cycling. Dr Rog didn't walk round with a centrifuge, testing everyone, for the very simple reason that we weren't up to anything. Can you imagine if the doc had been spotted wandering round the velodrome with blood-measuring equipment? That would have aroused suspicion.

British Cycling's sprint coach, Jan van Eijden, had been through exactly the same thing. He'd been kept out of the World Championships in 1999 with a high haematocrit and had been able to demonstrate that he had a naturally high level.

The German doctor Olaf Schumacher had been doing some research into haematocrit levels in track riders and had shown that the way we prepared for a major event, with a heavy, consistent workload, followed by a period of rest in the week leading up to the championships, meant that there was a greater risk of haematocrit levels rising as a percentage as plasma volumes decreased during the taper. He argued that track and road cycling are completely different sports physiologically and so the same rules should not apply.

Unfortunately for me, this all sounded like excuses. The

people who had made their minds up about me had made their minds up.

I knew very little about my own haematocrit level other than that it had been recorded at about 42 or 43 per cent after hard blocks of training or racing when I was at Cofidis. When I'd been concentrating on the track, it had been higher. I found out that at the Commonwealth Games in Melbourne two years earlier, I'd been in the high 48s.

The next day, I rode from home to the velodrome to have my blood test. When I got to the track, I saw Steve Peters, British Cycling's psychiatrist. He said, 'If you've nothing to hide, hold your head up and look people in the eye. Don't go down to the track centre or hang around with the riders, but don't hide away. Sit in the stands, wander round the velodrome.'

So that's what I did. I watched some of the racing and I walked around and people were so kind. They came up to me and told me they believed me and supported me.

When I was at home, I couldn't watch a lot of the racing on television. I knew the Great Britain team were tearing it up, winning gold medal after gold medal. Brad Wiggins won the pursuit, the boys won the team pursuit and then Brad and Cav won the Madison.

On another trip to the velodrome for one of my voluntary blood tests, I had a meeting with Brailsford and Steve Peters, with Dr Rog joining in by conference call from his office on the other side of the track. It was like being a fly on the wall.

Dave was asking what would happen if the test came back positive for EPO and Dr Rog was saying: 'But it's not going to.'

I sat there listening to this conversation about me, thinking: 'Jesus Christ! I am here, you know.'

A couple of days later, the UCI's urine test results came back.

They were negative for EPO and showed no other suspicious signs. I knew they wouldn't.

The regular blood tests I gave every couple of days showed my haematocrit was between 45 and 48, partly due to the fact I'd been riding my bike a bit, partly because of the stress, I suspect.

I saw Dave in the track centre and said to him: 'Now the EPO test has come back negative, can you turn the thumbscrews off a bit?'

British Cycling presented my data to the UCI and at some point later that year, the UCI dropped the haematocrit rule. Pim Ligthart, a Dutch rider who'd also been over the limit on the first day of the World Championships, and I were the last two riders to be 'rested' as a result of that rule.

But mud sticks. People thought because I'd ridden for Cofidis, I'd obviously been round the block. I made the mistake of reading the internet forums, where judge, jury and executioner seemed present. No matter how supportive the great majority of people were, each negative comment hurt. Reading the comments was killing me. It was the injustice of it. I'd sit up late at night reading through the comments pages and every time I saw someone accuse me of being a cheat, it was like a fresh blow to the stomach. All of them anonymous, all of them without access to any of the facts, many of them writing with the certainty and authority of people who'd been there and knew what was going on. In the end, I'd had enough and I replied to a few people. I told some of my critics to get in touch and I'd happily talk to them, but no one took me up on the offer.

A couple of weeks after the World Championships, we went to a family wedding at Alnwick Garden in Northumberland, in the beautiful wooden treehouse restaurant there (Europe's largest treehouse, apparently). I was miles away. My mind was still churning over the events of the previous fortnight. What if I'd waited a bit before having my test? What if I'd sat down on the floor and let everything settle? What if I'd drunk a glass of water straight after I'd got up that morning? Any one of those small things could have made a difference.

With my mind whirring, I got up from the table and went to get some fresh air. As soon as I got outside, I threw up over the side of the treehouse. I was in a bad way. I couldn't handle what had gone on. The tears were streaming down my face. I went back in and sat with Vicki and picked at the rest of my meal. Later that night, as I drove us home, I began crying again. She made me pull over and let out all the emotion.

My reputation was in tatters, but I knew I'd done nothing wrong. When I tried to explain complex science I didn't truly understand, it sounded like excuses. When I said I didn't know how it had happened, it sounded like I was dodging the question.

Sat there in the car, on the side of the road, Vicki made me call Steve Peters again. We arranged to meet the next day. I told him I'd been on internet forums and he said, 'That's the last thing you should do. If you know the truth, what does it matter what other people think?'

But it does matter what other people think. A year or so later, I was hours away from agreeing to go on the BBC show *Hole in the Wall*, the one presented by Dale Winton where celebrities dress up in a silver skinsuit and have to make themselves into the right shape so that the advancing wall can't knock them into the swimming pool. You must've seen it. Anyway, my agent rang and said the producers had been on Wikipedia and had read about my high haematocrit level and decided I wasn't right for the show. They thought it meant I'd been doping.

The point isn't about missing out on an appearance on *Hole in the Wall* – let's face it, I probably had a lucky escape – but the fact is, it's always there on my Wikipedia page.

I can't change what people think, so I have to follow Steve Peters' advice and say: 'I know the truth.'

# 18

# Skinsuit Champion

I never considered quitting cycling after the World Championships and the stigma of the haematocrit test result. Not for a moment. After two weeks, I got my licence back and immediately I wanted to race. I still believed I could be on the plane to Beijing.

Tom Southam and I got stuck into racing on Britain's roads. Just the two of us versus the rest; we loved the fact the odds were against us. In the springtime, we were trying to get a place in the Rás, a stage race in Ireland that has a brutal reputation. It would have been the perfect race to help me get into the sort of form I needed to make the Olympic squad but, unfortunately, the race was for teams of six riders, not two. Tom and I tried to get a composite squad made up of a group of individuals together, but there wasn't time to get it sorted.

Instead, we packed our bikes in the car and headed to Belgium to ride a series of *kermesse* races. The *kermesse* scene has broken the spirits of many a British rider over the years. *Kermesse* means 'festival' in Flemish, but in cycling terms the *kermesse* races are tough circuit races held in towns and villages all over the country. We went for about ten days, knowing we could race every day if we wanted. It was bike racing at its simplest. Put the bike in the boot of the car, turn up at a bar or café and pay the entry fee, smash it all the way round the circuit for a couple of hours, collect your winnings (if there were any), and do the same again the next day in another town.

We had a ball. I won the first race, then the second. By the time we were sitting on the start line before the third race, we had gained a bit of a reputation. Someone asked Tom, 'Which one of you is Rob Hayles?'

Tom pointed to me and the guy said, 'How long are you here?'

'Another week.'

Early in that race I was riding on the front and this Belgian lad came alongside me and said, 'Why don't you fuck off back to England?'

There were guys out there who made a decent living riding these races and picking up the prizes, and they didn't like a couple of foreigners turning up and spoiling it.

I got in the break again and another of the Belgian lads offered to buy the race from me for 200 euros. He rode off the front and I let him go, then pretended to chase for a bit without closing the gap, then took the sprint for second place to get ourselves a bit of extra cash.

When we went back to the café to get my winnings, we bumped into the first lad and I said, 'Are we allowed to stay another week, or do you still want us to fuck off home?'

He looked a bit sheepish and said, 'No, no, you're welcome. It's just your style of racing makes it really hard for everyone.'

Tom laughed at him and said, 'We're not racing to make your life easy though, are we?'

\*

Tom and I got on brilliantly, on and off the bike. I'm not sure what he thought when we'd met up before our first race. We were staying in a bed and breakfast and we met for dinner. There was me with a plate of nachos, chips and a pint of Guinness, while he had a salad.

The day before the National Championships in Yorkshire, we went to the supermarket to buy the food we'd need for the race. That night I sat in the bathroom, gluing new tyres on to his wheels. It was like it had always been. Racing hard, looking after myself and enjoying it. We didn't have a manager, as such. Julian Winn was the manager of the Halfords team but he spent all his time with Nicole and the women's squad. We only saw him once that season, on the morning of the Premier Calendar race in Abergavenny, the week before the National Championships. It went up and over this massive climb in the Brecon Beacons, and Winny said to me, 'You'll never get round here, Rob!' Talk about a morale boost.

Winny wasn't wrong. I did get dropped on that climb, but I was riding so strongly I managed to get back up to the leaders on the flat. I knew my form was good for the National Championships.

Having won national titles on the track and in time trials (twenty-one of them, I believe, in the course of my career), I thought the road race crown would top the lot. Many of Britain's best riders have won that championship. Look at the roll of honour and it's a who's who of the toughest and classiest riders: Keith Lambert, Les West, Phil Edwards, Sid Barras, Bill Nickson, John Herety, Paul Sherwen, Sean Yates, Malcolm Elliott, Robert Millar, Matt Stephens, John Tanner, Roger Hammond, Dave Millar.

I felt I was in good enough form to win the title, the course suited me and I was fired up. I also had a not-so-secret weapon at my disposal.

All season, I had been riding road races in a one-piece skin-suit, just like we wear in the track events and time trials. When I turned up to my first race for Halfords, someone said to me at the start, 'This isn't a time trial, Rob.'

'We'll have to see about that,' I replied.

I didn't mind that people took the mickey out of me, because I felt it was giving me an edge. I'd called Chris Boardman and said, 'We obsess over making sure we're as aerodynamic as possible for a race that lasts a minute or four minutes, but when we go out and do a five-hour road race, we're happy to wear a baggy jersey. Why?'

Boardman agreed with me. People might think this is an example of a marginal gain but for me it was a big gain. I knew from all the hours I'd spent riding in the wind tunnel – testing bikes, equipment and kit for British Cycling – that the benefits stacked up. When I wore the skinsuit in the race, I could feel the difference. I was faster through the corners and on the descents and so over a five-hour race I knew I was saving a lot of energy.

I asked Winny, who would be managing the women's team in Beijing, 'Have you thought about putting Nicole in a skinsuit?' Cooke did wear a skinsuit and I know for a fact the watts she saved by being a little bit more aerodynamic helped make the difference between her winning Olympic gold and silver. Having said that, it wasn't exactly a new idea – the Irish rider Stephen Roche had worn a skinsuit for a mountain stage of the 1985 Tour de France – but there was still a lot of resistance to it.

Anyway, I won the 2008 national road race title in unconventional style. I attacked on a descent and they didn't see me again.

Being national champion on the road was one of the proudest moments of my career and, with Dave Brailsford and Shane

Sutton following me in the car as I soloed to victory in the grounds of Duncombe Park, I knew I hadn't done my chances of getting on the plane to Beijing any harm. When I came off the podium in my new national champion's jersey, Shane said, 'See you on the track tomorrow morning at 8.30.'

But after four days of training and testing at Manchester velodrome, the guillotine fell on my Olympic dreams. Shane has never been one for spinning out the bullshit. He just called me into his office and gave it to me straight: 'You're not going to the Olympics, Rob.'

Shane is an abrasive character and he clashes with people, but when he first came on board, I thought he was great. I just think that over time I became immune to his methods. He had his favourites, and because he didn't feel I needed him, I wasn't one of them. But I will say this for him, when it comes to saying it how it is, he doesn't pussy-foot about. He'd be perfect running an abattoir.

Knowing I'd miss the Olympics was a bitter blow. I asked if the haematocrit test was a factor and, although they insisted it wasn't, I'm not so sure.

It's probably no coincidence that I won the two races I entered on the weekends the 2008 Olympic Games cycling was on. For a start, my entire season had been structured so I hit my peak in mid-August. And for another thing, I had a lot of frustration to burn off.

We were just rolling out for the Tour of Pendle Premier Calendar race in Lancashire when someone on the side of the road shouted out that Nicole had won the Olympic road race. Seven days later, a couple of hours after Ed, G, Paul and Brad had qualified for the team pursuit final, I was racing at the Goodwood motor racing circuit in the Surrey League Five-Day stage race. I emptied the tank that day, winning by more than a minute. The tenth-placed rider was over 11 minutes behind. I pumped my fists as I crossed the line and, although it wasn't Beijing and the Olympic Games, I was still being paid to race my bike. There are a lot worse things to do for a living.

As soon as I'd been left out of the Olympic squad, I decided I wouldn't watch the Games because it would be too painful, but when I wasn't racing, I watched everything I could. Although it did hurt that I wasn't there, I was over the moon for them all when they won gold medal after gold medal.

At the end of the season, John Herety and Simon Mottram approached me with an attractive offer. They wanted me to join the Rapha team. The Rapha clothing company was one of the success stories of Britain's cycling boom and the chance to ride for John again, while passing on my experience to the younger riders, really appealed.

But Shane urged me to stay at Halfords. 'Stay in the British Cycling system, Rob, there's more opportunities for you here.'

I knew what was happening. They needed me to stay or else the Halfords sponsorship was in jeopardy. Shane had an emotional gun to my head and it worked. I turned down Rapha and they signed Tom Southam instead.

Over the winter, I was back out with the Great Britain squad, touring the track World Cup events and trying to score points for World Championships qualification. I went to Cali in Colombia, then Beijing and finally Copenhagen, which turned out to be the final time I wore the national team's colours.

Very few riders get the opportunity to call time on their own careers in the way they want to. Look at Paul Manning – he had the right idea. He won Olympic gold, went to the podium, put his arms in the air and said, 'Thank you very much.'

My final ride for Great Britain in Copenhagen was in the

Madison final, with young Pete Kennaugh from the Isle of Man. We'd been flying in qualifying but I geared-up for the final and never got going. Then Pete crashed and our race was over.

A couple of weeks later, I met Brailsford at the Holiday Inn near Manchester velodrome. It was the same hotel where he'd told me that I had failed the haematocrit test, so it wasn't exactly my favourite place in the world.

There wasn't a lot of small talk and I knew what was coming. He said, 'We've looked at everything and we've decided you're not going to the World Championships.'

Although he didn't say, 'That's it, Rob, time at the bar, you're off the squad,' we both knew what he really meant, and I appreciated that he had made the effort to tell me himself, rather than leave it to Sutton.

I was disappointed, of course, but I thanked him for everything he'd done. I felt like it was probably time. I'd fought and fought for a couple of seasons and there wasn't a lot of fight left any more. I still believed I could do a job at the top level – but athletes are conditioned to believe that they belong in the team, even when the evidence is suggesting otherwise.

I wasn't ready to stop being a bike rider and I still felt I could do more, but I had to accept that, almost twenty years after that call-up to represent Great Britain in Brno, it was the end of my national service.

# 19

# Heading for Home

There was still life in the old dog. I'd never got too big or been too proud to pin a number on my back in a local race and get stuck in. But it was strange knowing that the security blanket of being funded by the national squad was about to be whipped away from me. We joke about it, but being a part of British Cycling is like being institutionalized. Once you're shoved out of the velodrome door, you come out blinking into the light. The velodrome had been my second home, my office, and now I had to find something else to do.

As soon as Dave Brailsford told me I was not going to the World Championships, I decided to announce that I was retiring from the national team. It felt better, somehow, to take charge of the situation and make that decision publicly, rather than sort of skulk away into the corner. Then I texted Chris Boardman, head of the Secret Squirrel Club, to ask if I could carry on doing the testing and development work for him in the wind tunnel.

Jason Queally and I had been British Cycling's guinea pigs for a couple of years. It was quite convenient for me because the wind tunnel they used was in Southampton, not far from where my parents live. When I was a funded rider, it was part of my job. I'd go down there and try out new bikes, wheels, handlebars, clothing, helmets, shoes or whatever it was they were developing in the wind tunnel. It was hard work because it required the mental stamina to keep putting the required effort in to ensure the test was reliable. I couldn't just go through the motions or the experiments would be pointless. And for me, it was good training.

I had to sign a confidentiality agreement to prevent the secrets getting out. It means there's not much I can say about the actual tests we did in the tunnel, or the things we discovered, but if you look at the bikes and kit the squad used in Beijing, you might be able to spot a few innovations. Most of it was pretty simple stuff: the long overshoes the riders wear on the track, for example, were a result of testing in the tunnel which showed they were more aerodynamic.

Once I had retired from the squad, I carried on as a freelancer on a day rate, which was peanuts compared to the cost of using the wind tunnel, which worked out at about £17 per minute, I think. I shudder to think how much time I've spent in the wind tunnel working for the greater good – it's days of my life pedalling like a hamster in a wheel but it was time well spent.

All that secret work was a huge factor in Great Britain's success. Boardman, being the type of character he is, didn't come out and take the credit for orchestrating all that, but there's no doubt that some silver medals were turned into gold by some of the innovations.

Ever since making that balsa-wood catamaran as a boy, I've always loved tinkering with bits of kit myself, seeing how I can improve things. It was hardly *the* decisive factor in Cav's 2011 World Championship road race triumph, but his helmet did play a supporting role, and I can claim some credit here. I had the idea of filling in the vents in the helmet to make it more aero-dynamic. Call it my own marginal gain for Cav.

I spent 2009 racing for Halfords, and the creation of the Tour Series early that summer was another blessing. We had a really busy time with two city centre criterium races per week for five weeks. It was like being a travelling salesman, driving up and down the country from Milton Keynes to Exeter and Peterborough to Blackpool. In fact, some of the lads who had full-time jobs used to turn up straight from the office and get changed out of their shirt and tie and into their cycling kit.

I was on tenterhooks because Vicki was pregnant again, and overdue. For about a fortnight, I was never closer than four hours from home. One day, I got home late from a long trip and was absolutely exhausted. I had just got into bed when Vicki said she thought it was time: 'Come on, Rob, we've got to go to the hospital.'

'Oh bloody hell, we'll go in a bit,' I said, before rolling over and going to sleep. I know, that sounds like the sort of thing my dad would have done.

A couple of hours later, she woke me up to say her waters had broken. Fergus was born later that morning.

Fergus's arrival coincided with the moment when the fairies came one night and took away our angelic, sweet Maddie and replaced her with a right little madam, so we had our hands full for a while. I rang my mum and said, 'I know what you went through with me, now, and all I can say is I'm so, so sorry!'

I found bike racing a difficult habit to kick, even though I was in my late thirties. At the beginning of 2010, Jim McFarlane of Endura, the Scottish cycle clothing company, and former national champion Brian Smith offered me the chance to carry on racing but combine it with being a team manager.

Everybody I spoke to told me it couldn't be done.

And they were absolutely right.

Endura were ambitious and they had assembled a decent squad of young riders, with Ian Wilkinson and Jimmy McCallum offering a bit of experience. They'd also signed Alexandre Blain, a talented and maverick Frenchman who had spent a couple of years with Cofidis. We also had Garry Beckett to help me out as joint team manager. Garry was one of the most respected *soigneurs* around and had worked for British Cycling on and off for years.

The race programme was mostly based in Britain but Stephen Roche had offered Brian the opportunity to base our training camp at his hotel down in the south of France. Roche had also wangled us an invite to a few early season French races, including the Tour of the Mediterranean and the Tour du Haut Var.

The weather at the training camp was atrocious. I was training in the morning but turning back earlier than the other lads to work on all the logistical things that needed to be done. I had this utopian idea of how I wanted to run the team. I wanted to empower the riders, give them the chance to take control of their own destiny and have a say in what they did. I wanted to treat each person like an individual. The older riders could use the benefit of their experience, and the younger ones I'd give a bit more guidance to. In the evenings, I took the lads into a meeting room and used the white board to run through a few of the basic things I'd learned about training, racing, recovery and bicycle equipment during my career. Some of them seemed to enjoy it, but I'm not sure they all took it in. A few glazed over.

Although I was trying my best, I didn't get the feeling it was going too well. Then, one morning, when the weather was so bad that we couldn't go out to train, I took charge. I split the team into two groups and set them a specific workout to do on the turbo trainers. It was just a stock session taken from my memory banks.

But they got on with it and really seemed to enjoy it. Later on Garry said to me, 'They're bike riders, Rob, they just want to be told what to do and when to do it.'

As head of selection, it wasn't hard to leave myself out of the team for the Tour of the Med. My training had been compromised for weeks and I knew that even in great form, I'd have taken a kicking. I'd been there, done that. It was time for someone else to dive in and see how they got on.

I left Garry to take charge of the team at the Tour of the Med and because our new Endura team car wasn't ready, we had to ask Roche if he could sort something out. The car he got for us was an ancient BMW 5 Series with 300,000 kilometres on the clock. There was barely any tread on the tyres and the seats had worn so much that the springs were poking through.

A couple of weeks later, I went down to the south of France for the Tour du Haut Var and spent a couple of days in this old wreck of a team car with Garry, then we had another training camp to prepare for the Tour of Murcia in Spain.

Although I'd only been in the job a couple of months, I knew it wasn't going to work out. I couldn't train properly, and I wasn't managing well enough either. Towards the end of the training camp, the riders decided to go out for a few beers and one of them, Ian Wilkinson, said, 'Are you one of us or one of them tonight?'

I wanted to go for a beer and be one of the lads, but I knew my authority as a team manager would take a hit if I did.

On the last morning, I had to sit down with every rider and talk through their race programme for the first half of the season. I hated having to disappoint people. I had to tell Ross Creber, our young Scottish rider, that he wasn't going to ride either of the first two Premier Calendar events of the season, and he told me that he had to ride them or else he wouldn't qualify for any funding from Scottish Cycling. I had to leave riders out of the Tour Series squad or tell them they wouldn't be getting a taste of the European stage races we'd been invited to.

My mind went back to all those meetings with Doug, Shane and Dave over the years, and I realized that it was never personal, even though as a rider I found it hard not to take it that way. It's as tough a job running a cycling team as riding in one.

I wanted to say to my riders, 'Look, here's the pie chart, there's not enough pieces to go round, so you're missing out. I'm sorry about that, but what would you do?'

In the end I rang Jim and told him I wanted to return to being a rider before I let anyone down badly.

Other opportunities were coming my way. I started commentating for Eurosport and BBC Radio Five Live, and, in 2011, I began advising the Italian Ivan Basso on his time trial training and his position on the time trial bike. This was proof of how far Great Britain had come as a cycling nation. Just a few years previously, the thought of one of the world's traditional powers, ingrained in their own cycling culture, turning to us for advice would have been unthinkable. Around the same time, I started talking to Cav about working with him, riding the scooter for him during training and looking after him on a day-to-day basis.

Eventually, I had to call it a day. I still loved racing but I couldn't carry on being a cyclist just because I loved the lifestyle. I had to bring the curtain down and move on to the next part of my career, and I knew the perfect place to do it.

The National Hill-Climb Championship was held at Long Hill, ten minutes from my house, on 30 October 2011, a month after Cav's victory in Copenhagen. Long Hill was one of the climbs I had regularly used to test my form during the latter years of my career. Now it would host my final race as a professional bike rider.

It took me just over 13 and a half minutes to ride the 4.4-mile climb and I was cheered every inch of the way. Whether the crowd were out to say farewell or not didn't matter. As far as I was concerned, they were there for me. I finished 14th. Afterwards, I put the bike in the back of the car and went to the bowls club HQ at the bottom of the hill for a cup of tea and a slice of cake before heading home.

After two world titles, three Olympic medals, a Commonwealth Games gold medal and countless bike races all over the world, that was me done. I loved every minute of it.

# Epilogue

Saturday, 27 October 2012. It's almost a year to the day since I last raced a bike and I arrive at the Sir Chris Hoy velodrome in Glasgow. Just over the way is Celtic Park, the huge football stadium; but the brand new velodrome, built for the 2014 Commonwealth Games, doesn't look out of place. It's just the name over the door that causes me to do a double take. Sir Chris Hoy. I knew him when he was just plain Chris. In fact, I beat him when he was just plain Chris, although he *still* pretends not to remember.

Knowing Sir Chris as I do, he's probably incredibly proud, very grateful, but also slightly embarrassed at having a velodrome named after him, but I can't think of anyone who deserves it more. The knighthood, the Olympic medals and the world titles haven't changed Chris a bit.

The same cannot be said for cycling in Britain. Everything has been transformed in the past twenty years. The sport has gone from the dingy backwaters to the mainstream spotlight. And Chris is one of those who was there at the beginning, as I was.

I've barely ridden a bicycle since I retired from racing. I don't miss the training. I miss the laughs and the café stops and the pursuit of victory, but I don't miss the hard work and the bad weather and the fretting over my form.

Jimmy McCallum has invited me to Glasgow to help mark the official opening of the Sir Chris Hoy velodrome and attend the Braveheart Cycling Fund dinner. Despite the millions that have flooded into cycling in Britain, organizations like the Braveheart still have a vital role to play. They give young Scottish riders a helping hand when they need it most. A bit of funding from the Braveheart might help nudge one or two talented youngsters on to the British Cycling Academy. It might help unearth the next Sir Chris, Graeme Obree or Robert Millar.

I've been asked to take part in an exhibition race on the new track. I thought it would be quite a casual, low-key affair, but after seeing the number of cars in the car park, the adrenaline starts to course through the veins and my mouth goes a bit dry. Then I step inside and hear the crowd. It's noisy and sounds like a full house.

Now I'm really panicking.

I'd agreed to do this because I thought it would just be a bit of a knock-about on the track, a laugh, not a serious race. I'm way out of shape for a race. But I'd do anything for Chris, and because it's for him, I wanted to make sure I didn't embarrass myself. I did two twenty-minute sessions on the rollers and an hour on the road last week in a last-minute attempt to remind my legs what to do.

I get changed into my kit and then sit in the track centre and take out my clippers and set about the year's worth of hair on my legs. I can't race with hairy legs. I'm not a complete amateur!

Then, with the nerves jangling, I get on the bike and roll round the track.

The first of two events is an elimination race, so I go to the front and set the pace until my legs give way. I slip to the back of the group and I'm called out.

Next up is a Derny race, with each of us cyclists paced by a motorbike. The ultimate Six-Day showstopper challenge. For the first fifteen laps of the forty-lap race, I feel great. I'm swooping up and down the banking like it's yesterday. I even contemplate putting in an attack.

And then I catch a glimpse of the lap board. We're only half-way.

Then my year out catches up with me. I'm out of breath and everything hurts like I'm in the Olympic Madison final. I have to shout to my Derny driver to get him to slow down a bit.

It's agony, and I'm loving it. I never thought I'd get to do this again in front of a capacity crowd, let alone in a velodrome named after Sir Chris Hoy.

And when it is all over, I get off the bike and my legs buckle under me like a new-born foal.

In those last twenty laps my whole career flashed in front of my eyes. I wouldn't have changed a thing. In fact, I'd do it all over again.

*'Go on, giz another go.'*

# Career Achievements

## Track

Olympic Games

Bronze medal, team pursuit 2000 (Sydney)
Silver medal, team pursuit 2004 (Athens)
Bronze medal, team pursuit 2004 (Athens)

World Championships

Silver medal, team pursuit 2000 (Manchester)
Bronze medal, individual pursuit 2000 (Manchester)
Silver medal, team pursuit 2003 (Stuttgart)
Silver medal, team pursuit 2004 (Melbourne)
Silver medal, individual pursuit 2004 (Melbourne)
Gold medal, team pursuit 2005 (Los Angeles)
Gold medal, Madison 2005 (Los Angeles)
Silver medal, team pursuit 2006 (Bordeaux)

## Commonwealth Games

Silver medal, team pursuit 1994 (Victoria, Canada)
Silver medal, team pursuit 1998 (Kuala Lumpur)
Silver medal, points race 1998 (Kuala Lumpur)
Gold medal, team pursuit 2006 (Melbourne)
Silver medal, individual pursuit 2006 (Melbourne)

## National Championships

National kilometre champion 1993, 1994
National Madison champion 1994, 1995, 1997, 1998, 1999
National points race champion 1996, 1997, 1998, 1999, 2000
National individual pursuit champion 1997, 1998, 1999, 2000

# Road

National road race champion 2008
National criterium champion 2000
PruTour stage winner (Edinburgh) 1999

## Premier Calendar

Second, overall standings 1997

# Time trials

National 10-mile time trial champion 1994, 1996, 1998
National 25-mile time trial champion 1998

# Index